THE ROLEX LEGACY

ROLEX
GMT-MASTER II
SUPERLATIVE CHRONOMETER
OFFICIALLY CERTIFIED
SWISS MADE

THE ROLEX LEGACY

The history of Rolex through 120 seminal and rare watches

JAMES DOWLING

ACC ART BOOKS

BASE 601 MILE
TELEMETER
ROLEX OYSTER
CHRONOGRAPH
ANTIMAGNETIC

CONTENTS

INTRODUCTION

The year 2025 marked 120 years since Hans Wilsdorf and his brother-in-law, Alfred Davis, opened the doors of Wilsdorf & Davis. Ten years later, they changed the firm's name to Rolex. The story of the company and the people behind it forms the heart of this book. I have chosen to break it down into 12 chapters, each covering one decade and starting with a summary of what was happening both within the company and in the world around it, and how the latter often influenced the former. The book is also about my 40 years of collecting, so it contains watches I have chosen to illustrate the company's progression. I am sure everyone who reads it will, at some point, think to themselves, 'Why didn't he include...?' Not all of the watches shown here are horologically or commercially important, but they are here for two reasons:

a. because each is a step on the road to where Rolex is now,
b. because I picked them.

The self-winding watch is more than 200 years old, and the waterproof watch over 100 years old, but we tend to think of them both as Rolex inventions. That's because while Rolex did not invent them, it did develop, refine and market them. In many ways, I like to think that Hans Wilsdorf and Steve Jobs would have seen each other in themselves; Jobs was not a computer scientist and Wilsdorf was not a watchmaker – but they were both excellent marketers. Apple did not invent the MP3 player but made the iPod a huge success; Jobs did not invent the mouse icon interface but made the Mac the computer of choice for creatives; and he did not invent the touchscreen phone, but look at the iPhone now. The crowds outside Apple stores every year remind me of the annual online frenzy as Rolex drops its new collection. The truth is that you can buy a touchscreen phone affordably and a new watch at a very low price, and they will do their job perfectly adequately. Wilsdorf and Jobs turned consumer items into luxury products for which clients will pay a premium price.

While Wilsdorf may not have invented the waterproof watch or the automatic one, there is one area where he was a groundbreaker – accuracy. He pursued precision in watches relentlessly, a quest which started long before he moved to London to found Wilsdorf & Davis. The first-ever advertisement for Rolex, from 1914, talks about achieving a Kew certificate for timekeeping, and for the next 40 years that was the principal focus not only of Rolex's advertising, but also of the company itself. While everyone knows the words 'Oyster' and 'Perpetual' and what they represent, few know about the Superbalance, the free-sprung early Datejusts or the 'Kew A' watches of the late 1940s. But each of them was an incremental step along the way to accuracy. Today, the Parachrom hairspring, the Chronergy escapement and the Syloxi hairspring are other incremental steps which have made the modern Rolex the most accurate mass-produced watch in the world. Most watch brands are perfectly happy to regulate their watches to the Swiss chronometer standard of -4 to +6 seconds a day; Rolex guarantee its models to -2 to +2.

With the 2025 launch of the Dynapulse escapement, Rolex has achieved what few brands have dared to think of, a mass-produced, lubrication-free, chronometer escapement. For Rolex, it's a radical step, rather like the one Apple took in 2010 when it launched its in-house processor chip. It shows that Rolex, the firm known for incremental development, can take radical steps now and then, just as it did when it made the self-winding, waterproof, chronometer wristwatch unremarkable. Nobody knows what the next steps will be, but I am sure of only one thing – they will be superlative.

Please note: dimensions given are diameter for circular watches or length for rectangular watches. Dates given are for the watch examples shown, not the date of introduction.

CHAPTER ONE

1905–1915

ROLEX

1905–1915

THE WRISTWATCH CENTURY

How Hans Wilsdorf and Rolex rewrote timekeeping.

The story of the 20th century is, in many ways, the story of the wristwatch. From the trenches of World War I to the lunar surface, the wristwatch was a silent witness to humanity's defining moments. And no brand is more entwined with this narrative than Rolex. Yet, to understand Rolex, we must first understand its visionary founder, Hans Wilsdorf – a man whose life was as precise and deliberate as the timepieces he created.

Hans Wilsdorf's story is often reduced to a few bullet points: born in Germany, educated in Switzerland and later relocated to London, where he co-founded the firm Wilsdorf & Davis in 1905. But these facts barely scratch the surface. To grasp his genius, we must journey further back – to the early 19th century, when his grandfather, Karl Traugott Wilsdorf, left Saxony (the heartland of German watchmaking) for Bavaria.

At the time, Germany did not yet exist as a unified nation. Bavaria was a Catholic stronghold, culturally distinct from the Lutheran austerity of Saxony – a divide that shaped Hans's upbringing. Born in March 1881, he grew up in Kulmbach, where his father managed a prosperous hardware business. His mother, Anna Maisel, came from the town's wealthiest family, who were the owners of a renowned brewery. Yet Hans was an outsider: a Protestant in a Catholic town, a bright student in a rigid system, and an orphan by the age of 12 after both his parents died within a year of each other.

Shipped off to boarding school in Coburg, 50 kilometres (31 miles) away, Hans mastered English, French and mathematics – skills that would later prove invaluable. Coburg's ties to Britain (through Prince Albert, Queen Victoria's consort) exposed him to Anglophone culture, while a Swiss classmate's stories ignited his fascination with Switzerland. But first, like all Bavarian men, he endured three years of compulsory military service. Opting for the Einjährig-Freiwilliger programme, he completed his duty in just one year, likely in the Engineering Corps like his elder brother – a choice that spared him frontline combat and honed his technical mindset.

In 1900, Wilsdorf left Bavaria forever, and settled in La Chaux-de-Fonds, Switzerland. His first job was with a pearl exporter, where his fluent English landed him correspondence work. But his true calling emerged when he joined Cuno Korten, a watch exporter supplying retailers across the British Empire.

At the time, watch branding was virtually non-existent. Retailers such as Tiffany and Bailey, Banks & Biddle dictated that their names appear on dials, while manufacturers remained anonymous. Wilsdorf saw an opportunity: accuracy as a selling point. Without permission, he began testing movements from each batch, identifying the rare few that kept near-perfect time. Submitting these to observatories,

← Rebberg, 1912 (see page 16).

The story of the 20th century is, in many ways, the story of the wristwatch. From the trenches of World War I to the lunar surface, the wristwatch was a silent witness to humanity's defining moments.

he secured chronometer certifications – a feat unheard of for mid-priced watches. His employers rejoiced, but Wilsdorf stored the lesson for later: precision could defy convention.

By 1903, Wilsdorf recognized London as the epicentre of global trade. He arrived in the city when the British Empire was at its height, and at a time when commerce ruled supreme. After a brief stint with an unknown watch importer, he partnered with Alfred Davis in 1905, founding Wilsdorf & Davis at 83 Hatton Garden, in London's jewellery district.

Its first products were not wristwatches but travel clocks – compact, leather-cased timepieces for the era's burgeoning number of railway travellers. Yet competition was fierce, and Wilsdorf pivoted to ladies' wristwatches, leveraging Swiss-made cylinder escapement movements. These early pieces bore no distinguishing marks until 1907, when British hallmarking laws required imported watches to carry a sponsor's mark – the now-iconic W&D cartouche.

The turning point came when Wilsdorf visited Jean Aegler's workshop in Bienne, Switzerland. Aegler specialized in petite, high-quality movements – perfect for wristwatches. Defying logic, Wilsdorf placed an enormous order (reportedly worth hundreds of thousands of Swiss francs), likely backed by Davis's finances.

The partnership was transformative. In 1910, Aegler's 11-ligne movement earned the first-ever chronometer certification for a small wristwatch from the Bienne Observatory. Four years later, another Aegler movement survived the Kew Observatory's brutal 45-day trials – a test designed for naval deck watches. By then, World War I had begun, and men were abandoning pocket watches for rugged wristwatches.

By the end of the war, Wilsdorf & Davis had rebranded as Rolex and relocated to Switzerland to avoid postwar British taxes. The Aegler partnership endured, formalized in 1913 with an exclusive deal for the British Empire. (Aegler retained ties to Gruen in the US, a subplot in Rolex's later rivalry with American brands.)

Hans Wilsdorf and Jean Aegler – both young, fatherless and obsessed with precision – had rewritten the rules of horology. The wristwatch was no longer a novelty but a necessity, and Rolex was its undisputed champion.

→ An early lady's 9ct gold Half-Hunter-style wristwatch, with a fired enamel dial and fitted with a Britannia Ltd expanding bracelet.

1907
LADIES' WATCH

The very first wristwatches ever sold by Rolex were gold ladies' models, very similar to the watch shown on the right.

- **Model number: No model number**
- **Date: 1907**
- **Dial: Brass, white fired enamel**
- **Movement: 8¾ ligne Rebberg**
- **Case material: 9ct gold**
- **Dimensions: 27mm**

When Alfred Davis and his brother-in-law Hans Wilsdorf (see page 11) opened Wilsdorf & Davis in London's Hatton Garden in 1905, some men were already wearing wristwatches, but they were few and far between. The wristwatch was essentially a feminine object, as much a piece of jewellery as a timepiece, yet even so, few women wore one. But things were about to change with the rise of the working woman. At the turn of the century, around one-quarter of women in the UK were employed, but the vast majority either were in domestic service or worked in factories and neither of these groups needed or could afford a wristwatch. However, a new cohort of women, the daughters of the middle classes, began to enter the workplace and they found employment in roles which had not previously existed, working in the new department stores or as secretaries and typists in commercial offices. They needed a watch as there were trains and omnibuses to catch, appointments to schedule, telephone calls to note the time of and, with decent wages, they could afford a watch.

Thus, it made sense for Wilsdorf & Davis to concentrate on the women's market and they had a significant advantage – their relationship with Aegler (see page 12). In an early advertisement for the firm, the business was called 'Vve. Jean Aegler' (vve is short for *veuve*, the French word for widow), meaning that the company was actually named 'Widow of Jean Aegler'. The advertisement was in French except for one phrase which was in French and German, to reach a wider audience: *Montres pour dames and Damenuhren* or 'Women's watches', for that was the firm's speciality.

Most small movements of this period used cylinder escapements, but Aegler was one of the few firms that specialized in small lever escapement movements. Cylinder movements had one advantage: watches that used them could be much slimmer than ones with a lever escapement. But to Wilsdorf the advantages of the lever watches – better timekeeping and less frequent servicing – far outweighed this benefit.

The vast majority of women's watches featured just an hour and a minute hand, usually blued steel to make them easily visible at a glance on a white enamel dial. The creativity lay in the design of the case and bracelet. Early cases were almost always 9-carat gold, often pink gold, and while most were round, square and octagonal cases are frequently seen. The sides, and sometimes the bezels, were engraved with floral or Greek key patterns. These watches were sometimes fitted with silk or leather straps, but the vast majority were supplied with expanding bracelets. At this time, Rolex (or Wilsdorf & Davis as it was then) did not put its name on the dial, and so it was the aesthetics of the case and bracelet which sold the watch. This is why we see so many different case designs from this period – the tiniest difference in style could make a sale.

→ These early ladies' watches almost always had fired enamel dials, but this one is rather special with the hand-painted Roman numerals and the XII in red enamel. Britannia Ltd were the English makers of the expanding bracelet, and Rolex was one of the first firms to fit these bracelets as standard.

VICKERS
AUCKLAND

1912

REBBERG

The relationship between Wilsdorf & Davis and Aegler bears fruit as wristwatches for men take on a prominent role during World War I.

- **Model number: No model number**
- **Date: 1912**
- **Dial: Brass, black fired enamel, radium numerals**
- **Movement: 13 ligne Rebberg**
- **Case material: Sterling silver**
- **Dimensions: 35mm**

The thing which changed everything for Wilsdorf & Davis was when Wilsdorf decided to only use movements from the firm 'Les fils de Jean Aegler, fabrique Rebberg', which translates as 'Sons of Jean Aegler; Rebberg factory'. This raises the question: does the phrase 'Rebberg factory' relate to the location of the factory in the Rebberg section of Bienne, or was it the factory which made Rebberg watches? We may never know, but what we do know is that it was at some point after 1906, when the two sons of Jean Aegler assumed the running of the firm, that Wilsdorf travelled to Bienne and placed his large order with Hermann Aegler, who he specifically mentions in the Vade Mecum.

The first order was for ladies' and men's wristwatches fitted with leather straps. It seems that W&D had no problem in selling them, as soon after this first order, Hans was making regular trips to Bienne, placing larger and larger orders with Hermann Aegler, and before long he was able to place the largest order ever given for wristwatches. In his writings, Hans says that the order 'amounted to several hundred thousand Swiss Francs'. This was obviously a very large sum of money, but it is important to realise that, at the time, Switzerland was primarily an agrarian society with concomitant low wages and a currency which was valued at around 25 Francs to the Pound Sterling, meaning that 100,000 Swiss Francs was a little over £4,000. Wilsdorf states 'several hundred thousand' without listing an actual amount, but we know that it was 200,000 or more, otherwise he couldn't use the word 'several'. So let's assume that his initial order was 500,000 Swiss Francs, which was around £20,000. Nowadays this wouldn't even buy you an entry-level Audi, but over a century ago, this was a huge sum of money, sufficient to buy four full-size steam locomotives.

Wilsdorf & Davis bought movements from Aegler in several sizes, ranging from 7''' to 13''' (''' meaning 'ligne'). The Rebberg movement was very successful because it was one of the first industrially produced movements available in several sizes, but all with identical plate layouts. In the period between their first deal and the end of the 1920s, Rolex became Aegler's largest customer, but Aegler wasn't one to put all his eggs in one basket and he continued to sell movements to other firms. Aegler advertisements from the time mention Rolex, but also Rebberg and Final as two other brands that were made by them. And in 1912, this fact was acknowledged when the firm's name was changed once again; now it was 'Les fils de Jean Aegler, fabrique de montres Rebberg, Final & Rolex', or 'The sons of Jean Aegler, manufacturer of Rebberg, Final & Rolex watches'. It is interesting to note that the in-house brands get top billing above Rolex. This is now descending into farce, but the following year the firm's name was changed once again; it became simply 'Aegler SA'. SA is short for Société Anonyme, meaning it was incorporated as a limited company with shareholders, and one of those shareholders was Hans Wilsdorf.

→ **Rebberg movements were at the heart of almost every early Rolex, although Aegler sold these movements to many other watch manufacturers and also sold complete watches themselves. Both practices ceased by the mid-1930s, and the firm only made and sold movements to Rolex from then on.**

ROLEX

1915

VARIATIONS ON A THEME

The first attempts at disconnecting wristwatch design from pocket watch design.

- **Model number: No model number**
- **Date: 1915**
- **Dial: Brass, white fired enamel, black numerals**
- **Movement: 13 ligne Rebberg**
- **Case material: Sterling silver**
- **Dimensions: 36mm**

→ Although sweep seconds hands had been seen on pocket watches for more than a hundred years by this point, they were very much a novelty on wristwatches. Rolex actually charged a substantial premium over the cost of a subsidiary seconds watch until the late 1930s. The case shown here is a perfect example of a reduced-scale pocket watch, with visible hinges for both the case back and bezel.

The first wristwatches for men could be regarded as either scaled-up ladies' watches or scaled-down pocket watches. They featured a uniform three-piece design: the case centre held the movement, dial and hands, while the case back and the bezel held the glass and were attached to the centre by hinges.

This design had been around for over a century and functioned well for pocket watches. But pocket watches lived a privileged life compared with early wristwatches. Snug in a waistcoat pocket, sitting upright in one position, they were usually kept at a constant temperature and protected from the environment.

The life of a wristwatch was different: it was exposed to the elements, never in one position for more than a few minutes and subject to the jolts and bangs of everyday life. No wonder early men's wristwatches had a poor reputation and needed more frequent servicing than the pocket watches of the day. One of the biggest dangers to the wristwatch was contact between the glass and a solid object, and so, once again, systems which had been used for pocket watches were miniaturized for the wristwatch. Both Hunter and Half-Hunter designs (see page 68) were produced. The former used a solid cover over the dial, which was opened by pressing a button in the centre of the crown or just below it, and the spring-loaded lid would flip up, enabling the time to be read. This was remarkably inconvenient as both hands were required to tell the time and to close the lid, but the major problem was that this design essentially negated the advantage of being able to tell the time at a glance – you might as well use a pocket watch. The Half-Hunter also had a sprung lid over the glass, but a porthole in the centre enabled you to see the hands, and the position of the hours was reproduced on the cover so that all the benefits of the wristwatch were retained.

What if you already had a watch and wanted to protect it? This was where the watch grille came in. An external frame was attached to the watch strap. It consisted of a grid of horizontal and vertical metal rods which made it difficult, but not impossible, to read the time. The grille could be removed if the watch no longer needed the protection. These came into wide use during World War I, and it is interesting to note that the first-ever Swiss patent granted to Hans Wilsdorf, number 77129, was for a watch grille design. Unfortunately for Hans it was awarded to him six days after the armistice was signed at Compiègne.

DINGWALL

1915

TRENCH WATCHES

No longer an affectation or a luxury, the wristwatch becomes an essential item in the trenches of World War I.

- **Model number: No model number**
- **Date: 1915**
- **Dial: Brass, white fired enamel, black numerals**
- **Movement: 13 ligne Rebberg**
- **Case material: Sterling silver**
- **Dimensions: 36mm**

→ This is a good time to define what a trench watch is. Horological historian David Boettcher's definition is 'the two principal features are luminous dials and unbreakable crystals, and the ultimate is a wristwatch with a luminous dial, unbreakable crystal and waterproof Borgel case'. I am certainly not going to argue with the first two; my only query on the final point is that not all screwed cases were made by Borgel.

While some British Army officers might have worn a wristwatch in the early days of World War I, their use had not yet become widespread due to their lack of accuracy. Small watches are inherently less accurate than large ones as their ability to keep time is governed by the balance wheel. A large balance wheel has greater inertia than a smaller one and, therefore, is much less likely to be affected by movement and occasional shocks. Thus, pocket watches were inherently more accurate than the new-fangled wristwatch. For Wilsdorf and his potential clients, this was the biggest hurdle to overcome – an inaccurate watch is probably less use than no watch at all. Wilsdorf could not overcome the basic prejudice that wristwatches were essentially a feminine adornment, but he could overcome the opinion that they did not perform accurately.

As early as 1909, Wilsdorf convinced Aegler, his movement manufacturer (see page 12), to choose the best-performing ladies' sized movement from a recent batch and adjust it to perform as well as possible. On 22 March 1910, the observatory at Bienne, Switzerland, awarded a chronometer certificate to an 11''' 25mm diameter watch produced by Aegler. This was the first chronometer certificate ever awarded to a watch of this size – essentially a lady's fob watch movement. Wilsdorf publicized the event widely in the press.

The relationship between Aegler and Wilsdorf & Davis was formalized in 1913 when Aegler agreed that Wilsdorf & Davis would have the exclusive right to use its movements in Britain and its empire. The agreement was not global because Aegler was already working with the Gruen watch company in the US and did not want to end that relationship.

Almost as if to celebrate the new working relationship, and its dependence on the UK and the British Empire, Aegler submitted another watch (perhaps even the same one) to the King's Royal Observatory at Kew, London, for testing. This tiny lady's movement was subjected to the same tests as tourbillons and karrusels, yet it still achieved the coveted 'A' certificate. The tests took 45 days at three different temperatures and five positions and, on 15 July 1914, the watch completed them successfully and the certificate was issued. Less than two weeks later, the world was at war.

1915

TRENCH WATCHES

It has always been known that 'conflict breeds creativity', and while everyone knows about the tanks and airships of World War I, it also accelerated the evolution of the wristwatch.

- **Model number: No model number**
- **Date: 1915**
- **Dial: Brass, white fired enamel, black numerals**
- **Movement: 13 ligne Rebberg**
- **Case material: Sterling silver**
- **Dimensions: 35mm**

When Wilsdorf & Davis began in 1905 (see page 12), the wristwatch was almost exclusively a feminine object, and even then not many women owned one. The only men who wore one were officers in the British Army, and they were few and far between. Prior to World War I, Britain maintained a rather small standing army – almost all of the nation's military resources were poured into the Royal Navy.

If they were thought of at all, men's wristwatches were considered to be dainty and to lack accuracy. Men carried a pocket watch snug in the lower pocket of their waistcoat, and used a precious metal chain to attach it to a nearby buttonhole. Compared to the much larger movements in pocket watches, the wristwatches of the day were small and inherently inaccurate. The only downside to the pocket watch was that using it was inconvenient. Checking the time meant reaching across the body, extracting the watch, reading the time and then replacing the watch in the pocket. In stressful situations this was not always possible. The earliest known military users of wrist timepieces were British infantry officers fighting on the northwest frontier of India in the 1880s. They put their pocket watches in leather holders which were attached to leather wristbands known as wristlets. Over the next two decades, as officers were dispatched to the next hot spot, they took their wristlets with them, other officers saw them, quickly grasped their convenience and purchased their own. British cavalry officers in the 1880–81 Boer War in South Africa quickly caught on to the idea and were often photographed wearing wristlets.

By 1911, South Africa was one of the two locations outside the UK and Switzerland where Wilsdorf & Davis had offices (the other being Yokohama, Japan). They found a ready market for their early wristwatches in Africa and India, tropical locations where it was really too hot to

→ The Half-Hunter case shown here is a miniaturized version of the pocket watch style. It was especially popular during World War I, as the cover and its secondary glass gave some protection to the watch glass and the enamel dial below. The danger to the watch wasn't so much from enemy action as from knocking against solid objects during everyday use.

wear the three-piece suit which was the necessary uniform if one carried a pocket watch. These markets were probably among the first where male civilians adopted the wristwatch, as distinct from the wristlet.

World War I was not just the first industrialized conflict, it was also the first synchronized one – a war dependent on timing. Artillery barrages had to happen simultaneously across the field, and – more importantly – they had to cease at precisely the same time so that the attacking infantry would not fall victim to their own fire. For this reason, the wristwatch became an essential item that an officer needed before going into battle.

Officers were given £50 to equip themselves with all the items needed and were expected to purchase a wristwatch from this outfit allowance. Men in the other ranks who wanted one relied on gifts from family or friends. I have seen several watches from this period with engravings indicating that the watch was a gift before the wearer embarked for the front. Newspaper advertisements promoted the wristwatch as the ideal gift for a soldier, and by the end of the war a sizeable proportion of the men who returned did so wearing one. The man's wristwatch had arrived.

1915

FIRST CALENDAR

Only ten years after Wilsdorf & Davis was founded, and 30 years before the Datejust was launched, Rolex sold their first calendar watches.

- **Model number: No model number**
- **Date: 1915**
- **Dial: Brass, fired white enamel, radium numerals**
- **Movement: 13 ligne Rebberg, sweep seconds**
- **Case material: Sterling silver**
- **Dimensions: 35mm**

→ A common feature seen on many of these early silver wristwatches is the oversized 'onion' shaped crown in gold-coloured brass, with deep flutes. This design enabled easy winding and setting under all circumstances, although its large size meant that it could easily be caught on clothing.

One of the things which makes collecting Rolex watches so challenging is that it is almost impossible to arrive at a fixed conclusion. It is not just that the accepted wisdom is often wrong, it is that at the moment you think that you understand something, the narrative changes.

For example, the accepted dateline for the Rolex calendar watch is:

- 1945 Datejust
- 1947 DatoCompax
- 1950 Moonphase
- 1956 Day-Date

In November 1945 the reference 4467 Datejust had the honour of being the firm's first calendar watch. It was launched to celebrate the 40th anniversary of Rolex's foundation.

But that was not really true. The first Rolex calendar watch had been sold 30 years earlier, in 1915. Based on the classic Rebberg 13''' movement, it featured a sweep seconds hand – unusual for this period – and a central calendar hand that pointed to the date numerals which were arrayed around the extreme periphery of the dial. To the best of my knowledge, this was one of the first wristwatches with four concentric hands on the centre pinion. Oddly, the calendar hand – for reasons yet unknown – revolves around the dial in an anticlockwise direction. This may well have been the first wristwatch with four centrally mounted hands, but it was most definitely the first with three hands going in one direction and another in the opposite direction. I guess that it was mechanically simpler to do it this way.

The four examples of this watch that I have seen were all sold in the UK and have Swiss and UK hallmarks dating to 1915/1916. But the case numbers do not seem to be in any sequence, which makes me think that they were made to order. What I do not understand is that, while they were obviously more expensive than regular watches from the period, none of the watches I have seen were cased in gold – they were all sterling silver – which was the least expensive case material at the time.

I believe that these were custom orders because every one of them is unique in some way. For example, the first one I saw had an unsigned dial. It was a simple enamel dial with the nice touch of a red 12 but, unbelievably, the winder was at 9. Without a doubt, this makes it the earliest left-handed Rolex ever produced. The second one had a conventional case hinged at the front and back, an interesting Rolex signature on the dial and very prominent radium Arabic numerals and hands. The most recent one was identical to this watch, but it lacked the name Rolex on the dial.

CHAPTER TWO

1916–1925

ROLEX
OBSERVATORY
SWISS MADE

1916–1925

ROLEX LEAVES LONDON

Wartime taxes and import duties force Rolex to move to Geneva.

Hans Wilsdorf had come to London for commercial reasons. When he arrived in 1903, London was the centre of the British Empire and the trading hub of the world, and Britain and Germany were allies and friends. Queen Victoria had married into one of the German royal families – the Saxe-Coburg-Gotha branch – and six of her nine children would marry into other branches. Britain's 'natural' enemy was the French, with whom it had been intermittently at war for almost a thousand years. It is worth remembering that British and Prussian troops fought together to defeat Napoleon at Waterloo, and while the Prussians defeated France in the Franco-Prussian War of 1871, Britain stood on the sidelines. When that war was over, the German princely states then united under Prussian leadership to form the German Reich (empire). Britain viewed this new continental power as a counterweight to Russia and France, both of whom had previously threatened British expansionist policies. Germany was seen as a fellow liberal constitutional monarchy and was respected for its poets, musicians and philosophers.

It was in this atmosphere that many Germans came to England. They worked principally as waiters, but many of the more enterprising individuals opened butchers' shops, specializing in sausages. However, all of this changed when the new German emperor, Wilhelm, decided that he was not satisfied with having Europe's strongest army; he also wanted Europe's strongest navy and embarked on a battleship building spree. This immediately presented a challenge to the Royal Navy's centuries-old domination of the high seas, and British public opinion began to swing against Germany. Then two things happened: Britain began to build a relationship with France under the new king, Edward VII, resulting in the Entente Cordiale of 1904, and the editors of British newspapers began a virulent anti-German campaign in which each vied with the other to emphasize the danger Germany posed to the British Empire.

While London had been a welcoming place for Wilsdorf when he arrived in 1903, a decade later, even before the outbreak of war, it was no longer a nice place in which to be German. Realizing this he took British nationality in 1912, a year after his marriage to his English secretary, Florence Frances May Crotty.

On the outbreak of World War I, British public opinion swung from hostility to outright hysteria, with newspapers declaring that there were between 60,000 and 300,000 German spies in Britain, even though the pre-war German population in the UK never rose above 40,000.

Once the war began and the German army advanced into the Low Countries, reports of (real or imagined) German atrocities in Belgium reached the newspapers. This news then combined with the prevailing wave of anti-German sentiment, boiling over into acts of mass

← **Rectangular Watch, 1925** (see page 38).

At the start of World War I, Wilsdorf & Davis was an Anglo-German-owned firm, headquartered in London [. . .] At the end of the war, Rolex was a Swiss firm based in Geneva, casing movements made in Bienne, focussed on wristwatches and selling to the world.

civil disobedience. German-owned businesses were vandalized, anti-German riots erupted, and thousands of German civilians were arrested and interned. Under these circumstances, a business with a German name faced a significant handicap; thus, the name Wilsdorf & Davis was discarded and the business rebranded as Rolex, a trademark that had been registered in 1908 as a brand name but never as a business. The first step had been taken.

Mass conscription in World War I by all the combatants produced armies numbering in the millions; and so it became necessary to co-ordinate the movement of men, munitions and materials tightly. To facilitate this, the British army issued pocket watches to its officers. They proved to be useful for staff officers and supply officers; however, the men who needed them the most, the ones on the front line, found that they were less than utilitarian – retrieving a pocket watch from under the layers of clothing worn in the trenches was no easy matter. This became obvious very quickly, and by 1915 a wristwatch headed the War Office list of equipment a British officer was expected to own when leaving for the front.

No one knows who wore the first wristwatch during World War I, but it was most likely an officer in the British Army who was serving with Empire troops.

Before the turn of the century, British cavalry officers serving in north-west India had purchased leather devices which enabled a pocket watch to be worn on the wrist. These were much more efficient than carrying the watch in a waistcoat pocket but, due to their size, were cumbersome and restricted the flexibility of the wrist on which they were worn. When these officers were transferred to South Africa to fight in the Boer War (1880–81), other officers saw a watch being worn on the wrist, and immediately grasped the benefits of a watch which was always visible and subsequently purchased their own leather watch holder.

Within a year of the outbreak of World War I, wristwatches were common among officers and were also being purchased by non-commissioned officers such as sergeants and corporals. The male wristwatch had arrived, and Rolex was one of the principal beneficiaries.

In 1915, to raise funds for the war effort, a tax was introduced on the import of luxury goods. Unfortunately for Rolex, this included wristwatches. The tax of 33.3 per cent was charged on items imported into Britain, even if they were destined for subsequent export. As much of Rolex's production was destined for the Empire, this placed an unbearable burden on it, so the decision was made to open an office inside Aegler's Bienne factory in Switzerland. Previously the movements had been checked and then cased at the company's London office; this work was now carried out in Switzerland for all watches, not just those destined for export from the UK, which now (of course) never touched British soil.

Britain's first budget after the end of the war raised personal taxes to such a level that Wilsdorf left Britain for Switzerland. He settled in Geneva where he opened an office and relocated the people who had been checking and casing the Aegler movements. The head office remained in London but from this moment on, Rolex became a Swiss firm.

At the start of World War I, Wilsdorf & Davis was an Anglo-German-owned firm, headquartered in London, importing pocket watches, clocks and wristwatches and selling to the British Empire. At the end of the war, Rolex was a Swiss firm based in Geneva, casing movements made in Bienne, focussed on wristwatches and selling to the world. And if you want an accurate and concise description of the company today, that is one that will certainly suffice.

→ A Rolex UK magazine advert from the 1920s, issued after Rolex moved to Switzerland. Notice that ladies' watches are very much in the majority – just the rectangular watch at the top of the advert is a men's watch.

1916

CHANGING CASES

With factories and coal fires everywhere, wristwatches needed protection not from water, but rather from the ever-prevalent dust: here is an early attempt.

- **Model number: No model number**
- **Date: 1916**
- **Dial: Brass, fired enamel, radium numerals**
- **Movement: 13 ligne Rebberg**
- **Case material: Sterling silver**
- **Dimensions: 36mm**

If asked, most people would say that Hans Wilsdorf's two greatest inventions could be summed up with the two words 'Oyster' and 'Perpetual'. He popularized waterproof and self-winding watches and those two words are on the dial of pretty much every Rolex sold today. But I would argue that his greatest invention was not those two, but rather one which can be summarized in another word found on the dial – 'chronometer'.

Wilsdorf knew that a wristwatch could not become ubiquitous unless it was accurate, and making it waterproof and automatic were essential for this. Having a hermetically sealed watch was important for accuracy. This is why.

Back in the early 1920s, when Wilsdorf and his team began their horological experiments, watch lubrication had hardly moved on since Abraham-Louis Breguet said, 'Give me the perfect oil, and I will give you the perfect watch', almost 200 years before. Most of the oils used came from natural sources, either seed or animal oils; sperm whale oil in particular was highly valued. The oil should allow the wheel teeth to slide easily past each other, but the problem was that any dust or dirt that entered the watch would be attracted to these natural oils and settle on them. Before long – a matter of a few months – the oil would turn into a kind of waxy grinding paste and tiny sections of the teeth would be worn away, settle in the paste and make it more abrasive. Eventually the movement would gum up as the paste solidified.

Wilsdorf realized that preventing dust from entering the watch case was as important as – if not more important – than making it waterproof. A waterproof watch was not really a big priority – nobody ever swam wearing a watch back then – but it was a unique selling point that differentiated Rolex from all the other brands. It also meant that the watch would also be dust- and dirt-proof. So, from as early as 1915, Wilsdorf began to experiment with ways to protect his movements.

Waterproof pocket watches had been available for years; François Borgel had been making screwed pocket watch cases since the early 1890s. When the wristwatch came along, Borgel made smaller versions of his case for these new movements. Many firms adopted them, including Longines, Zenith and Rolex. I have seen an example of a Borgel-cased Rolex wristwatch with a UK hallmark for 1911/12, meaning that these watches were distributed well before World War I. Its unique construction consisted of three components: a cup-shaped main case which replaced the case centre and back of a conventional watch; a screwed metal ring which held the movement, dial and hands; and a bezel which was attached to the screwed metal ring. The crown protruded from the case body and had two positions. In the regular state, it allowed the watch to be wound, and it could also be pulled out, allowing the bezel and movement to be unscrewed and removed. There were three possible areas where dust or moisture could enter: the join between the bezel and the case, the crown and the push pin. However, all had some degree of protection: the milling on the bezel allowed it to be screwed tightly against the body, while the crown was pulled tight against the case tube by a spring, and the push pin was kept secure by a strip of sprung steel holding it in its default position. All in all, the Borgel case was as impermeable as could be expected for the time.

→ The coin edge-style milling on the front and back of this case enabled the watchmaker to use their fingers to screw the two components tightly into the case body, thereby making it dustproof. It's obvious that this style of milling was the inspiration for the milling on the early Oysters. The big breakthrough was designing a tool which enabled the front and back to be screwed much tighter than ever possible just by hand.

60
10
20
30
40
50

1923

NURSE'S WATCH

Wilsdorf spots a gap in the market and designs a watch to fill that gap. Is this the first Rolex 'tool' watch, the ancestor of the Submariner and GMT-Master?

- **Model number: SN3564**
- **Date: 1923**
- **Dial: Brass, white fired enamel, black numerals**
- **Movement: 13 ligne Rebberg**
- **Case material: Sterling silver**
- **Dimensions: 35mm**

It comes as no surprise to anyone who knows me that I am drawn to the more unusual watch specimens. During World War I and the following years, Rolex made tens of thousands of wristwatches powered by the ubiquitous Rebberg 13''' movement. Of these, 99 per cent were silver- or gunmetal-cased wristwatches, known as 'Trench watches'. But not this one – this was designed for nurses. It has only one lug, and was attached to the front of a nurse's uniform, using pins, a ribbon or a leather tab, hanging upside down but still quickly readable.

The design meant that there was little chance of dirt, bacteria or any other contamination to find a hiding place, as was possible with a wristwatch, which – by its very design – would be much closer to the patient during treatment.

The whole watch looks strange – it only has one lug and the subsidiary seconds hand is in the 3 position, rather than the conventional 6. This dial layout is a consequence of using a normal wristwatch movement turned through 90-degrees anticlockwise. It places the winder in the 12 position and the seconds at 3 and, in order for this to work, a special dial was produced. Like most dials of this period, it is porcelain with a high gloss outer surface and a matte centre. However, unlike most wristwatches of the period, it is a one-piece dial with the subsidiary seconds simply printed on the dial surface. Wristwatches often used a two-piece dial where the subsidiary seconds dial was a separate component, inserted into a hole in the dial. This was a much more complex method of construction, but it allowed the seconds dial to be sunk below the surface of the dial and this then permitted the seconds hand to be below the surface of the main dial, allowing the hour and minute hands in turn to be lower, reducing the overall height of the watch. But not on this watch.

What I also find interesting about it is that this is a utilitarian watch, designed to

→ **Cases like this were completely handmade, although some machinery was used during the process. The separate components would be individually produced before all being given to the case maker, who assembled the hinges and soldered on the large strap lug before completing the final step of fitting the glass.**

be used while doing a specific job – it has no other reason to exist. So, you might expect a pragmatic design. Instead it has painted Roman numerals, which are quite small and the most delicate fleur-de-lys hands; it is almost as if the guy who designed it – and it would have been a guy – thought to himself, 'This is a woman's watch, so it needs to be pretty'.

And that is a big part of why I love this watch; it is a study in contradictions. It is a watch for a woman, but it is as big as a man's watch. It needs to be easily read to fulfil its role, yet it uses delicate, almost spidery, hands and numerals, requiring more than a quick glance. But, more than anything, I love it because it is a classic example of Wilsdorf (see page 12) seeing a gap in the market and quickly filling it. He had either seen, or been told about, nurses pinning the strap of a wristwatch to their uniforms, making it easy to glance at the time while their hands were otherwise occupied. He modified the existing wristwatch case, rotated the dial through 90 degrees and it became the subject of Swiss Patent 109,335 – one of his very first patents.

1924

HERMETIC

One of the first attempts at making a wristwatch waterproof. While it worked, it proved cumbersome to use and was eventually superseded by the Oyster.

- **Model number: 937**
- **Date: 1924**
- **Dial: Brass, white fired enamel**
- **Movement: 9¾ ligne Rebberg**
- **Case material: Sterling silver**
- **Dimensions: 32mm**

Prior to the introduction of the Oyster, Rolex had experimented with several case designs. All of them differed from the Oyster in one major aspect: they were designed and made by specialist case companies. Even if they were signed 'Rolex' inside the case back, they were not exclusive to the company.

Throughout the late 1910s and into the mid-1920s, the multitude of independent case makers in Switzerland tried dozens of ideas for new forms, but I am going to focus on three that Rolex used. They were all very different but had one thing in common – they used a one-piece case, thereby eliminating one entry point for external substances.

The Borgel (see page 32) case also used a monocoque case with a screwed bezel, but the movement, dial and hands were attached to the bezel. These three kept the movement in its normal location but differed in every other aspect.

Pretty much every two-piece case had a screwed removable bezel similar to the Borgel one, but an interesting design from the start of the 1920s did not. It used a case back that screwed into an integrated case and bezel. It might have been aesthetically pleasing, but I think that it was worse from a functional point of view. The single 'seam' was now at the wearer's wrist where perspiration, flakes of skin and other detritus might be found. I have only seen a couple of examples of this design, so I think I can easily classify it as a failure.

→ The Hermetic should be seen as just one of many stepping stones Rolex walked on during their efforts to produce a wristwatch which was not only waterproof, but also easy to use. The main problem with it, in the eyes of Rolex, was that the design was also used by several larger competitors. Rolex wanted their own unique design, so that they could stand out from the crowd.

The next design was the 'Neo-Borgel' design. The layout was identical to the Borgel, with the movement and other parts attached to the screwed bezel. But it omitted the push-piece at 4 used to set the hands. The Borgel case had a two-position winder: the first wound the movement, the second either allowed the bezel to be unscrewed or – if the push-piece was actuated – to set the hands. This design had a three-position crown and the final position enabled the bezel to be unscrewed.

The final design pretty much got it right, except that it was remarkably inconvenient in daily use. The Hermetic protected the watch by containing the entire timepiece inside a monocoque cup-shaped case with a screwed bezel. However, this meant that to wind the watch the bezel had to be unscrewed, placed to one side, the watch swung out on its hinge and wound. Then the process had to be carried out in reverse to close the case. There was one other problem with this design: the cases were made from silver or gold, both quite soft metals where the daily unscrewing of the bezels meant that the milling would slowly wear away until it was almost gone. Once the milling had been removed it proved impossible to create a moisture-proof seal.

1925
RECTANGULAR WATCHES

Wristwatches started to move away from being shrunken pocket watches, and case and dial design began to take on much more important roles.

- **Model number: 2536**
- **Date: 1925**
- **Dial: Brass, matt silvered, raised gilt numerals**
- **Movement: Calibre HW**
- **Case material: 9ct gold**
- **Dimensions: 38mm**

Nowadays, I estimate that 90 per cent of all watches sold are essentially round. This makes sense as the dials are circular and so are most movements. This was the case when Rolex was still Wilsdorf & Davis as they were simply scaled-down versions of the pocket watch movements that manufacturers were used to producing. But simply scaling down a pocket watch movement brought problems. While most of the components in a movement are tiny, there are two vital ones where bigger is better. The winding barrel and the balance are both circular – if you place these two circles inside another circle (the case), you can see that each of the smaller circles has to measure less than half the diameter of the larger circle. In fact, in a watch movement they need to be even less than half the diameter to make space for the centre post that holds the hands.

Making both the balance wheel and the winding barrel small has detrimental effects on the performance of the watch. A tiny balance wheel has little inertia, and so is easily affected by movement and position, while a small winding barrel cannot contain enough coiled energy to keep a watch running for an acceptable length of time.

The first wristwatches were purely functional, and when World War I (see page 23) was over, style regained its place in society. Everything from architecture to women's fashions changed quickly – and watches were not left behind. Until the 1920s, most watches were circular

→ The word 'Observatory' on the dial is a clever piece of marketing by Hans Wilsdorf. By the 1920s Rolex were well known for being one of the few wristwatch firms sending their watches for chronometer testing. These tests were done at astronomical observatories, which were among the few places where super accurate clocks were used. By putting 'Observatory' on the watch it implies that the watch has been tested, but it hadn't.

or a variation of it, while some were octagonal and others were tonneau- (barrel-) shaped. The era saw the arrival of the first wristwatches that broke the mould. These were rectangular or square but used existing circular movements, which limited their design. If a watch is much longer than it is wide, but still uses a circular movement, the small seconds dial will no longer be at the bottom of the dial, but somewhere between the centre post with the hands and the base of the dial. Many early rectangular watches solved this problem by omitting the subsidiary seconds hand and dial altogether; this was not popular as the major role of this hand was not to keep track of the passing seconds, it was as an assurance that the watch was still running.

Style is an inherent component of fashion, as is change, and the introduction of shaped watches gave manufacturers and retailers the opportunity to offer the style-conscious public something new and different. Normally form follows function, as it had been with round dials and watches, but now function followed form as watch manufacturers embraced the shaped watch and began to design movements to fit them.

CHAPTER THREE

1926–1935

P. ORR & SONS
MADRAS & RANGOON
ROLEX OYSTER
SWISS
MADE

1926–1935

THE MOST IMPORTANT DECADE

The decade which saw the launch of the Prince, the Oyster and the Perpetual.

It is obvious that during this period, the Rolex Oyster was the firm's most important launch. But it was not the watch itself that changed the company's fortunes, rather how Hans Wilsdorf promoted it.

On 7 October 1927, Mercedes Gleitze was the first Englishwoman to swim the English Channel. She wore a Rolex Oyster on a subsequent Channel swim, but her relationship with the company was not restricted to this one event. In fact, she was featured in Rolex advertising and catalogues for over half a decade, as she was one of the most prominent sporting personalities of the 1920s and '30s. Like Rolex, she was an outsider, but she was also an individualist who created her own publicity and nurtured her fame carefully. As a solo record-breaking distance swimmer there was no team framework within which she could operate, no challenger swimming alongside her who she could vanquish in an equal contest, and no regular events she could compete in. As a result, she chose her challenges carefully, briefing the press herself and building the suspense as to whether she would complete the task or not.

Mercedes was a natural fit for Rolex. Not only were her many swims great publicity for the Oyster, but there was the undoubted additional advantage of the fact that she was both attractive and happy to pose in her swimsuit. This was at a time before the pin-up became common, when images of scantily dressed young women rarely appeared on the front page of newspapers. But when there was an excuse to run such an image, newspaper editors were more than happy to do so. This perhaps explains why there were more front page images of Mercedes in US newspapers than of baseball player 'Babe' Ruth, at a time when both were at the height of their careers. Ruth was a US-only phenomenon while Mercedes never swam in the US, but her image was splashed across the country's front pages. And whenever she was mentioned, Rolex would try to have an advertisement nearby.

With his sponsorship of Mercedes Gleitze, Wilsdorf realized that it was not the ability of the celebrity to break records that was important, what mattered was their ability to generate publicity and to be in the public's eye. While swimming was a great match for the Rolex Oyster, it was not inherently glamorous or heroic. And so Wilsdorf scanned the newspapers and the cinema newsreels before deciding to focus his attention on aviators. They were the astronauts of their day and regularly featured on the front pages. Plus they had major advantages over Gleitze. First, they were mostly male, and Wilsdorf still needed to get men to wear wristwatches. Second, there was an element of danger in these flights. Nowadays we treat long-distance flights as just another form of public transport, but in the late 1920s and 30s, these flyers were taking their lives in their hands, and were seen as modern adventurers. Third, most of the

← Oyster Octagon, 1928 (see page 52).

In 1927, everything slotted into place for Rolex. It had a unique product, nationwide points of sale, and national advertising in the daily newspapers which all had a widespread readership.

long-distance flights were from London to far-flung corners of the British Empire, exactly the places where Wilsdorf wanted the Rolex name to be promoted. And, finally, it is worth noting that almost all of these early aviators were from the upper classes and so made a Rolex watch seem even more aspirational.

The earliest link I have been able to find between Rolex and aviators is a 1930 advertisement for the Oyster. It mentions various sports personalities. As well as Gleitze there was the Australian cricketer Don Bradman and the Scottish swimmer Jabez Wolffe (although Rolex misspelled it Woolf). Capt. Barnard is also listed. This was Charles Barnard who flew a Fokker F.VII from Lympne (a couple of hours outside London) to Karachi (then in Imperial India) and back in eight days, covering over 16,000 km (10,000 miles) to establish a new world record.

Not long after this, advertisements appeared mentioning New Zealand-born Arthur Clouston (usually referred to as Flying Officer Clouston) and his record-breaking flights to South Africa, Australia and New Zealand. While Clouston was hardly a member of the aristocracy, he was an aspirational figure. The son of a mining engineer, he learned to fly while in his 20s and, over the years, rose to the rank of Acting Air Commodore in the Royal Air Force (RAF). Then there was Alexander Henshaw, who was also a Rolex testimonee. Henshaw was the son of a wealthy English landowner, who bought his son his first plane before he was 20. Henshaw obtained his pilot's licence shortly afterwards and began to enter air races, many of which he won. But I get the feeling that the races did not present much of a challenge to young Alex, so he decided to try his hand at long-distance flying records; aged just 27 he secured three world records for the London–Cape Town (South Africa) flight, one for each leg and another for the round trip. All of these pilots and their testimonial letters and cables were quoted in Rolex newspaper advertisements of the period as part of a campaign in which every advertisement bore the title, 'TIME FLIES' in bold capital letters. Then, there was Owen Cathcart-Jones, who had an excellent pedigree. He became an officer in the Royal Marines at the end of World War I and then joined the RAF in 1925. A daring flyer, he was renowned for both his low-level aerobatics and his long-distance flying. He was the first man ever to make a nighttime landing on an aircraft carrier. At the end of his flight to Australia, he telegraphed Rolex, congratulating them on the performance of his watch during the trip, which went from a European winter to an Antipodean summer, with every other conceivable weather pattern in between. He took several long-distance records over the years, to say nothing of other men's wives. Married six times, it is difficult to know if he made more frequent appearances in the divorce or the bankruptcy courts.

But equally important during this period was Wilsdorf's insistence that every Rolex watch must have the company name on the dial. This may seem bizarre to us now, but prior to this the majority of watches only bore the retailer's name there. Wilsdorf wanted the Rolex name on the dial because he had begun a nationwide advertising campaign, spending more than £1,000 a month (equivalent to well over £50,000 now) in national newspapers. This was one of the first nationwide advertising campaigns for any watch brand. It was no use having a brand if you did not have a nationwide advertising campaign. Otherwise, how would your prospective clients hear about your product? In 1927, everything slotted into place for Rolex. It had a unique product, nationwide points of sale, and national advertising in the daily newspapers which all had a widespread readership. Rolex was in the right place, at the right time and with the right product.

↗ This model is called the Rolex Prince Classic in 9 carat gold. The white bars framing the dial are platinum. This watch is shown on its original cushion with an advert from the period (see page 50 for more on the Rolex Prince).

1926

FIRST OYSTER

This was the watch that changed everything – Rolex could now differentiate themselves from every other watch on the market. Wilsdorf has his first celebrity ambassador.

- **Model number: No model number**
- **Date: 1926**
- **Dial: Brass, fired enamel, radium numerals**
- **Movement: 10½ Hunter**
- **Case material: 9ct gold**
- **Dimensions: 32mm**

What most people never realize is that Hans Wilsdorf, the founder of Rolex was never a watchmaker, even though he was obsessed with watches all his adult life. Rather, all his legal documents give his profession as 'merchant', someone who buys and sells. This is important to understand, because for the 50-plus years that he ran the firm it did not make watches from scratch, as it does now; it assembled them. Movements were bought from one firm, cases from another, as were dials, bracelets and all the other components. Rolex was able to take commonly made items and assemble them into something special, and this happened because Wilsdorf was excellent at spotting a gap in the market and filling it. Nowadays we would call him a marketing genius, and nothing exemplifies this genius more than the story of the Rolex Oyster.

Wilsdorf knew that the biggest problem in making a wristwatch watertight was the winding crown. In the 19th century, the pocket watches used by explorers were fitted with screw-down caps over the winding crown. This cap was attached to the body of the watch by a small chain, but the system was clumsy and necessitated a very tiny winding crown to fit under the screw cap. This design was, incidentally, reintroduced by Cartier in the 1990s with its Pasha model.

We have already discussed the Hermetic cases (see page 36) where the watch was fitted inside another screwed case, and an astute reader will have noticed that both of these were early attempts focused on protecting the crown as the most obvious point for the entry for unwanted detritus.

What was required was a method of securing the crown and making it waterproof itself, and in May 1926 fate intervened. Wilsdorf would have made it a habit to scour the entries in the Swiss patent register for anything he thought that he could use, and patent 114948, filed by two gentlemen from La Chaux-de-Fonds, Paul Perregaux and Georges Perret, certainly fitted that description. This was for a winding crown that screwed down onto a threaded tube that protruded from the case. As the crown was in the normal position and unencumbered by a cap or an extra case, it was much easier to use and therefore much more likely to achieve sales success. Wilsdorf lost no time in acquiring the patent from its owners and within months the Rolex Oyster was on the market.

→ It is common to think of the Oyster as a revolutionary watch, but I like to think of it as evolutionary. Look at the milling on the bezel, just like the black dial Rebberg on page 33. The large 'onion' crown is just like the First Calendar watch on page 25, and the dial and hands look just like the ones on the Nurse's Watch on page 35.

1927

OYSTER POCKET WATCH

This is probably the craziest watch ever made by Rolex – it is a mystery as to why they were made or who might possibly use them. But they had an interesting postscript.

- **Model number: No model number**
- **Date: 1927**
- **Dial: Brass, silvered, enamel numerals**
- **Movement: Montilier 663**
- **Case material: 9ct gold**
- **Dimensions: 47mm**

→ I think of this as the strangest watch ever produced by Rolex. Despite thinking about it for over thirty years – which is when I first encountered one – I am still unable to think of a situation in which a waterproof pocket watch would be better than a waterproof wristwatch. Or, to be honest, any conceivable use for a waterproof gold pocket watch.

Rolex's success was down to one thing – Hans Wilsdorf (see page 11). He had an uncanny ability to spot a gap in the market, real or imagined, and create a product to fill it. In many ways, he was like Steve Jobs, co-founder of Apple; neither was technically qualified, but both focused on the product's user rather than the technology inside. But even visionaries make mistakes, and Wilsdorf's albatross was the Rolex Oyster pocket watch. Launched simultaneously with the wristwatch, it is probably the least discussed product ever made by Rolex.

So, why did Rolex make it? What was the gap in the market that Wilsdorf saw?

The watch was launched in the first half of 1927, or that's what the hallmarks in every example I have seen state. By 1926, the man's wristwatch was in the ascendancy and pocket watches were seen as old-fashioned and formal. A man living in a humid climate might need a waterproof pocket watch, but humid zones are also very hot and carrying a pocket watch is best done in a waistcoat, which was not suitable attire for the tropics. More confusing is the fact that the pocket watch was evidently much more expensive than a wristwatch. All the Oyster pocket watches I have seen were made from 9-carat gold – every one of them – and there is a lot more gold in the much larger watch. But the main reason for the price difference was the movement: the wristwatch used the Aegler-built 10½''' Hunter movement. The workhorse of the Aegler output, it was proud to be industrial and robust. The pocket watch, on the other hand, used a Montilier calibre 663 16¾''' 17j movement, which was beautifully finished with many of the jewels in screwed gold chatons. It also had a micrometer regulator and a steel end piece to the escape cock. All of these signs are of a very high-quality movement, most likely costing at least four or five times that of the Aegler one.

The short and sad life of the Oyster pocket watch can be demonstrated by the fact that the 1928 catalogue gives a whole page (page 14 of the catalogue) to the Oyster wristwatch, showing both case styles and with sweep and subsidiary seconds. Pages 16 and 17 of the catalogue show fourteen different styles of pocket watch, but there is no sign of the Oyster one. It seems that the lack of demand for a waterproof pocket watch and its high cost doomed the Oyster pocket watch. Like all Oyster watches, the case number was stamped in the case; wristwatches began at 20,001, while pocket watches began at 2,000,000. I have never seen an Oyster pocket watch with a serial number higher than 2,000,4XX, leading me to believe that the total production was 500 or less. Definitely one of the rarest of all Rolex watches, but today – as in the 1920s – nobody wants them.

ROLEX
OYSTER

1928

PRINCE

The first Rolex watch with both a unique case design and a movement specially designed for accuracy. Rolex now had a flagship watch aimed at the top of the market.

- **Model number: 971**
- **Date: 1928**
- **Dial: Brass, gilt finish, black enamel numerals**
- **Movement: Calibre TS**
- **Case material: Sterling silver**
- **Dimensions: 44mm long**

Ever wondered why wristwatches are circular? Because pocket watches were almost all round and, as early wristwatches were essentially shrunken pocket watches, it made sense to copy the format. But as wristwatches became more popular wristwatch makers began to question the logic of following the old ways and began to experiment. And Rolex was not going to be left out of this new trend. In August 1926, Aegler filed the patent documents for the design of a new movement that was almost twice as long as it was wide – 32.7 x 16.9mm. It allowed the components to be arranged in an unusual layout: the mainspring and winding barrel were at one end and took up almost the entire width, while the balance wheel and escapement were at the opposite end. There were several advantages to having both items oversized: a large, heavy balance wheel was the best way to guarantee accuracy, and a giant mainspring meant that at a time when you expected to wind your watch every day, the watch had an advertised autonomy of 56 hours.

But it was not just the movement that was unusual. At the time, almost all watches had a standard dial layout: the hour and minute hands were on a post in the centre of the dial and a small constantly running seconds hand was at the 6 position. The purpose of this tiny hand was not to measure the time elapsed in seconds – it was much too small for that purpose and in the 1920s if you needed to time something to the second you used a pocket watch-sized chronograph. No, the principal job of the little hand – known in French as *trotteur*, or trotter in English – was to reassure you that your watch was still running. But Rolex and Aegler wanted to show off the accurate movement they had developed and so the dial had a radical design – it was essentially split in half horizontally. The top half showed the hours and minutes while the seconds were displayed in their own sub dial which occupied almost as much acreage as the hours and minutes. This was a wristwatch that could be used to time things to the second, and it resulted in the Prince – the name Wilsdorf bestowed on the watch – becoming known as the Doctors' Watch.

A watch with such a radical movement and dial layout deserved an unconventional case, and it got one. It was possible to purchase a Rolex Prince with a simple rectangular case, called the Classic – the majority were cased in the newly designed Brancard case (this was the French word for stretcher). It consisted of a simple rectangle for the movement and dial with two long poles on each side of the case to form the lugs. These poles were shaped so that they were narrow at the centre of the watch and flared out as they reached the top and bottom. It was a radical, sensuous – almost voluptuous – shape, unlike anything on the market at the time.

→ The outstanding feature of the Rolex Prince is the uniquely shaped case. These were made in Geneva by a number of specialist case-making firms, principally Robert Meylan and Genex. What I find interesting is that both firms eventually ended up being owned by Rolex Geneva.

1928

OYSTER OCTAGON

By offering two different Oyster case designs, Wilsdorf increased his chances of making a sale. With different dial options and sweep or subsidiary seconds layouts, Rolex spoiled you for choice.

- **Model number: No model number**
- **Date: 1928**
- **Dial: Brass, fired enamel, Arabic numerals**
- **Movement: 10½ Hunter**
- **Case material: 9ct gold**
- **Dimensions: 32mm**

On pages 50–1, I give the accepted history of the case. However, more recent research brings this account into question. David Boettcher's article in the December 2010 issue of the National Association of Watch & Clock Collectors Bulletin stated that the patent was transferred from Perregaux & Perret to Charles-Rodolphe Spillmann, who owned a case-making firm in La Chaux-de-Fonds, Switzerland, on 19 July 1926. Then, five days later, it was transferred from Spillmann to Wilsdorf personally, interestingly not to Rolex. Another five days later, on 29 July, Wilsdorf registered the trademark 'Oyster' and the package was complete; the case, crown and name were all in place.

However, Spillmann was much more than an intermediary used by Wilsdorf to conceal his interest in the patent. I think that Spillmann took the Perregaux & Perret patent to Wilsdorf and explained to him that combining this crown with a variation of the three-piece cases that Wilsdorf and he knew about would result in the world's first waterproof watch. While I have no proof for this theory, inside the case back of all these watches you will see a small hammerhead at the bottom. This is a Swiss case maker's stamp, and inside it is the number 136, which indicates that C R Spillmann & Cie of La Chaux-de-Fonds made the case. This mark can be found inside almost all early gold Rolex Oyster cases indicating that this single maker was responsible for them all.

The most common shape of the case is known as a Cushion and was used by Rolex and others from the second decade of the 20th century. Rolex continued to use it until the end of World War II. The Oyster was also launched in an alternative case style, the Octagon, shown here, which was never as popular as the Cushion and lasted less than a decade in the firm's catalogue.

The design of the case is interesting, as the movement is not attached directly to the case body. Instead, the case is composed of three parts: a central case body to which the lugs are attached, and a separate screw-on bezel and case back. The movement, dial and hands are held in a metal ring with external screwed threads, and the ring has a hole at the 3 position and a pin at the 9 position. The ring is inserted into the case body and the pin at 9 fits into a corresponding hole in the case body. The crown and winding stem are then fitted into the hole at 3 and the bezel and case back are screwed into place.

At this time Rolex's advertising emphasized that it did not use cork or leather gaskets in its watches, stating that it used metal-to-metal contact. While this was true, it did use a gasket inside the case back and under the bezel to ensure a perfect seal. But these were made from a thin circle of lead, which when screwed down moulded to accommodate any irregularities in the machined surface of the case back. The gasket could only be used once, but it was the secret weapon which contributed to the success of the Oyster as it ensured that the case was watertight. Most previous gaskets were made from oiled leather or heavily greased string. When these dried out, the gaskets were no longer effective, so potential clients were wary of any system using gaskets, which is why Wilsdorf made the claim he did.

← Look at the two watches on the left and you will see two different placements for the words 'Rolex Oyster' – the one on the far left has it written above the seconds and space for the retailer's name at the top. The layout seen on the black dial watch was for retailers who weren't prepared to order in a large enough quantity to have their name on the dial.

ROLEX CHRONOMETERS confor
with this Official definition.
ROLEX OYSTER Imperial
CHRONOMETER. 18 Rubies
No. 105 Stainless Steel
,, 106 9ct. Gold
,, 107 With large centre
seconds hand
ROLEX OYSTER
Royal
15 Rubies jewelled
a very flat and elegant model
No. 109 STAINLESS STEEL
,, 110 9ct. Gold Cambree
shape
ROLEX OYSTER Aviator
15 Rubies jewelled
No. 108. 9ct Gold STRONG CASE
BLACK DIAL with markings
and hand of
Admiralty Grade luminosity
Centre seconds hand
specially suitable
for Airmen
ROLEX OYSTER
Small Models for Ladies
15 rubies jewelled
The ideal watch for all women
WATERPROOF—DUSTPROOF
POWDERPROOF
ROLEX OYSTER
Duchess
Strong sporting and everyday
watch with leather straps
No. 119 Stainless Steel

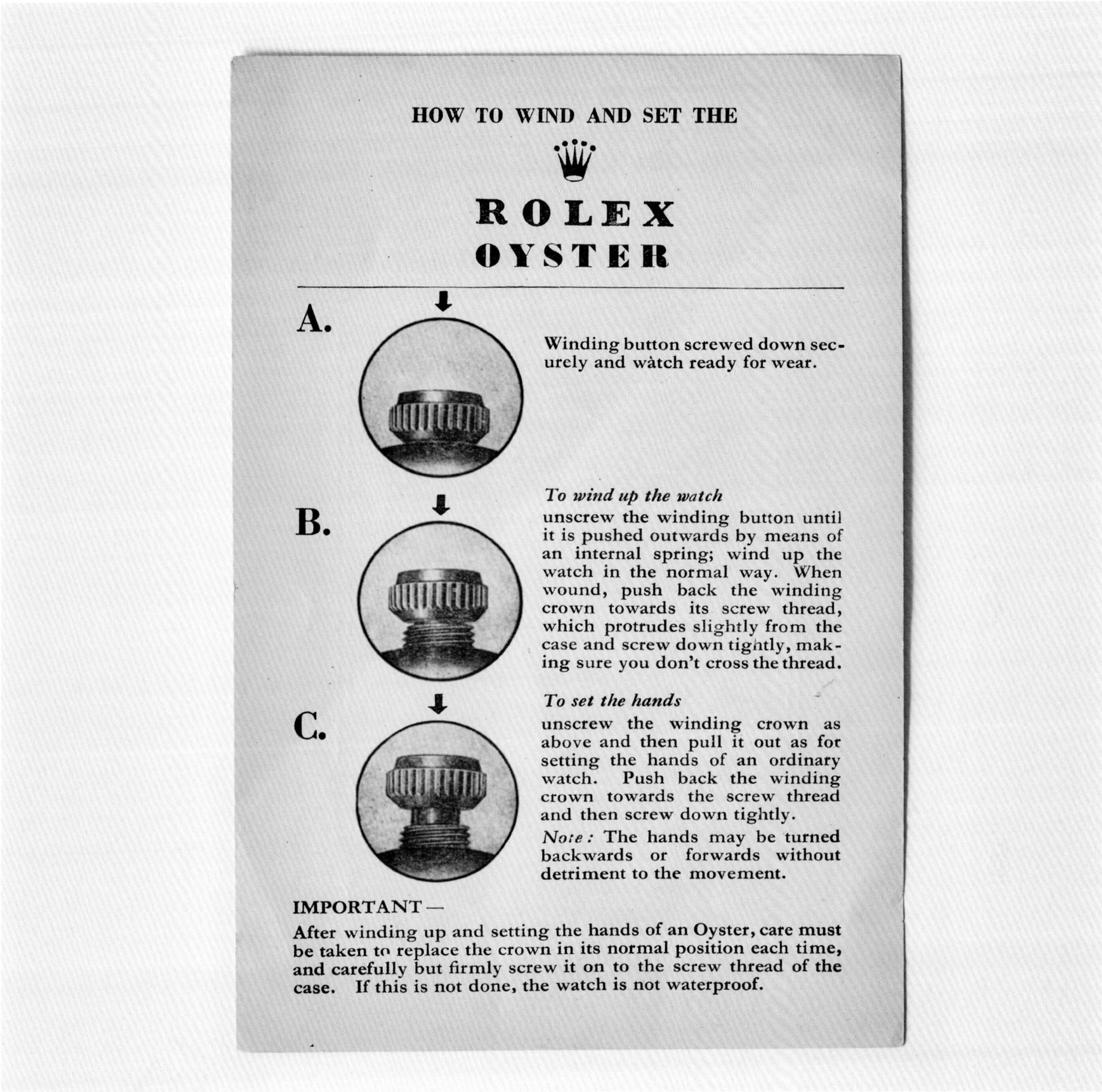

HOW TO WIND AND SET THE

ROLEX
OYSTER

A.

Winding button screwed down securely and watch ready for wear.

B.

To wind up the watch
unscrew the winding button until it is pushed outwards by means of an internal spring; wind up the watch in the normal way. When wound, push back the winding crown towards its screw thread, which protrudes slightly from the case and screw down tightly, making sure you don't cross the thread.

C.

To set the hands
unscrew the winding crown as above and then pull it out as for setting the hands of an ordinary watch. Push back the winding crown towards the screw thread and then screw down tightly.
Note: The hands may be turned backwards or forwards without detriment to the movement.

IMPORTANT —
After winding up and setting the hands of an Oyster, care must be taken to replace the crown in its normal position each time, and carefully but firmly screw it on to the screw thread of the case. If this is not done, the watch is not waterproof.

← A page from a 1934 Rolex sales brochure, showing three different case styles for the Rolex Oyster and two smaller versions for ladies.

↑ A 1935 instruction leaflet provided with a new Rolex Oyster. This gave the client detailed instructions on screwing the crown, unscrewing the crown, setting the time and winding the watch.

1934

FIRST BUBBLEBACK

The watch that originated Rolex case design language for the next 90 years, and which changed wristwatch movement design for ever.

- **Model number: 1858**
- **Date: 1934**
- **Dial: Brass**
- **Movement: Calibre 520**
- **Case material: Stainless steel, yellow gold**
- **Dimensions: 32mm**

Developed in 1931 and introduced in 1934, the first Rolex Oyster Perpetual movements were basic manual wind 8¾''' Hunter movements with a frame bolted onto the back of the main plate. Inside the frame were a couple of gear wheels that were linked to a gear which sat directly above the winding spring barrel. The semi-circular rotor was attached to the frame by a centrally mounted pivot. There was another gear on this pivot and it meshed with the other gears. As the inherently unstable rotor swung around its axis, the rotation of the gears on the pivot was transmitted to the winding spring. Although it only wound the mainspring while moving in one direction, the fact that the heavy rotor was almost always in motion meant that the owner had to wear the watch for just six hours a day to provide the mainspring with sufficient power to run it for 24 hours.

The adaptation of the manual movement into an automatic one was a design by Emil Borer (see page 68), who was Hermann Aegler's nephew and the firm's technical director. His brilliant idea was not only to adapt an existing movement, but also to make the automatic winding mechanism a module that was held on to the base movement by just two screws. To make things even easier for the watch repairer, instructions for removing the module were engraved (in both English and French) on the body of the automatic mechanism itself.

The first problem to arise with the new Perpetual was that it proved to be too efficient, getting to a fully wound state much faster than Borer and Aegler had imagined. Because the watch was based on an unmodified manual 8¾''' Hunter movement, the winding mechanism continued to try to wind the watch when it was fully wound, putting extra strain on the mainspring. This was solved by fitting a clutch between the rotor and the winding gears. These first Perpetuals are easy to recognize. If you wind them using the crown, the crown will cease rotating any further once the mainspring is fully wound.

By making the winding system a module which sat on top of the basic manual movement, Borer solved the problem which had dogged previous attempts to make an automatic wristwatch; they were incapable of being hand-wound. Every previous self-winding wristwatch, from the Harwood to the Wig-Wag to the Rolls, had no facility for manually winding the watch. This raised two questions in the minds of prospective buyers. The first was 'How do I know the watch is actually running?' This was relevant because several early automatic watches lacked a seconds hand which would show that the movement was working. And the second was 'What do I do when the watch stops?' The only solution was to shake the watch vigorously to impart some motion to the balance wheel and the movement to transfer energy to the mainspring. The new Perpetual movement was so efficient that it rarely (if ever) needed winding if worn constantly, but the fact that it could be hand-wound gave owners much-needed reassurance.

The sales success of the first Perpetuals was aided greatly by the fact that Rolex was an established firm with widespread distribution. All the other firms which had previously introduced automatic watches were newcomers to the market and so not only had to persuade customers to purchase the watches but overcome the much greater hurdle of convincing jewellers to stock an untried brand.

The clutch on the winding mechanism was only the first of many Rolex and Aegler innovations to be made over the next few years. Developments in the manual Hunter movements were almost immediately fitted to the Perpetual. This was followed by a new aerodynamic Superbalance wheel. Advances in machining allowed for the mass-production of chronometer-grade movements, which were fitted with additional jewels (often in chatons)

↑ The watch that genuinely changed Rolex; what was special about it was that it wasn't special. It was a watch you strapped on your wrist and forgot about. It asked nothing from the wearer, was autonomous and looked just like every other wristwatch in the store. All other early automatic watches looked different, as if they were making a statement, but not the Bubbleback – it just sat on your wrist, unobtrusively, and did its job.

and micrometre adjustments for the regulation. But the most visible change was the attempt to reduce the height of the watch. The edge of the rotor was machined with double angles to allow the case back to be domed rather than flat (hence the name, 'Bubbleback') and this immediately made the watch sit lower on the wrist.

1935

EARLY CHRONOGRAPHS

As Rolex focused on the Oyster and the Perpetual, Wilsdorf saw chronographs as a diversion from the company's goals and so initially put little effort into them.

- **Model number: 3484**
- **Date: 1935**
- **Dial: Brass, gilt finish, radium numerals**
- **Movement: Valjoux 22, signed Rolex**
- **Case material: 18ct gold**
- **Dimensions: 35mm**

→ Nowadays, when we think of Rolex, the Daytona is one of the first models which comes to mind. But back in the 1930s, chronographs were among the last things Hans Wilsdorf was thinking about. I get the feeling that he almost had to be dragged – kicking and screaming – into producing them. These early ones show very little imagination or creativity, they simply exist.

Chronographs were irrelevant to Hans Wilsdorf (see page 11). He ignored them for the first 30 years of the company's existence, but by the mid-1930s he was forced to notice them. In 1936 the firm introduced five chronographs – four wristwatches and a pocket watch. Rolex was forced into this launch by the popularity of its competitors' wrist chronographs, particularly Longines and Breitling. Longines introduced its first wrist chronograph movement, the 13.33Z, in 1913, and its first watches not long after, while Breitling launched its first wrist chronograph in 1915.

The competition had a 20-year start on Rolex, but if clients were asking for chronographs, Wilsdorf was not going to let them go elsewhere. Looking at the five launch models, it is interesting to note how old-fashioned they were. For example, only one of them had the twin pusher configuration we take for granted nowadays. The remainder used the old single pusher in the winding crown layout, which was nowhere near as convenient as the more modern layout.

It is easy to understand why Wilsdorf had no interest in chronographs. They were not waterproof, nor were they self-winding, and they could not be regulated to chronometer standards – the three pillars on which Wilsdorf was building the Rolex brand.

But Wilsdorf was, above everything else, a merchant, the profession he listed on every legal document he ever signed. In simple terms, he bought stuff and he sold the same stuff for a profit. It is important to remember that Rolex did not make the movements, cases or dials. It bought all the components it required from suppliers and added value by assembling them into watches and advertising them worldwide. So if people demanded chronographs, and there was money to be made from them, Wilsdorf wanted some of it.

Because Rolex did not make any of the components, it was easy to produce these new watches. Valjoux was happy to supply its calibre 22 and 23 movements – as used by Breitling and many others – and the usual suspects provided the cases, dials and hands. But, judging by the small number of the early chronographs which have surfaced, it seems that they were not very popular. As the movements could not really be changed, Rolex played with the only external component that it could change, the case. Over the next few years it introduced watches with flexible lugs, teardrop lugs, coin-edged cases and even fan-shaped hidden lugs. None of this seems to have made a difference. Rolex chronographs from this period are rare, and because they do not have Oyster cases to keep out dust and moisture, the dials and movements are usually not in the best condition.

BASE 60 1000M
ROLEX
SWISS
MADE

CHAPTER FOUR

1936–1945

ROLEX OYSTER
PERPETUAL
VERGA
CHRONOMETRE
SWISS MADE

1936–1945

COMMERCE AND CONFLICT

The German occupation of Europe forced Rolex into finding new international markets, bringing them to the United States for the first time.

The outbreak of World War II in 1939 had a profound impact on Rolex. Wilsdorf was born in Germany but had left his homeland at 19 and never returned. He moved to Switzerland and then London before returning to Switzerland. By the time war broke out, the 58-year-old had spent two-thirds of his life outside Germany. Although like Switzerland Wilsdorf could have remained neutral, he chose to align himself with Great Britain, the country whose nationality he had adopted 28 years before.

Rolex had primarily focused on Britain, its Empire and continental Europe. However, within a year of the outbreak of the war, Switzerland was nearly surrounded by German-occupied nations, making exports to Britain and its Empire virtually impossible. France, another significant prewar market, was now occupied and its citizens were more concerned with survival than luxury watches. Despite these challenges, two neutral countries – Spain and Portugal – offered a glimmer of hope. Although both nations were led by Axis-leaning dictators, they allowed Swiss firms to ship products to their ports, from where neutral-flagged vessels could transport goods globally. However, Nazi submarines targeted ships bound for combatant nations, making it risky to transport goods to British outposts. As a result, Rolex shifted its focus to the United States and Latin America, the only accessible markets.

Before the war, Rolex had avoided the US market due to an agreement with the Gruen family. Gruen, which manufactured movements in Bienne, Switzerland, shared the ownership of the Aegler factory with Rolex. Both companies sold nearly identical watches – Gruen's Techni-Quadron and Rolex's Prince. While there is no written evidence, it is believed that the two firms agreed to divide markets: Gruen would focus on the US, while Rolex would concentrate on the British Empire and Europe. The partnership dissolved when Gruen relinquished its shares in Aegler, freeing Rolex to enter the American market. However, Rolex lacked infrastructure there, and an earlier distribution deal with Abercrombie & Fitch had failed. But with its primary markets closed, Rolex had little to lose by establishing a US operation.

Rolex had a flourishing operation in Canada, meaning that they were not exactly newcomers to the North American market. But the US was different; this was the first time that Rolex had attempted to enter a country with a flourishing wristwatch industry of its own. The wristwatch had gained mass acceptance in the US much sooner than in Europe. Americans were more accepting of new ideas and the wristwatch was new and fashionable, and US manufacturers regularly introduced new case styles – such as deco and streamline – to reflect current trends.

American manufacturers had a crucial advantage over Swiss ones. As in

← Bubbleback, 1938 (see page 68).

In Europe, Rolex became popular among Allied pilots [...] These pilots adopted British traditions, including wearing Rolex Oyster watches.

Switzerland, most watch companies only made the movements and bought cases, dials and other components from outside suppliers. And American case-making companies were expert at producing complex gold-filled cases. These were made of a base material, usually brass or steel, with sheets of solid gold formed over the top and bottom. They have the same appearance as solid gold, are much more resistant to wear than gold plate, but are much less expensive than solid gold. These watches were stylish, fashionable and comparatively inexpensive, meaning that they would be replaced much more frequently. This in turn kept production numbers high and unit costs low.

Swiss companies also had to contend with the fact that the US watch industry had persuaded the US government to impose duties on imported watches, and the highest duties were on watches with 18 jewels or more. Additional duties were charged on adjustments for timing and temperature. In other words, in an attempt to keep them out of the US market the duties were aimed directly at high-end Swiss watches.

Transporting watches from Switzerland to the US during wartime was complex but feasible. Trains carried goods through neutral Vichy France to Spain or Portugal, where neutral ships transported them to Central and South America. From there, the watches were easily shipped to the US. This route became heavily utilized as American watch manufacturers shifted production to military equipment. Companies including Elgin, Hamilton and Waltham shifted to manufacturing marine chronometers, bomb fuses and aircraft instruments. This left the civilian market wide open for Swiss imports, which dominated despite logistical challenges and high tariffs. Despite wartime tariffs, Swiss watch imports surged. With full employment and rising wages, Americans had more disposable income but fewer goods to purchase due to rationing. Watches became popular gifts for engagements and weddings, further driving demand. By 1945, the US had imported 30 million Swiss watches or movements.

I mentioned earlier that watches destined for the US initially went to South America; but not all of them immediately left for the US – a large proportion stayed there. Like the US, South America prospered during the war from its role as a major supplier of raw materials to the Allies. Before and during World War II, Argentina was one of the richest nations in the world. In the inter-war period, Parisians would say that someone was as 'Rich as an Argentinian', and by the end of the war the country was running such a trade surplus that it redeemed its entire national debt. And so Rolex established its first Latin American office in Argentina's capital, Buenos Aires, well before World War II began, and its expansion throughout Latin America started. Some of the most desirable 'Double Name' Rolex watches bear the names of Latin American retailers. Serpico y Liano in Caracas, Venezuela, and Joyeria Rivera in Havana, Cuba, were just two of the fabled names which sold Rolex watches before and during the years of conflict.

In Europe, Rolex became popular among Allied pilots. The Royal Air Force (RAF) formed three squadrons—71st, 121st and 133rd—composed of American volunteers who had joined the fight against the Nazis. These pilots adopted British traditions, including wearing Rolex Oyster watches. Although the RAF issued standard models, many pilots purchased Oysters with their own money, viewing them as a symbol of their connection to aviation pioneers. One such American pilot was Chuck Yeager, a 32-year-old captain who wore a manual-wind Rolex Oyster during his service. After the war, Yeager joined the US Air Force's Flight Test Division at Wright Field, Ohio, and wore the same watch when he piloted the Bell X-1 rocket plane to break the sound barrier in 1947.

The war also influenced watch design. At the start of the conflict, British Army-issued watches measured 31–32mm in diameter. By 1945, British-issued Waterproof Wrist Watches (WWW) had grown to 35–37mm. Rolex, attuned to market trends, followed suit. In 1945, the company introduced the Calibre 720, a 10½''' Perpetual movement, which later powered the iconic Datejust – a watch that would redefine Rolex's legacy.

↑ Rolex model 3525 Monobloco. This was the most often requested model by British and Commonwealth officers in German prisoner-of-war camps.

1938

BOY'S OYSTER

Moving on from the Cushion and Octagon Oysters, Rolex developed a new design for their most popular models, with the movements remaining the same.

- **Model number: 2765**
- **Date: 1938**
- **Dial: Brass, silvered, Arabic numerals**
- **Movement: 10½ Hunter**
- **Case material: Stainless steel**
- **Dimensions: 31mm**

I wrote in the previous chapter about how the first Bubbleback movements (see page 56) were modifications of existing Aegler movements (see page 16). But what is not so widely known is that the cases for these first models were modifications of existing ones. By the mid-1930s, the original three-piece cushion Oyster case (see page 52) had all but disappeared, replaced by a model nowadays known as the Viceroy (see inset). This had a flat-topped tonneau-shaped case surmounted by a round bezel. The bezel was fixed in place, and there was a screwed case back to allow access to the movement. These watches were available in a variety of materials: steel, a steel case with a gold bezel and crown, or all gold. I believe that these were the first Rolex models to be available in a mixture of steel and gold. Rolex had produced two-tone watches previously, but these were made from different colours of gold.

Stainless steel was invented just before the start of World War I, to solve the problem of naval gun barrels wearing out after only a few hundred rounds being fired. This resulted in a lack of accuracy that was deadly for a warship. Replacements could take weeks, so the search was on for corrosion-resistant steel. But the start of the conflict put further research and development on hold while all efforts went towards winning the war. Thus, it was not until the early 1920s that stainless steel first hit the market, and not as gun barrels but as knives and forks. Medical instrument makers also picked up on the new material, as it was resistant to corrosion and kept a sharp edge even after high-temperature sterilization. The finest medical instruments came from Switzerland, which in turn influenced the use of stainless steel in Swiss wristwatches. Stainless steel's resistance to corrosion also made it ideal for inexpensive wristwatch cases. The non-noble metals such as nickel or gunmetal used previously for watch cases corroded quickly when exposed to perspiration. A 1937 Rolex advertisement describes the new case material as 'of the appearance of platinum and will not discolour. The steel used with gold gives a very distinguished appearance to the case.'

→ Hans Wilsdorf became a British citizen in 1911 and remained one until his death. He was a British patriot and a fan of the royal family, as can be seen by the names of Rolex models from this time. The Prince was followed by the Viceroy, the Oyster Imperial, the Oyster Princess, the Oyster Duchess, the Oyster Royal and the Oyster King Chronometer. It was the latter watch, a tonneau shape like the Viceroy but with the smooth bezel reaching to the edges of the case, which became the base for the Bubbleback. As the King Chronometer was wound manually, it had a flat screwed back. To accommodate the rotor and the winding gears, the flat back was replaced with a deeply domed one, giving the new watch its nickname.

ROLEX OYSTER
SPEED
EXTRA PRECISION
SWISS MADE

1938

BUBBLEBACK

Aesthetics take hold at Rolex as new case and dial designs for the Bubbleback are introduced. The first Bubblebacks go for chronometer testing.

- **Model number: 3372**
- **Date: 1938**
- **Dial: Brass**
- **Movement: Calibre 620**
- **Case material: Pink gold**
- **Dimensions: 32mm**

It is easy to see the introduction of the Rolex Perpetual movement (see page 56) as a radical move. However, it was simply another step in Rolex's gradual evolution. After all, the first perpetual movement was simply a self-winding module bolted onto the back of an otherwise standard 8¾''' Hunter subsidiary seconds movement. This movement was a scaled-down version of the most popular Rolex movement, the 10½''' Hunter. The name 'Hunter' comes from pocket watch terminology: a Hunter pocket watch had a sprung hinged cover over the dial and glass to protect them when the wearer was riding on horseback. This was released by pressing a button in the middle of the winding crown and was usually activated by the thumb of the right hand while the watch was being held in that hand. To ensure that the dial was in the correct position to be read when the cover was opened, the winding crown was at the 3 position. Conventional wristwatch movements followed this setup, with a winding crown at 3 and the subsidiary seconds at 6. They are known as Hunter movements.

The adaptation of the basic movement into an automatic one was designed by Emil Borer, who was Hermann Aegler's nephew and the technical director of the firm. His brilliant idea was not only to adapt an existing movement, but also to make the automatic winding a module held onto the base movement by just two screws. To make things even easier for the watch repairer, instructions for removing the module were engraved (in English and French) on the body of the automatic mechanism itself.

The first problem to arise with the new Perpetual was that it proved to be too efficient, getting to a fully wound state much quicker than Borer and Aegler had thought. And, because the watch was based on an unmodified manual 8¾''' Hunter movement, this meant that the winding mechanism would continue to try to wind the watch when it was already fully wound, putting an extra strain on the mainspring. This was solved by fitting a clutch between the rotor and the winding gears. These first Perpetuals are easily distinguished by the fact that when you wind them using the crown, the crown will cease rotating any further once the mainspring is fully wound.

→ This watch is a symphony in pink. The blued steel hands are the only components which are not pink; the dial, the case and the bracelet are all resplendent in the colour. This is a model 3372 with a flat bezel with stamped hour markers and finely milled concentric lines. It was retailed by the now closed Verga store in Rome, who have nothing to do with the current Verga Milan.

ROLEX OYSTER
PERPETUAL
VERGA
CHRONOMÈTRE
SWISS MADE

The ROLEX OYSTER PERPETUAL CHRONOMETER

No. 100 Stainless Steel
,, 101 9ct. gold heavy case
,, 102 18ct. ,, ,, ,,
,, 103 With large centre seconds hand.
Also made in smaller sizes

THE ROLEX OYSTER PERPETUAL

(Self-Winding)

is a true Chronometer, registering precise time within the narrow limits laid down by the rules of Swiss Government Testing Stations, in all conceivable positions and in extremes of climates.

An official Certificate giving the daily variations during a 14 days trial in 5 positions and extreme temperatures is supplied with every watch.

Unless the quality of every component part of the movement is of the very finest, as well as the workmanship throughout, it will fail to pass this extended official test. The Certificate is therefore a valuable and impartial guarantee of lasting quality. THE ROLEX PERPETUAL movement is jewelled in 18 finely polished red rubies, ensuring all pivots running almost without friction. Epicycloidically shaped teeth of wheels enable the same to engage and disengage freely.

The mainspring itself is made of the best tempered steel and an infallible tension and elasticity test carried out with Rolex Patent machines, guarantees its immunity against breakage under stress and temperatures.

The power carried evenly from source by teeth and pinions to the escapement, is effectually absorbed by the Balance or fly-wheel.

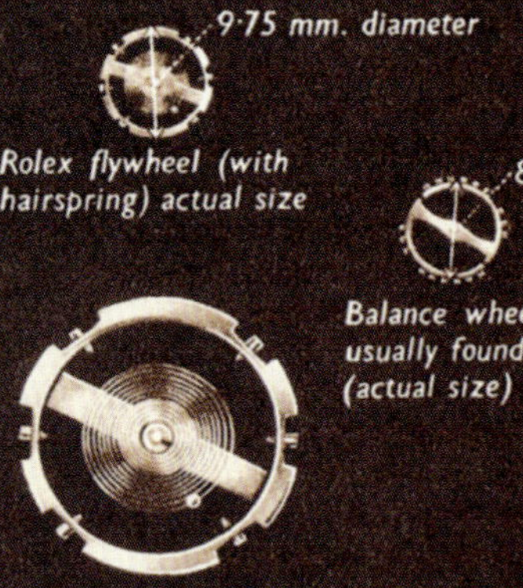

AERO-DYNAMIC SUPER-BALANCE.
PATENTED IN ALL COUNTRIES

The ROLEX PERPETUAL is fitted with a fly-wheel or balance wheel of great ingenuity. It is made of one solid piece of non-magnetic metal, with six recesses in its rim for regulation screws, instead of being made of delicately poised metal rims of brass and steel, which bend so easily! The great advantage of this solid balance is, easy replacement of the staff, namely of that part which breaks when you drop your watch. The rim of the balance wheel not being studded with screws, as all other balances are, a much larger diameter is obtained which assures a much more powerful swinging motion, therefore greater accuracy—especially on the wrist.

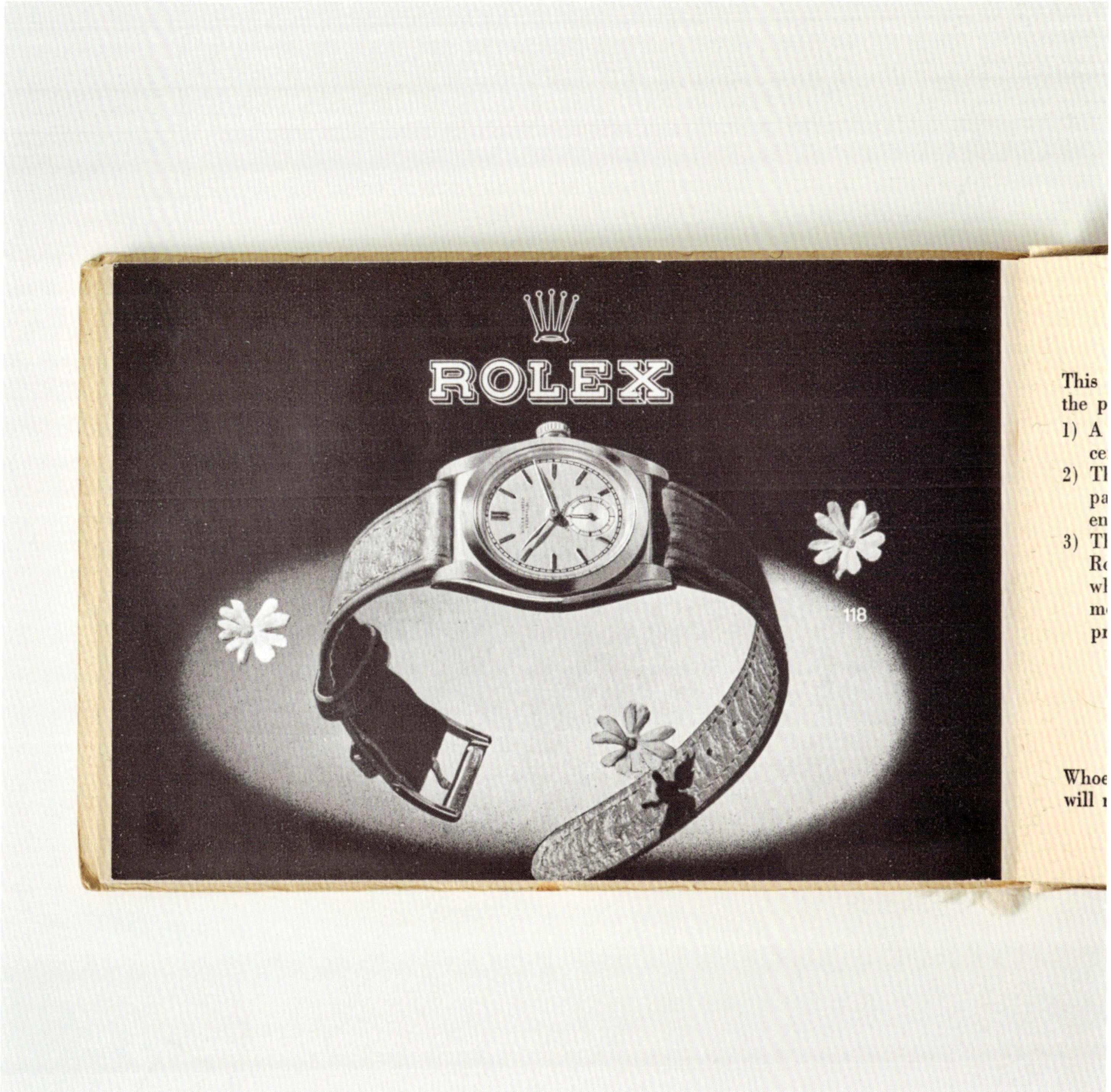

←↑ Another page from the 1934 Rolex brochure (left). This full page extols the benefits of the newly launched Oyster Pertpetual, or Bubbleback. It's interesting that the basic movement is shown with the automatic module removed. Above is a 1936 Canadian brochure also showing the first model of the Bubbleback. The watches shown in both brochures differ only by the style of numbers on the dials.

1940

PANERAI

Rolex finally finds a role for the Oyster Pocket Watch as Italian Navy divers perform the world's first underwater frogmen attacks using midget submarines.

- **Model number: 3646**
- **Date: 1940**
- **Dial: Brass dial, matt black, radium numerals**
- **Movement: Rolex/Cortebert calibre 618**
- **Case material: Stainless steel**
- **Dimensions: 46.5mm diameter**

Rolex does not make a lot of mistakes, but in the late 1920s it really messed up, and the firm's attempt to correct the error led to the Panerai watch you see here. You might well ask, what is a Panerai watch doing here? The answer is simple: for the first couple of decades of their existence, all Panerai watches were made by Rolex.

In 1926–27, Rolex launched the Oyster wristwatch (see page 46), the watch that had a bigger impact on the watch industry than anything that preceded it. But what is almost completely unknown is that the Oyster wristwatch was launched simultaneously with what was, undoubtedly, Rolex's biggest commercial failure to date: the Rolex Oyster pocket watch (see page 48). It did not take long for the company to realize that the pocket watch was a commercial disaster, but Wilsdorf was not going to let the watches go to waste. He removed the attachments for the watch chain and the dials, rotated the watch 90 degrees clockwise, attached a new dial with the subsidiary seconds now at the 9 position, and finished them with wide wire strap attachments soldered at the 12 and 6 positions. These revised models entered the 1934 catalogue as Oyster wristwatches, reference 2533.

Meanwhile the Panerai family in Florence was running two businesses: Orologeria Svizzera, a prestigious watch retailer in the shadow of the Duomo, and G. Panerai & Figlio which made instruments for the Regia Marina, the Italian Royal Navy. The Regia Marina was the first navy in the world to use free divers in an offensive capacity; however, for the divers to operate in teams they needed a watch in order to co-ordinate their actions. Since the introduction of the Rolex Oyster, several other firms had introduced watches which were notionally waterproof, but all were too small to be read underwater in the dark in treacherous conditions. But when Giuseppe Panerai saw the 1934 Rolex catalogue – Orologeria Svizzera was a Rolex agent – he realized that this could be the answer to the Regia Marina's requirements.

On 24 October 1935, Rolex sent a package containing one of the new reference 2533 watches to Florence. Like the original pocket watch it sprang from, it was made from 9-carat gold and equipped with a 16¾''' movement from Montilier, a high quality movement with 17 jewels, most of them in screwed chatons. It also had a snail-shell micrometer regulator and a Breguet overcoil blued hairspring. They were timed to six positions at all temperatures (although the watches were only tested at three temperatures).

The watch was extensively tested by the Regia Marina and must have passed these tests, because on the 20 December 1938 Orologia Svizzera submitted another order to Rolex, this time for 15 of the reference 2533 watches incorporating a number of changes. The order was for steel watches fitted with dials supplied by Panerai, but the most important feature is stated on an invoice from 7 March 1939: 'Oyster acier spéciales pour scaphandriers', meaning 'Oyster, steel, specially for divers'. These early Panerai watches, made completely by Rolex, are the first true divers' watches ever made.

The second invoice from Rolex stated that the dials were supplied by Panerai, which had developed a method of dial construction for its instrument gauges. These dials were made from two brass discs – the lower one was thickly coated

with a radium and phosphor paste and the upper one had the outlines of the quarter hour numerals and bars for the remaining hours punched out so that the luminous material shone through the apertures. The thicker the paste was applied, the brighter it shone, and this method allowed a much thicker paste layer to be applied to the dial than if it had been painted on in the conventional manner. As these watches were to be used underwater, Panerai wanted an even brighter luminosity. So, instead of a brass top disc, it used celluloid, probably on the assumption that the luminosity would shine through it. However radium generates heat as well as light and the celluloid warped, which stopped the hands from rotating, so the dial on almost every one of these early Panerai watches has been replaced.

→ The first diver's watch was made by Rolex for the Panerai family business in Florence. The shape of the case resembles that of the classic Oyster (see page 46), but expanded to 50mm.

← The inside of the case and the movement are stamped with the Rolex name.

1941

ZEROGRAPH

The most spectacular dead-end from Rolex; their first in-house chronograph movement and their first watch with a rotating timing bezel, yet it went absolutely nowhere. One of the great 'might have been' watches.

- **Model number: 3346**
- **Date: 1941**
- **Dial: Brass, silvered, radium Roman/Arabic numerals**
- **Movement: 10½ ligne Hunter, modified**
- **Case material: Stainless steel**
- **Dimensions: 32mm**

→ The Zerograph(e) was produced in tiny quantities during World War II, yet despite the miniscule production numbers – less than 25 have ever appeared – it appeared with three different names. Zerograph and Zerographe were most probably destined for Anglophone and Francophone markets, but what are we to make of those ones signed 'Centregraph'? Destined for those living in the middle?

The Rolex Zerograph or Zerographe – the optional 'e' at the end of the name seems to denote whether or not the piece was sold in the Anglophone sphere of influence – was the watch that could have changed everything for Rolex. It used the company's first in-house chronograph movement and its first rotating timing bezel. The Zerograph, launched in the midst of World War II, predated the 4130-powered Daytona by 60 years and the Turn-O-Graph by almost 15 years.

The movement, case and dial are all masterpieces in their own right, but I think that the movement is the undoubted star. Aegler took the regular 10½''' Hunter movement and added new parts – a couple under the dial and four or five on the visible side – to convert the basic subsidiary seconds movement into a flyback Chronostop one. The sweep seconds hand is the continuously running type until the button at 2 is pushed; this causes it to return to the 12 position, and it remains there for as long as the button is held. As soon as the button is released the seconds hand starts moving again. This feature has a dual use, it can either be used to synchronize the seconds hand with a time signal, or it can be used as a chronograph in conjunction with the rotating bezel. To use it as a chronograph, the bezel is rotated so that the 0 is aligned with the minute hand, enabling the watch to measure events lasting up to one hour.

The case is the standard 32mm boy's-size Oyster with the addition of the push-piece at 2 and the unique rotating bezel marked from 5 to 55 with double red bars at 60. The bezel rotates in either direction and, unlike the only other contemporary wristwatch with a rotating bezel, the Longines Weems, it does not have a locking device to hold it in position. Weems pattern watches were made by other manufacturers for the British Royal Air Force during World War II, but I believe that Longines were the originators of the style.

Most Zerographs appear to have been fitted with the Roman/Arabic dial – Rolex referred to this style as the error-proof dial. They were considerably thicker than other dials and the numerals, Roman for the 10, 11, 1 and 2 and Arabic for the 4, 5, 7 and 8; 12 was designated by an inverted triangle while the other quarter-hour indices were horizontal bars. But the defining feature was that these indices were stamped deep into the dial's surface before being filled with the radium paint. This allowed much greater quantities of luminous material to be applied, making the dial and hands much more visible in the dark.

ROLEX

1942

BUBBLEBACK

Gradual evolution takes root at Rolex as the Bubbleback gains a metal bracelet and the case design evolves, as does the movement inside.

- **Model number: 5010**
- **Date: 1942**
- **Dial: Brass, matt white finish, full Arabic numerals**
- **Movement: Calibre 620**
- **Case material: Stainless steel**
- **Dimensions: 32mm**

It's obvious that the principle benefit of an automatic watch over one that is wound manually is that you do not suffer the inconvenience of having to remember to wind it, and it performs that function for you too. But those are really fringe benefits, the real advantages are improved accuracy and the need for less servicing. This is why.

If the automatic movement means that the watch spends most of its time with the mainspring fully wound, then a constant level of torque is released by the mainspring and that significantly improves accuracy. Also, if the watch now winds itself and is accurate, then there is rarely any need to unscrew the Oyster crown. This means that the chances of dirt, grit or moisture contaminating the movement and its lubricants are massively reduced and so the need for servicing is reduced.

The quest for a watch that wound itself had been going on for centuries when, 240 years ago, Swiss watchmaker Abraham-Louis Perrelet introduced a pocket watch that wound itself thanks to the motion of the wearer when walking. Within a couple of years both Abraham-Louis Breguet and Louis Recordon produced watches with the same feature. But the big problem for them was that pocket watches normally remain in one upright position in the wearer's pocket, so there is little motion imparted to them. This meant that the self-winding system was rarely efficient enough to keep the watch fully wound, and so they fell out of favour. While the waistcoat pocket was a sheltered and almost static location for a watch, the wrist was the complete opposite. It is likely the part of the body which moves the most and is usually exposed to the elements, and so the wrist was probably the silliest place imaginable to place such a delicate instrument. But it was the ideal place for the Oyster Perpetual (see page 56) and, in many ways, its development was really the birth of the wristwatch as we know it now.

The Oyster Perpetual, rather than the Rolex Prince (see page 50), was the flagship of the Rolex range, and was priced accordingly; in the 1934 catalogue the 18 carat Prince was listed at 27 guineas (£28.35, €33.72 or $35.47), while the 18 carat Oyster Perpetual was 38 guineas (£39.90, €47.45 or $50), a substantial premium. From the outset, the Oyster Perpetual was available in the full range of materials: steel, steel and gold, and 9, 14 and 18 carat gold. Before long it became available in different looks as well. The first variation was the reference 3372, which was introduced at the end of the 1930s. The hour indices were machined into its flat, engine-turned bezel. But as it went on sale, World War II began and the demand for luxury timepieces collapsed almost completely.

→ Within a few years of the launch of the Bubbleback it had matured and taken on many of the attributes we associate with modern Rolex watches; it had a sweep seconds hand – not a subsidiary one. The Rolex Coronet appeared on the dial and the Mercedes hour hand was now fitted. But perhaps most importantly, the watch was now fitted with an Oyster bracelet in the same material as the case.

ROLEX OYSTER
PERPETUAL
SELF WINDING
SWISS MADE

1942

PRISONER OF WAR WATCH

How the Bavarian-born Hans Wilsdorf chose sides during World War II. Thank goodness, he picked the good guys – and the eventual winners.

- **Model number: 3525**
- **Date: 1942**
- **Dial: Brass, cream paint, radium numerals**
- **Movement: Valjoux VX, signed Rolex**
- **Case material: Stainless steel**
- **Dimensions: 35mm**

Even though Wilsdorf (see page 11) was born in Germany, he became British at the age of 30 and, despite living in Geneva longer than anywhere else in his life, he remained British in both nationality and deed. He could have become Swiss and maintained a neutral stand towards the war raging all around Switzerland. Instead he made a substantial statement about where he stood, which was very much on the side of Britain and the Empire. There was not much he could do to aid Britain itself or its armed forces, but there was one group of British combatants he could help: the prisoners of war held by the Germans. Working in co-operation with the International Committee of the Red Cross, also based in Geneva, he arranged for Rolex watch brochures to be delivered to all the Oflags (Offizierslager, or officer camps) run by the German Army for Allied officer ranks and the Stalag Lufts, run by the Luftwaffe for Allied aircrew officers. His offer to the prisoners of war was that they could choose any Rolex watch from his catalogue, and the watch would be delivered to the officer via the ICRC, which was allowed to send packages to the camps and make visits. The icing on the cake was that the watches would not have to be paid for until the war was over.

I do not know exactly when the programme commenced. The earliest watch delivery I have seen is in 1941, and I assume that deliveries continued until close to the end of the war in 1945. It is not known exactly how many watches were delivered via these channels, but in an April 1943 letter to Captain Robinson, held in Oflag VII-B, Wilsdorf writes, 'As we have a large number of orders in hand for officers, there will be some unavoidable delay in the execution of your order, but we will do the best we can for you.' This shows that quite a few officers took advantage of the offer. While writing to Captain Robinson in Oflag VII-B, Wilsdorf may not have known that

Robinson was incarcerated just outside Eichstätt, less than 100 miles from where he was born and grew up, in Kulmbach.

By this time, Wilsdorf and his wife were the sole owners of Rolex, so it is unlikely that this programme could have existed without his knowledge and active participation. Further evidence for this can be gleaned from the fact that Wilsdorf signed every letter to a prisoner of war with his own hand and, once the war was over and the recipients began to repay their debts, Wilsdorf dictated and signed every letter to these proud owners. Unlike the wartime letters which were form letters with handwritten or typed entries for the variables, each of these post-war letters is individual.

→ The chronograph model 3525 is often nicknamed the Prisoner of War watch, but the truth is that the majority of watches that Rolex shipped to the British and Commonwealth prisoners were not chronographs, but rather stainless steel Oyster Royal manual-wound watches. Although, I have encountered one officer who was either very wealthy, or perhaps just greedy, who ordered one of each to be delivered to him.

1945

¼ CENTURY CLUB PRINCE

Eaton's was the largest department store chain in Canada and these watches were presented to employees who had worked for the firm for 25 years.

- **Model number: 1490**
- **Date: 1945**
- **Dial: Sterling silver, black enamel numerals**
- **Movement: Calibre TS**
- **Case material: 14ct gold**
- **Dimensions: 42mm long**

One of the more unusual versions of the Rolex Prince was the ¼ Century Club. These Prince watches were awarded to members of staff of the Canadian department store, T. Eaton Company Limited, who had completed 25 years of continuous service. The company started the club in 1919, when it was 50 years old and around 60 members of staff qualified. Obviously, the first members of the club did not get a Rolex Prince; they received a gold pocket watch of unknown make. Starting in around 1928, the Prince was introduced for those who wanted the more modern look of a wristwatch. By 1944, when the club was 25 years old, there were more than 4,200 members, with many of the women opting for an engraved diamond ring or a smaller-sized watch than the Prince. The ring or watch was not the only benefit given to those who qualified; on their special day they received gifts from their department and an additional six weeks' holiday on top of their normal allocation.

These watches are extremely unusual in that the dial does not bear the name 'Rolex'. In its place is the name 'Eaton' while the numerals 1 to 12 are replaced with '¼ Century Club'. The first watches given were small flared model 1490s in yellow 14-carat gold. During a short period in the mid-1930s Eaton's also gave out a small number of two-colour flared Princes; so far less than a dozen of these have been seen. These two-colour watches were the normal configuration: a yellow gold centre and white gold flares, although, one ¼ Century Club watch has turned up which has the reversed configuration – a white gold centre and yellow gold flares. This watch was given out in 1934 but is also unusual in that it is a large flare model, which had never been previously seen on a ¼ Century Club watch. It is even more unusual when we look at the model number and see it is a 1343. This, of course, is the model number for a straight sided Prince (see page 50). The number is followed by the letter A,

which means that it is a factory variation. All in all, a very unusual watch.

A very small group of individuals completed not a quarter century, but a half century. Members of the ½ Century Club received a platinum Prince. As I have a copy of the 1944 history of the club before me, which includes a list of all ¼ Century and ½ Century members, I can be sure that this is true, but I have never actually seen one of these ultra-rare pieces with their unique dials. Of the 4,200 ¼ Century Club members in 1944, only six were also members of the ½ Century Club.

→ The dials on these watches are very special, not just because of the text, but rather the way they are produced. The dial is solid silver and the numbers, text, minute and seconds tracks are engraved into the surface of the dial. This is filled with black enamel and fired. The dial is then polished flat and a clear lacquer applied to the surface. All 'print' is actually in the dial, not on the surface, so it can never rub off.

1945

DATEJUST 4467

Everything we expect of a Rolex today – waterproof, automatic, dial window for the date and a free-sprung, chronometer-rated movement – are features that were already present 80 years ago in the most important watch in the firm's history.

- **Model number: 4467**
- **Date: 1945**
- **Dial: Brass, gold-plated, gold indices**
- **Movement: Calibre A296**
- **Case material: 18ct gold**
- **Dimensions: 36mm**

→ This design is now 80 years old, but you can see the current Datejust in it. But it's the things which differ from today's model that catch the eye: the very fine milling on the bezel, the equally fine printing of the outer seconds track, the lack of a frame or a Cyclops lens on the date window, the tiny winding crown and the elegant hands and indices.

In November 1945, Hans Wilsdorf, head of Rolex (see page 12), held a party at Geneva's upmarket Hotel des Bergues. The party celebrated two events – one in the past and one which would change the future of the company for ever. The past event was the founding of Wilsdorf & Davis in London 40 years before; the other was the launch of a new watch. It was called the Jubilee but became better known by the name Datejust – which was not featured on the dials of these early watches.

The Datejust changed the company forever, in ways seen and unseen. The obvious innovation was that this was the first mass-produced 36mm-diameter watch from Rolex. Over the next half-century, this size became the standard for almost all men's watches from the firm, and it is still the most popular size. Less obvious was that the reference 4467 was the first mass-produced wristwatch with a free-sprung balance. Previously, these were only ever fitted to the most expensive pocket watches. Now, every Rolex produced has a free-sprung balance wheel. I know what you are thinking... 'What is a free-sprung balance?'

The normal method of adjusting the accuracy of a watch is to lengthen or shorten the length of the hairspring through an adjustable regulator fitted to the end of the spring. Free-sprung balances are adjusted using weights screwed into the rim or spokes of the wheel itself. Adjusting these screws

alters the inertia of the wheel. Think of the wheel as an ice skater spinning on the rink – if they move their arms out, they slow down; if they tuck them in tightly, they spin faster. The free-sprung balance is not so easy for a watchmaker to adjust, but it does allow a much more precise level of regulation than the conventional regulator.

The accuracy of the new balance was vital to Wilsdorf's vision of what the perfect watch should be. For 40 years he had striven to produce a watch which the owner would never need to touch and, with the Datejust, he had achieved his goal. If the watch was worn regularly, the Oyster crown never needed to be touched, so there was no chance of moisture or dust affecting the movement. The accuracy was guaranteed by the new balance assembly, so once again, there was no need to unscrew the crown to adjust the time. In fact, there should be only seven times in the year when a Datejust owner would need to adjust the watch; at the end of the five months with less than 31 days, and when clocks go backwards or forwards.

Wilsdorf's vision was correct. From the Turn-O-Graph (see page 100) to the Daytona (see page 154), no other watch ever came near the sales success of the Datejust. It has remained the best-selling men's Rolex watch for well over half a century.

CHAPTER FIVE

1946–1955

ROLEX
OYSTER PERPETUAL
SUBMARINER
10
20
30
40
50

1946–1955

THE 'TOOL' WATCH ARRIVES

Along with the most complicated wristwatches that Rolex had ever made.

The decade after World War II ended can now be seen as perhaps the most significant period in the history of Rolex. But at the time it must have felt like the end of the world. Its principal markets – Britain, its Empire and Europe – were devastated to varying extents, and most governments were focused on rebuilding and austerity, not the importation of luxury items – things that few could afford. The firm continued to focus on the US and Latin America which was extremely wealthy at this time. The continent had remained neutral during the war, but had supplied the Allies with beef, grain, minerals and other raw materials and grown rich from this trade.

In 1948, Hans Wilsdorf tempted André Heiniger away from his management role at Ebel and offered him the chance to run Rolex's Latin American operations. He made such a success of this that just four years later, in 1952, he was brought back to Geneva to become worldwide head of sales. With J P (Jean Pierre) Jeanneret who ran the publicity side of the business and Wilsdorf who was the strategist, Heiniger was the third of the triumvirate running the firm. Jeanneret's skill was in finding people with obscure interests or professions, working out how they could be of use to the firm and then building relationships with them. Two of the individuals he landed on are worth discussing. Dimitri Rebikoff, photographer, engineer and inventor, was one of Jeanneret's first contacts. Everyone knows Jacques Cousteau, and almost all of them know him through the films he made and the photographs that he took. None of these would have been possible without Rebikoff. He developed camera housings, lighting rigs, underwater vehicles and the first functional underwater flashgun. As an engineer, he did not just build things – from his Institute of Submarine Research in Cannes, France, he ran scientific experiments on all his projects to decide which design was best. When Rolex was planning to launch the Submariner (see page 102), Rebikoff and his institute were the right people to run the underwater tests, and so in early to mid-1953 the Institute ran well over 100 dive tests on the new watches. It also performed unmanned tests; watches were tied to ropes and lowered into the sea to depths as much as 121m (400ft). These tests were all performed on pre-production watches made to exactly the same specifications as the watches that were sold to the public.

Simultaneously, Jeanneret liaised with another individual who was preparing to go where no one had ever been – the very bottom of the ocean. Auguste Piccard was a Swiss physicist. He built a pressure-proof aluminium sphere and suspended it below a gigantic hydrogen-filled balloon to enable him to study the existence of cosmic rays. He and an assistant rode the device to a height of 22,860m (75,000ft). Then Piccard had his eureka moment – if the pressure-proof sphere could survive the near vacuum of near space (Piccard

← Submariner 6205, 1955 (see page 104).

The combination of Rebikoff's tests, Piccard's descent with the special watch and Jeanneret's flair for publicity meant that when the production watch, named the Submariner, was launched at the Basel trade fair the following year, it became a massive success.

was the first person ever to see the curvature of the earth) then it could most likely survive the pressure of the depths. So he began to design an underwater balloon. If you think about it, it is very easy to get to the bottom of the ocean, the hard part is getting back to the surface. He suspended his new sphere under a large tubular construction, which was almost entirely filled with petrol. Petrol is much lighter than the same volume of water, so the vessel would naturally remain on the surface. In order to descend, metal weights, which could be discarded on demand, were attached to the outside of the vessel.

On 26 August 1953, this new vessel, named the *Trieste*, descended to 3,543m (11,624ft) in the Mediterranean off the island of Capri. A very special Rolex watch that Jeanneret had convinced the experts at Rolex to produce was attached to the exterior of the vessel. It looked nothing like any watch the firm had ever produced: a massive slab-sided body surmounted by a crystal which rose vertically from the case and was capped by a hemisphere. Contemporary publications state that the watch case was tested at the Federal Institute of Technology in Zurich. I wonder whether it was actually made there, as I doubt that Rolex had any idea of how to build a case capable of surviving these depths. This is a mystery we will probably never know the answer to.

Where the special watch was constructed is irrelevant, because the combination of Rebikoff's tests, Piccard's descent with the special watch and Jeanneret's flair for publicity meant that when the production watch, named the Submariner, was launched at the Basel trade fair the following year, it became a massive success.

Another new watch, the Explorer 6350 (see page 98), was launched alongside the Submariner 6204 (see page 102). While this watch had not been to the bottom of the ocean, it benefitted from having conquered the world's highest mountain. Some members of the British team ascending Mount Everest wore Rolex watches, but neither of the two climbers who made it to the summit first did so (see Explorer, page 98). The New Zealander Edmund Hillary wrote a testimonial for the British firm Smiths, saying, 'I carried your watch to the summit. It worked perfectly,' and Smiths used this quote in its advertising. However, I believe that Rolex signed up most of the expedition's returning members. Certainly, Hillary and the expedition leader, John Hunt, both became prominent spokespeople for the firm. Early brochures for the Explorer show members of the Everest expedition in full mountain gear, and featured a quote from John Hunt. In simple terms, Rolex could outspend and out-promote Smiths in any market, and it did. By the time these two watches were launched, austerity in Europe was starting to slacken, and the US market was really taking off.

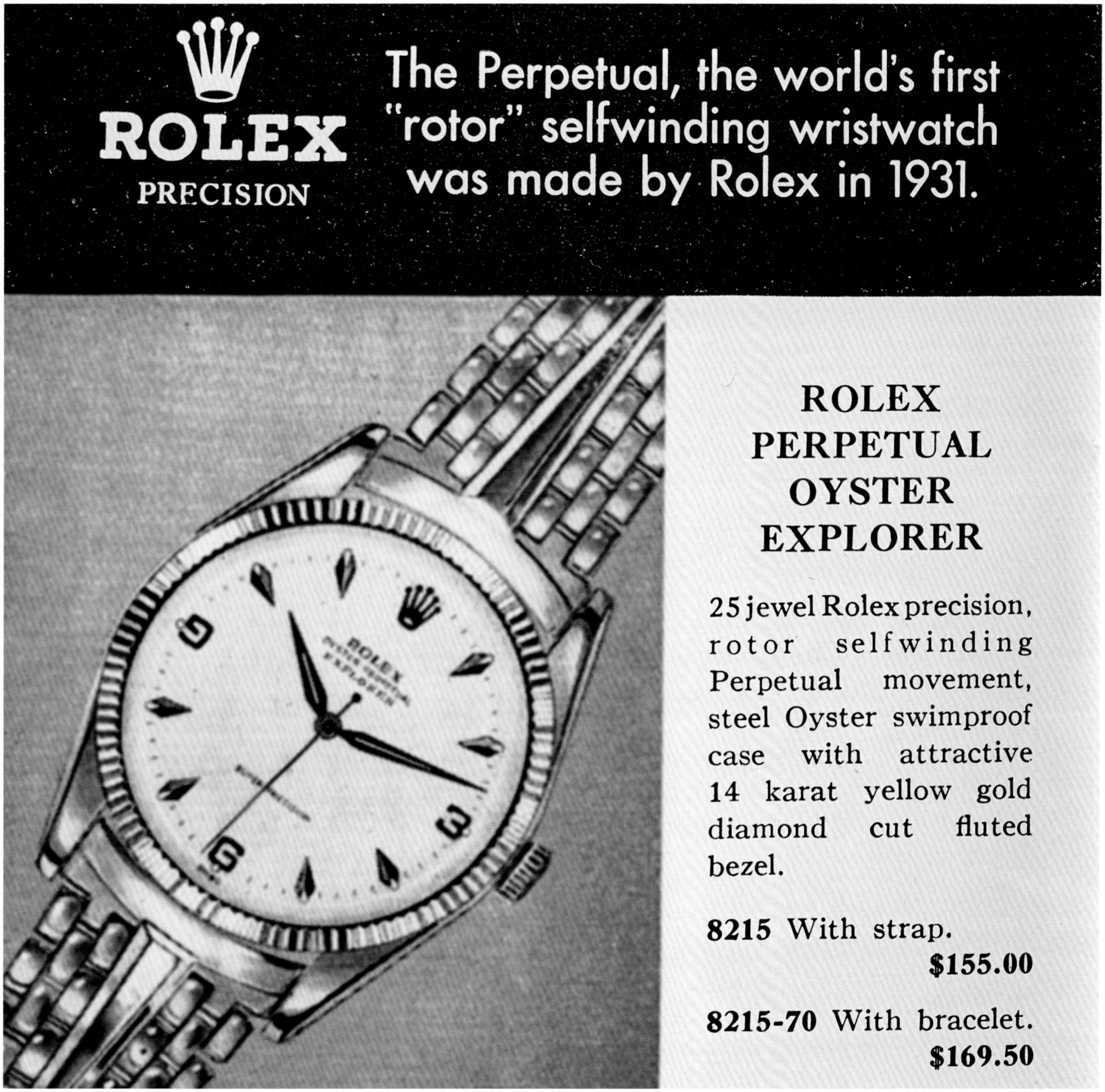

↑ A Canadian advertisement from the 1950s showing a version of the Rolex Explorer sold only in Canada. Notice the gold fluted bezel and the very unusual bracelet.

1950

HOLY YEAR JUBILEE

One of the very last of the original-style Bubblebacks was made as a special edition to commemorate a significant event in the calendar of the Roman Catholic Church.

- **Model number: 5010**
- **Date: 1950**
- **Dial: Brass, matt white finish, applied arrowhead indices**
- **Movement: Calibre 620**
- **Case material: Steel, gold bezel**
- **Dimensions: 32mm**

By making the winding system a module which sat on top of the basic manual movement, Borer had solved the problem which had dogged all previous attempts to make an automatic wristwatch: they were incapable of being wound by hand. None of the previous self-winding wristwatches had a facility for manual winding, and this raised two questions for buyers: 'How do I know the watch is actually running?' and 'What do I do if the watch stops?'.

While the Perpetual sold much better than other contemporary automatic watches, it was hardly an immediate sales sensation; it was priced at the very peak of Rolex's catalogue. An 18-carat new Perpetual was listed at 38 guineas (£39.18, €46.60 or $49), more than one-third more expensive than the company's previous apex watch.

Demand for simple, manual-wind steel Oyster watches continued. People had wound their watches by hand every day for centuries, so why pay a premium to avoid this minor inconvenience? Rolex tried a new tack – fashion. It focused on the aesthetics of the watch and introduced new case styles for the Oyster Perpetual. Known collectively as the 'hooded' models, they featured elongated downturned lugs, and the space between the lugs was filled with either gold or steel hoods in sundry patterns.

If World War I had made the wristwatch acceptable for men, then World War II made it ubiquitous. A side effect of this was that when wristwatches were only for the few, discretion was the norm, and so they remained small. But to be useful during wartime, watches had to grow in size to make them easy to read. Rolex acknowledged this by introducing a larger 10½ ligne version of the Bubbleback movement and fitted it to the new watch that became its flagship, the Datejust (see page 82), which was 36mm in diameter.

While these hooded Bubblebacks were no longer fashionable, they are, without doubt, some of the most exotic cases the brand has ever made for men's watches.

My particular favourite is the 3536, introduced towards the end of World War II. It has an unusual cylindrical case, concave bezel and huge curved hoods that fill the space between the straight lugs; it's probably the most Bauhaus-inspired Rolex Oyster Perpetual.

The new fashion for larger watches meant that the hooded Bubblebacks were a commercial disaster for the company; yet, because so few of them were ever made, they became sought-after by collectors. Towards the end of the 1980s, Japanese collectors drove the price of the rare variant, the 3599 all-steel Bubbleback, to almost US$100,000. This was at a time when the Paul Newman Daytonas (see page 154) were selling for between $12,000 and $15,000. But as Japan's bubble economy crashed, so did the Bubbleback market. Now the values of the Paul Newman and the 3599 are reversed. I often use this fact to counsel those who ask me what collectable watch they should invest in.

→ The 1950 Jubilee was held five years after the cessation of World War II hostilities and was seen as the Jubilee of reconciliation and forgiveness. The only place I have ever seen any mention of these watches was in an Italian Rolex advertisement from 1950, making these some of the last Bubblebacks ever produced.

← The Holy Year Jubillee watch in a Rolex advertisement from the period.

ROMÆ
ANNO SANCTO
GENERALIS
MAXIMIQUE
JUBILÆI MCML
ROLEX
OYSTER PERPETUAL
OFFICIALLY CERTIFIED
CHRONOMETER

1950

MOONPHASE 8171

One of the most unusual and attractive Rolex watches of the 1950s, but with the misfortune to be nicknamed after an Italian kitchen utensil.

- **Model number: 8171**
- **Date: 1950**
- **Dial: Brass, silvered paint, applied indices**
- **Movement: Calibre 270**
- **Case material: 18ct gold**
- **Dimensions: 38mm**

Rolex has always been an innovative company. By the end of the 1940s, it had an enviable list of original ideas in production: the Oyster (see page 46), the Perpetual (see page 56), the mass production of chronometers, and – its flagship – the Datejust (see page 82). But in 1949 it did something it did not usually do: it followed the competition. Everyone from Heuer to Movado was making triple calendar moonphase watches, and – for reasons that remain unexplained – Rolex chose to jump on this horological bandwagon.

Moonphase wristwatches first rose to prominence with the appearance of Patek Philippe's reference 1518 in 1941. At the time, this was the world's most complicated watch, a perpetual calendar chronograph with a moonphase indicator. The Patek 1518 was in a very different league to Rolex, but it set the format for almost every calendar moonphase watch that followed. Two windows in the dial, next to the 11 and 1 indices, showed the day and the month in abbreviated form, and a circular aperture at the 6 featured a bosom-like cutout with a rotating disc behind it. Two moons were printed on the disc which rotated once every 59 days so that each moon traversed the cutout in 29½ days, which is more or less a lunar month.

The watch which Rolex launched in 1949 – the reference 8171 – measured 38mm in diameter and was one of the largest watches in the catalogue at the time.

Powered by the 10½''' A295 or calibre 720, it was the largest version of the original Bubbleback movement, but this caused a potential problem. The A295 was a conventional 10½''' Hunter movement with the Borer-designed automatic winding system attached to the rear of the movement. It was already a substantial movement, but another module to handle the day, date, month and moonphase indications was added under the dial. The result was the bulkiest movement Rolex had ever made. In an attempt to make the watch more wearable, one of the firm's signature features was shelved, and the 8171 was introduced with a non-Oyster snap-back case.

The watch was launched in both steel and gold cases, and while the gold ones were sent to the observatories for chronometer testing, the steel ones had to go without. They were signed 'Precision' on the bottom of the moonphase aperture, while the gold versions were marked with the classic 'Officially Certified Chronometer'. The watch was not a success and had vanished from the catalogue within three years. But it paved the way for a rather more popular successor, which arrived in 1950, the Oyster Moonphase, reference 6062.

→ Italian collectors love to give nicknames to watch models – they are responsible for the 'Paul Newman' appellation, after all (see page 154). But the nickname given to the big moonphase is one of the most bizarre: the Italian for a large frying pan, 'Padellone'. OK, the watch is round, and at 38mm it is pretty large, especially for the 1950s, but could you imagine a UK collector asking another, 'Do you like my big frying pan?'

SUN
JAN
ROLEX
PERPETUAL
OFFICIALLY CERTIFIED
CHRONOMETER
SWISS MADE

1952

OYSTER MOONPHASE

The most desirable non-chronograph vintage Rolex. It is only in such demand because it was a veritable sales catastrophe when it was originally available.

- **Model number: 6062**
- **Date: 1952**
- **Dial: Brass, silvered paint, applied indices**
- **Movement: Calibre A260**
- **Case material: Stainless steel**
- **Dimensions: 36mm**

Only a year after the launch of the 8171 (see page 92), Rolex returned with another full calendar moonphase watch. But this time it was finally in an Oyster case. By using a movement with a smaller diameter, it was able to reduce the height of the movement; this also made the watch slimmer. The 10½''' A295 was replaced by the 9¾''' calibre 620, another variant of the original Bubbleback movement. Due to the smaller diameter of the movement, the new watch had a 36mm case, the same as the Datejust.

Given the reference number 6062, the new Oyster Perpetual Cosmograph was always a low-production model, but it was sold with a wide variety of dials. The most common one appears to have applied Arabic 3 and 9 numerals with applied arrowheads for the remainder of the indices. In around 1953 a new dial appeared with large, applied arrowheads for the 3 and 9; a small arrowhead at the 6; an applied coronet at the 12; and small applied stars for the remaining indices. Both of these dial designs were produced with a silver finish, or – for the 18-carat gold versions only, it seems – in high gloss black. But the rarest dial appears to have only been available on the 18-carat gold version. This was a version of the second dial, but instead of stars, small square diamonds were mounted on the dial.

It was the most expensive watch in the catalogue until the 1956 introduction of the Day-Date, by which time it was looking decidedly old-fashioned. Both the Datejust and Day-Date appear to have been more desirable than the 6062. In the 1958 Master catalogue, the ex-factory price of the 6062 was 900 CHF on a leather strap or 1,670 CHF on a gold bracelet. Meanwhile, the 6609 Datejust Turn-O-Graph was 921 CHF on a leather strap and 1,691 on a gold bracelet, and the 6611 Day-Date in 18ct yellow gold was 1,005 CHF on a leather strap and 1,855 CHF on a gold bracelet. The recently introduced platinum version of the Day-Date started at more than 4,000 CHF, and the top of the top-of-the-line version was almost 10,000 CHF. It was clear that Rolex no longer considered the 6062 Cosmograph to be its flagship watch. By the time the last ones were sold in 1961–62, the watch was two generations out of date. After a ten-year production run, the 6062 was long past its sell-by date; it was a sad ending for the most complicated watch in the Rolex catalogue but a reasonable facsimile would return for a short while as the Cellini Moonphase in 2017. That too, however, met an ignominious end after only five years.

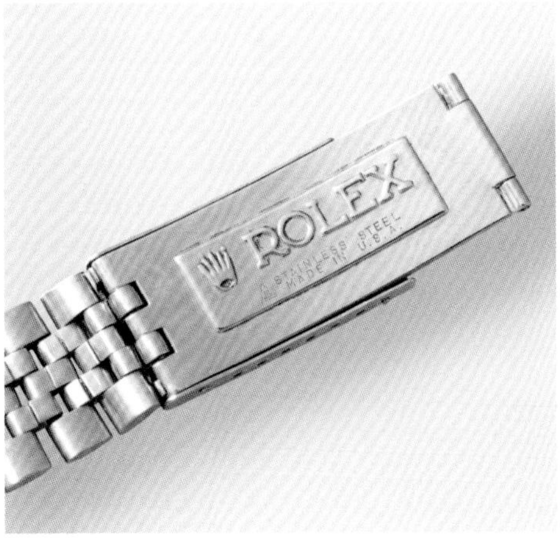

→ The model 6062 is proof that it is Rolex's commercial failures which go on to achieve greatness in the collector market. In many ways, this is the most un-Rolex like watch that Rolex ever made. Rolex make useful, functional watches; knowing the time is important, the date is useful, the day of the week is quite useful and the month even less so. But does anyone other than werewolf hunters need to know the phases of the moon?

ROLEX
OYSTER PERPETUAL
FRI
MAR
OFFICIALLY CERTIFIED
CHRONOMETER
SWISS MADE

1952

TRIPLE CALENDAR

Fashioned after the most complicated watch in the world, this watch has a very interesting history, encompassing the reconstruction of Greece after the Civil War.

- **Model number: 5036**
- **Date: 1952**
- **Dial: Brass, silvered, applied gilt indices**
- **Movement: Valjoux 72C**
- **Case material: 18ct gold**
- **Dimensions: 36mm**

When I talked about the Rolex Moonphase 8171 (see page 92), I mentioned how it owed a debt to the Patek Philippe 1518 with regards to its dial layout. While that is true, the subject of this essay owes its very existence to the 1518. Triple calendar chronographs passed through five different models over a 15-year production run. When the 4768 non-Oyster and 4767 Oyster versions were launched in 1947, it was one of the rare occasions when Rolex followed the market, rather than leading it.

Valjoux launched its 72C triple calendar movement in early 1946; Gallet's MultiChron Calendar model was the first to use the new movement, but many other brands such as Heuer and Eberhard were soon on the market. It was easy for Rolex to jump on the bandwagon: the movements were available, dials could be secured from Stern, Beyeler or Singer, and the cases needed only the slightest modifications.

The problem that Rolex and its dealers discovered was that similar watches with identical movements and functions were available from the competition at substantially lower prices. This might explain why the 4768 non-Oyster watch disappeared from the catalogue within 18 months, and only Oyster versions were produced from 1948. This allowed retailers to focus on the advantages of the Oyster case. But there was another problem: these watches – along with all other contemporary Rolex chronographs – were not really waterproof, as the pushers had limited protection against water ingress.

In 1948 the 4767 was replaced by the 5036. It retained the monobloc case and the unadjusted Valjoux 72C movement and the dial was updated slightly with more contemporary graphics and fonts. Plus the Rolex Coronet was no longer printed on the dial but was now an applied metal one above or below the day/month windows.

After only three years the 5036 was replaced with the new reference 6036.

→ This watch was awarded to Brigadier General Lancelot Edgar Connop Mervyn Perowne of the British Army who was appointed head of the UK military mission to Greece in 1951, which helped reorganize the Greek armed forces after the Civil War ended in 1949. By April 1952, the Greeks were in a fit enough state to join NATO and the British military mission was withdrawn at the end of the month.

Once again the only noticeable difference was the dial: the applied Rolex Coronet was now positioned either above the day/month windows or between them, depending on whether or not the dial had an applied numeral at 12. The other change was that the digits on the outer seconds track had disappeared.

In 1958 the final iteration of the Rolex triple calendar chronograph appeared. The 6236, still powered by the venerable Valjoux 72C but now in a new larger case, was fitted with a more prominent separate bezel and – of course – a revised dial. The digits on the outer seconds track made a return, while those on the subsidiary dials were no longer radial vertically aligned. And, most noticeably, the numbers 6 and 9 now had closed loops.

The 6236 lasted four years and its predecessor the 6036 for almost eight, so these are by far the most numerous of the four versions available. They are also the most sought-after by collectors. Gold versions in excellent condition and on original bracelets have sold for seven figures at auction. Evidence once again that Rolex's commercial disasters turn into future collectors' dreams.

1953

FIRST EXPLORER

The watch that didn't conquer Everest, but went everywhere else instead. The first real 'tool' watch from Rolex and, by far, the longest lived.

- **Model number: 6150**
- **Date: 1953**
- **Dial: Brass, galvanic black paint, radium indices**
- **Movement: Calibre A260**
- **Case material: Stainless steel**
- **Dimensions: 36mm**

The Explorer has the best back story of any watch made by Rolex. In a 1960s sales brochure the firm explained how '[it] was created specially for the first successful Everest expedition' and told the oft-recounted tale of how Tenzing Norgay and Edmund Hillary proudly wore their watches to the summit of the world's highest mountain. It is a great story and one that never fails to bring a proud smile to the face of any Explorer owner. Except for one tiny detail: neither Tenzing, Hillary nor anyone on that famed 1953 expedition wore an Explorer on Everest.

The truth is that both Norgay and Hillary did wear Rolex watches, and the Explorer was developed from the watches worn on Everest. The expedition was not sponsored by Rolex, and while the company did supply watches to the members of the climbing team free of charge, it did not give them to the Sherpas.

The watches worn on the Everest expedition were simple Rolex Oyster Perpetuals, with white dials and applied steel triangular indices with larger versions for the quarter hours. But they were not signed 'Explorer' and they did not look like them.

The actual watch that Hillary wore is now in the collection of the Beyer Clock and Watch Museum in Zurich. Its only differences from the standard specification were that the watches had an extra-long brown leather strap so that they could be worn over heavy clothing and the watches used a new, much less viscous lubricant to enable them to function in the extreme cold. While the strap never made it to production, the new lubricant did. It was the only change from the standard movement made when the first production Explorer watches hit the market a few months after the conquest of Everest. These bore the reference 6350 and may have been the most beautiful Explorers of all. They featured black dials with a gorgeous gloss black finish with an engraved honeycomb texture and gilt text. The watches were fitted with unusual hands, which only appeared on this model. They are parallel pencil-style hands with an extra heavy application of radium. The seconds hand on this model was also unusual in that the luminous dot was at the very tip, rather than inset from it.

The 6150 was a less expensive version of the Explorer. It was powered by the same movement and the only difference from the 6530 was that the dial bore the word 'Precision' in place of 'Officially Certified Chronometer'. The 6150 is notable for being the first Rolex Oyster Perpetual to be issued to British military personnel.

The thing which distinguished the 6150 from all the other Rolex watches was the layout of the dial. It was a deep black with a large luminous inverted triangle at 12, large luminous Arabic numbers at the remaining quarter hours and large luminous bars for the intervening indices. Introduced in late 1953, the dial remained essentially the same more than 70 years later. While the case and movement have changed with advances in technology (and, dare I say it, fashion), the layout of the dial is the only constant.

→ The watch shown here exemplifies everything I love about vintage watches. It is 70 years old but still usable as an everyday watch. But it is the details which make it stand out from the crowd; the 'fat' coronet, the gilt outer minute track, the 'puffy' luminous numerals whose hygroscopic binder has absorbed the moisture from the air, and more than anything, the minute hand with its hypodermic needle shape.

ROLEX
OYSTER PERPETUAL
PRECISION
SWISS

1954

TURN-O-GRAPH

Practically forgotten nowadays, this was the first mass-produced watch by Rolex with a rotating timing bezel and the first with the now-classic dial layout of luminous triangle, bars and dots.

- **Model number: 6202**
- **Date: 1954**
- **Dial: Brass, black galvanic paint, radium indices**
- **Movement: Calibre A260**
- **Case material: Stainless steel**
- **Dimensions: 36mm**

Rolex probably had its busiest year in 1953. It introduced the Explorer (see page 98) and the Submariner (see page 102), two watches which would go on to define what we mean by a sports watch. Somewhere in between these launches, it found time to introduce the 6202, under the bizarre name Monometer.

The Monometer was the watch that gave birth to the Turn-O-Graph, the Submariner, the Sea-Dweller and the GMT-Master (see page 128). The Monometer combined the waterproof case, automatic movement and rotating bezel for the first time. Its name is a combination of Greek words – mono means one and metre is derived from metron, meaning measure, so a Monometer measures one thing, in this case, elapsed time. And it did so with its rotating bezel.

The Monometer name only appeared on a few of these watches, as Rolex quickly realized that few of its clients either spoke or understood Greek, and the name gave no indication of the purpose of the watch.

Thus, within a few months of production starting, the Monometer name disappeared and the rest of the production run bore the name Turn-O-Graph. It was marketed as the easy alternative to a chronograph for the majority of tasks. The accompanying brochure claimed that it was 'The Watch with a Thousand and One Uses'. It added, 'Timing a transatlantic telephone call, the rate of a machine, a patient's pulse, the speed of a train, the development of a film – how often we long for a stopwatch on our wrists.' The brochure went on to say that a chronograph is complicated, expensive and unable to be made waterproof due to its buttons. At this time, Rolex listed four chronographs in its catalogue, and three of them had screwed backs and the word Oyster on the dial. However, they were not waterproof. The Turn-O-Graph could operate safely down to 45 m (150 feet) below the surface. I think, without meaning to, Rolex had touched on a point – we may like to believe that a chronograph on our wrist makes us an astronaut or a racing driver, but the truth is that the majority of chronographs are used to time cooking pasta or boiling an egg – functions equally easily performed by a Turn-O-Graph.

Powered by the reliable A260 automatic movement, which was getting pretty long in the tooth at this point, it was an enlarged version of the first Bubbleback movement launched 20 years previously. This in turn was based on the $10\frac{1}{2}$''' Hunter launched in the mid-1920s. Yet, despite its age, the A260 could still be tweaked to produce chronometer-certified performance. While most of the watches were delivered with the standard movement, the brochure stated that the watch was available in chronometer grade with a white or black honeycomb dial and a gold bezel. In 40 years of collecting, I have only ever seen two of these. That is probably because the 6202 may have had the shortest production life of any recent Rolex: it lasted just two years before disappearing from the catalogue.

→ I have always liked the 6202, but I am in the minority and I think that's because it lacks an image. We know what the Explorer, the Submariner, the GMT-Master and the Daytona all represent, but not so the Turn-O-Graph. Rolex called it the watch with 1001 uses, and that was its problem: it wasn't one thing or the other.

← A chronometer version of the Monometer.

ROLEX
OYSTER PERPETUAL
TURN-O-GRAPH

1954

SUBMARINER 6200/6204

The birth of a legend. The 6200/6204 Submariners weren't the world's first diving watches, but they were – by far – the most important. They introduced a look still present today in practically every dive watch, Rolex or not.

- **Model number: 6200**
- **Date: 1954**
- **Dial: Brass, galvanic black paint, radium indices**
- **Movement: Calibre A296**
- **Case material: Stainless steel**
- **Dimensions: 36mm**

→ The model 6200 Submariner is probably the least documented Submariner of all, and probably the most desirable. Was it launched with the 6204, or before, as the model numbers might suggest? Why so many dial variations and why make two models of the Submariner with different movements at the same time? So many questions but so few answers.

In 1953, the same year in which the Rolex Monometer was introduced, Jacques-Yves Cousteau published his book, *The Silent World: A Story of Undersea Discovery and Adventure*. Recreational diving became hugely popular and, in the US alone, there were more than 100 diving clubs. Rolex decided to exploit that interest with a watch made for divers. Undoubtedly the decision was hastened by their director of Public Relations, René-Paul Jeanneret, who was an enthusiastic diver.

The development of the first Submariner was not an arduous task. Essentially it involved taking the Turn-O-Graph (see page 100) and replacing the 5.3mm crown and tube with the more substantial 6mm version and the slim Tropic 10 crystal with the thicker Tropic 16. The bezel insert was replaced with one of a much simpler style, while the 6202 had individual dots for each minute. The new watch was given the model number 6204. It had the individual ten-minute divisions in block Arabics and bars for the intervening five minutes, but there were no other markings. Otherwise, it was the same watch, the A260 Bubbleback movement was identical, as were the oversized parallel pencil hands with their heavy luminous inserts. Even the seconds hand with its unusual lollipop dot at its tip was identical.

The big difference was the model name printed on the dial, or to be more correct, the lack of one. Bizarrely, the first editions of the watch had a perfectly placed block of black paint where the model name should have been. I assume that Rolex had chosen a name to which they did not hold the rights, or that a name was chosen and then dropped.

The year before Cousteau's book was published, his rival, Dimitri Rebikoff, who was based at the Institute of Submarine Research in Cannes, had published the less well-known *L'Exploration Sous Marine* (Underwater Exploration). Cousteau was one of the co-developers of the Aqualung (breathing apparatus) while Rebikoff concentrated on developing cameras, lighting systems and underwater propulsion devices. It was to Rebikoff and his institute that Rolex turned in early 1953 to test prototypes of the new 6204. They conducted 132 dives, going as deep as 61m (200ft) with it on one occasion, and subsequently attached the watch to a cable and lowered it to a depth of 122m (400ft), where it remained for an hour. For testing purposes, several dives were performed with the crown pulled out to the hand-setting position and it was during these dives that the new gaskets proved their mettle – the watches were unaffected by the deep water.

ROLEX
OYSTER PERPETUAL
SUBMARINER
SWISS

1955

SUBMARINER 6205

The Rolex process of gradual evolution is evident in the second model of the Submariner, introduced only a year after the first model.

- **Model number: 6205**
- **Date: 1955**
- **Dial: Brass, black galvanic paint, radium indices**
- **Movement: Calibre A260**
- **Case material: Stainless steel**
- **Dimensions: 36mm**

→ The 6205 used exactly the same case and movement as the 6204, but while the 6204 looked almost identical to the Turn-O-Graph, the 6205 was the first dive watch to adopt the now classic 'Mercedes' hour hand – and, in so doing, became the archetype for almost every Rolex tool watch which followed.

While Rolex USA was promoting the new watch on an almost one to one level, Geneva operated on a more global scale, and one with a Swiss accent. Professor Auguste Piccard was an unusual character. He was born in Basel, Switzerland, and was a professor of physics at the Free University of Brussels in Belgium. He held the world altitude record of over 16,154m (53,000ft) which he set in 1932 using a balloon he had designed himself. He then decided to explore the oceans, and convinced the Belgian National Scientific Research Fund (Fonds de la Recherche Scientifique or FNRS), which had paid for his balloon, to back the construction of a vessel which could independently descend to great depths and return to the surface without the aid of a surface ship and cable. His first bathyscaphe (as he named his creation) was called *FNRS-2*; his balloon had been named *FNRS-1*. Piccard was an entertaining character, immortalized by the Belgian cartoonist Hergé, as Professor Cuthbert Calculus in the Tintin comic books.

The *FNRS-2* made several successful dives and was sold to the French Navy after Piccard began to construct its replacement, the *Trieste*, named for the city where it was constructed. The *Trieste* was ready in August 1953 and soon began to dive to much greater depths than its predecessor. On the last day of September, Piccard and his son Jacques took the new craft down to a new world record depth of 3,168m (10,395ft) near the island of Ponza off the coast of Naples. We do not know if either of the Piccards wore a Rolex on the voyage, but a rather special Rolex Oyster was securely attached to the bottom of the *Trieste*'s hull. It was unlike any watch the company had previously made (or would make again). The massive watch measured 62mm from lug to lug and its case was surmounted by a hemispherical crystal rising more than 2.5cm (1in) above it. Today, such a watch would be considered unwearable, and in 1953 it was a behemoth, but it did the job. It survived the dive and gave Rolex tremendous material for the publicity it unleashed when the 6204 (see page 102) was launched.

The Rolex Submariner was revealed at the 1954 Basel Spring Watch Fair (now known as Baselworld). Blancpain showed its Fifty Fathoms diving watch at the same fair, and the argument as to which of the two invented the diving watch continues to this day. Both firms had been developing their competing models for at least a year, with tests going on in the Mediterranean and Switzerland. I do not believe that either firm copied the other, rather that they both saw an opening in the market. Blancpain was trying to build a watch to the specifications of a French Naval unit looking for a diving watch, while Rolex was looking to make a watch which would appeal to the burgeoning recreational diving market.

ROLEX
OYSTER PERPETUAL
SUBMARINER
50
10
20
30
40

1955

CLOISONNÉ

The most exotic and expensive non-jewelled dials ever fitted to a Rolex watch. Each was the result of weeks of artistry by a uniquely skilled craftsperson.

- **Model number: 6284**
- **Date: 1955**
- **Dial: White gold, cloisonné enamel**
- **Movement: Calibre A260**
- **Case material: 18ct gold**
- **Dimensions: 34mm**

→ Over the years I have seen many of these cloisonné dials and have had several confirmed as authentic by Rolex. But, despite over 30 years of research, I have never found a Rolex catalogue which lists them. This leads me to think that they were special-order pieces made for favoured clients. I would love to find a catalogue just to know what the additional cost was of one of these special dials.

The Hans Wilsdorf collection of pocket watches is the finest collection of Geneva enamel watches I have ever seen. They all feature enamel on the watch case, not the dial. Wilsdorf's love and admiration for the enameller's craft meant that, in the early 1950s, Rolex was one of the principal makers of watches with enamel dials.

Cloisonné dials are the most difficult to produce. Creating these miniature masterpieces involves a time-consuming technique that requires high artistry and years of experience. The design is lightly engraved onto the dial plate (white gold is usually used for its stability), then thin gold wires are attached to the dial, following the pattern and using an organic gum to secure them. The finished wire structure resembles a series of compartments (cloisonné is the French word for compartments). Each cell is then filled with coloured enamel powder, a mixture of silica (the principal component of glass) and colouring agents. This is fired in an oven at the temperature required by each colour of enamel – they range from 800 to 1,200°C. There is a high risk of the enamel cracking or bubbling if there are any contaminants or moisture in the enamel powder or on the dial. The gold wires and the gold dial plate have exactly similar coefficients of expansion when in the oven, but the enamel has a different one so – to prevent distortion while being fired – the back of the dial is also enamelled with a plain finish. The gum used to attach the wires to the dial burns off leaving no trace behind.

Once the dial has cooled to room temperature, it faces its next challenge; each enamel colour reacts differently to the heat, so they may rise to different levels, all – hopefully – below the wire cages separating them. The dial surface must be carefully polished so that the levels of all the compartments and the dividing wires are at the same height to create a perfectly smooth dial.

Now the dial faces another challenge: attaching the hour markers. Normally, these are fitted using small pins which go through tiny holes in the surface of the dial. Drilling these holes is a challenge as there is always a risk of the enamel (which is nothing more than coloured glass) cracking or shattering.

The process can take weeks and goes a long way to explaining the rarity of these dials. Rolex's cloisonné dials were made by Marguerite Koch and Charles Poluzzi, who both worked for the dial company Stern Frères. They were very expensive to produce and so were fitted only to the most expensive Rolex models – always solid gold Oyster Perpetual watches.

CHAPTER SIX

1956–1965

ROLEX
GMT-MASTER
SUPERLATIVE CHRONOMETER
OFFICIALLY CERTIFIED
SWISS

1956–1965

BIG CHANGES

Rolex welcomes the Day-Date and the GMT-Master and becomes a household name.

This was a decade of change. Hans Wilsdorf was ageing. In 1956, he celebrated his 76th birthday but rheumatoid arthritis severely limited his movements. In 1949 he had remarried and now wanted to spend more time with his new bride, his secretary Bertha 'Betty' Mettler. The day-to-day running of the firm was now in the hands of a triumvirate: René-Paul Jeanneret, André Heiniger, and Wilsdorf himself. Their responsibilities were public relations, sales and strategy, respectively.

Jeanneret was much more than just a PR guy; he was a relationship guy, and two of the relationships he built changed Rolex for ever. The first was with the American advertising agency J Walter Thompson (JWT). I will discuss the second one later as it was the JWT relationship which completely changed the public perception of Rolex in this decade. In the 1950s, Rolex advertising through JWT was performance-focused. It talked about the timing records the firm had won and expeditions where the watches had experienced extreme conditions and triumphed. These were the days when Rolex was still, very much, Wilsdorf's company. His name appeared at the bottom of every advertisement, described as either 'Founder and Chairman' or 'Governing Director'. But on 6 July 1960, Wilsdorf died. Nothing changed about the ownership of the company – it was still in the hands of the foundation he had established – but the management changed. The triumvirate became a duopoly.

One of the first things that Jeanneret did was to loosen the reins on JWT. Many years ago I worked in advertising myself, and I remember well the advice given out to young copywriters: 'Don't sell the steak, sell the sizzle'. In other words – do not sell the performance, sell the promise. JWT latched on to a quiet programme that Jeanneret had instituted immediately after the end of World War II. He had contacted world leaders and statesmen and offered them notable Rolex watches. In 1949 Winston Churchill was given a gold Datejust (see page 82), fitted with the 100,000th chronometer movement. Two years later Jeanneret gave Dwight D Eisenhower another gold Datejust, but this one housed the 150,000th chronometer movement. By this time Eisenhower was US President and Jeanneret wrote to assure him that there would be no commercial exploitation of the gift. Rolex did not need to publicize the relationship. These extremely newsworthy individuals were always being photographed, often waving their hand with their wrist nicely exposed for the ever-present cameras. They were then seen in newspapers and magazines or on the cinema newsreels with their watches on show. Consequently, everyone from NATO generals to European statesmen was gifted Datejusts and subsequently Day-Dates (see page 124). Rolex kept its word; not a single recipient was ever featured in any advertising or promotion

← GMT-Master, 1959 (see page 148).

The Day-Date, the Lady-Datejust and the Milgauss [...] none of these would have been the success that they were if it had not been for the structural and marketing changes which happened after the passing of Wilsdorf.

– but it was this programme which formed the foundation for a JWT advertising campaign which I believe changed Rolex for ever in the minds of the public.

This was the 'Men who guide the destinies of the world wear Rolex watches' campaign. It lasted over a decade and was revolutionary in that, while it showed statesmanlike figures signing documents, attending press conferences or entering 10 Downing Street, it never showed – or named – a single individual. To quote one of the advertisements, 'They are the people who feel the pulse of our time'. Rolex advertising had moved from performative to aspirational.

Rolex had promised the recipients of these watches that they would not appear in any promotional materials; the only request they had was for a signed 8x10in photograph. These were framed and then displayed along a corridor in the inner sanctum of the firm's Rue du Marché headquarters in Geneva.

As long as Wilsdorf was alive, the firm had remained on Rue du Marché, even though the building was much too small for a company the size that Rolex had become. But within a year of his death, land was purchased in the Geneva suburb of Les Acacias and construction began on what became Rolex's new world headquarters. The original head office in Geneva's Old Town had served it since Wilsdorf had moved to the city in 1919. But Rolex's 1960s incarnation was a very different incarnation. Rue du Marché was a couple of hundred metres away from Patek Philippe's similar turn-of-the-century factory on the lakefront. But Patek could rightfully claim to be an artisanal manufacturer; Rolex was now a modern industrial concern and needed suitable premises. Opened in 1965, the new building stated exactly how Rolex saw itself: it dominated the skyline, was unashamedly modern and was composed of two perfectly rectangular eight-storey blocks, each sheathed in glass, which was – of course – Rolex Green. It was as if Rolex was saying to the world, 'We are here, and we are serious'.

It was rather fitting that the new headquarters should open at the end of this decade, because it perfectly illustrates how much the firm had changed during this time. Yes, there were some major introductions: the Day-Date, the Lady Datejust (see page 132) and the Milgauss (see page 140) were all launched during this period, as was the firm's most important movement ever, the 15XX series (see page 146). But none of these would have been the success that they were if it had not been for the structural and marketing changes which happened after the passing of Wilsdorf. The Rolex of 1956 and the Rolex of 1965 were almost unrecognizable as being the same firm. And the progress did not stop there.

→ A sales tool from the 1950s, used by Rolex staff to demonstrate to retailers how the Oyster cases were made from a solid bar of Swedish stainless steel.

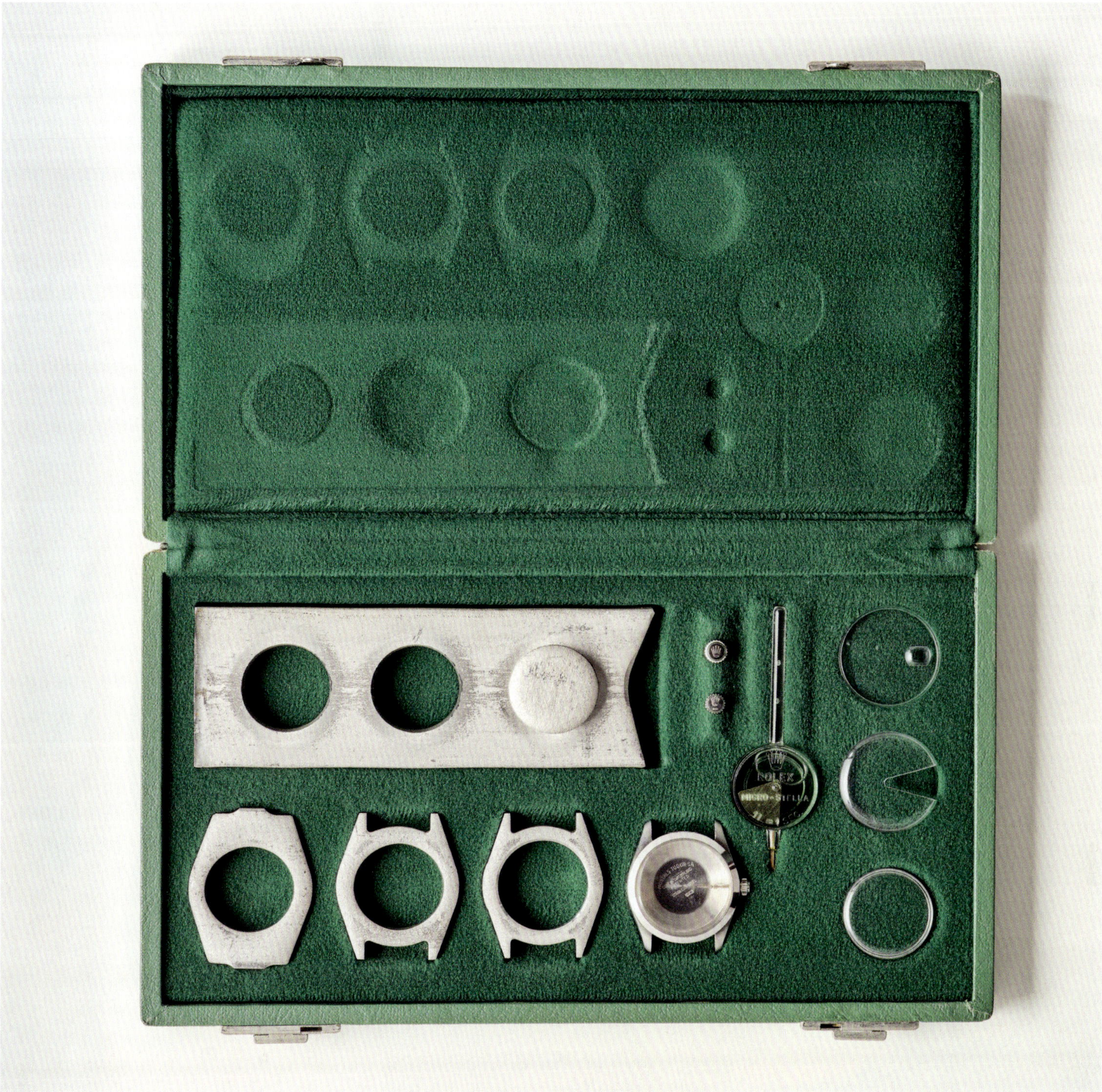
ROLEX

The World Famous
OYSTER Case

1956
PRE-DAYTONA

A classic transitional watch, the 6234 shown here uses the case, movement and pushers of the later 6238 but the earlier-style dial with superimposed telemeter and tachymeter tracks.

- **Model number: 6234**
- **Date: 1956**
- **Dial: Brass, silvered, applied gilt indices**
- **Movement: Valjoux 722**
- **Case material: Stainless steel**
- **Dimensions: 36mm**

I suppose I should start by defining exactly what a Pre-Daytona chronograph is. The generally accepted definition is an Oyster chronograph with three registers powered by the Valjoux 72. But this is my book, and I am going to use my definition, which is any Rolex chronograph with the word 'Oyster' on the dial.

The first watch that fits my definition is the reference 3525 two-register chronograph manufactured from 1939 to 1946. Produced in steel, steel and gold and in 18-carat gold, the 3525 was powered by the classic Valjoux 23VZ, a 17-jewel, manually wound, two-register chronograph calibre.

The Italian nickname for the 3525 – Monoblocco or Monobloc refers to its one-piece case body and bezel. In the Anglophone world it is usually referred to as the Prisoner of War watch (see page 78).

The dial had a 30-minute register at the 3 position and a running seconds subsidiary dial at the 9 position. It had adjacent tachymeter and telemeter scales on the periphery of the dial. Dials have been seen with a silvered finish as well as gilt, salmon and – most desirable of all – black.

It is probable that more of the 3525 were produced than any of Rolex's other two-register chronographs. Meanwhile its replacement, the 4500, may have had the shortest production run – around 18 months in 1946–47. The dial and movement were essentially identical to the 3525, but the case underwent a radical change. It was still a Monobloc case, but its silhouette had changed. It copied the tonneau shape of its contemporary, the Datejust, rather than the round case with attached lugs of the 3525. The 4500 was joined by the reference 4537, which was identical except for the new Valjoux 72 movement, which added a 12-hour counter at the 6 position. The 4537 is even more rare than the 4500, but is probably the most important chronograph produced by Rolex up until that date, because it became the prototype for every chronograph which followed up to the launch of the Daytona.

Every one of these chronographs followed the same layout, tonneau (barrel) case and three-register layout, and was powered by a variant of the Valjoux 72. The 5034, the 6034, and the 6608 all followed in the footsteps of the 4537, the case went from a monobloc to a three-piece, the movement had some minor changes with the addition of shock protection and, with the final version, the 6238, the dial was simplified. The cases and movements of the 6238 watches were identical to the first 6239 Daytonas, except for the bezel and dial. I have, over the years, seen several Daytonas with 6238 stamped between the lugs and inside the case back. I had always assumed that these were aftermarket conversions, but about ten years ago I saw a complete set including the invoice which stated 'Rolex Daytona chronograph' with the case serial number, so I can only envisage that these were made at the factory or the distributor.

→ **The 6234 is the transition between the vintage-style dial of the older models and the new tonneau case. With the blue tachometer track and the red telemeter one, it has a real vintage appearance. Look at the minute register on the right and the three slashes at 3, 6 and 9. These were for timing long-distance phone calls which used to be charged in units of three minutes.**

TELEMETER 1 MILE
BASE 1 MILE
ROLEX
OYSTER CHRONOGRAPH
ANTIMAGNETIC

1956

'KEW A' CERTIFICATE

One of the rarest, but least understood, watches ever to come from Rolex. It would be over 20 years before another firm attempted to mass-produce Observatory chronometers.

- **Model number: 6210**
- **Date: 1956**
- **Dial: Brass, white paint, applied gold indices**
- **Movement: 10½ Kew**
- **Case material: 18ct gold**
- **Dimensions: 36mm**

Rolex emerged from World War II in the best position it had ever been. Like the rest of the Swiss watch industry, it benefitted from the fact that the Allied nations' watch- and clock-making facilities had ceased civilian production to concentrate on making fuses for bombs and artillery shells.

But Rolex faced a problem. Founded in London, before the war it had focused on the UK and British Empire markets. In the aftermath of the conflict, Britain found itself in an economic chasm with no obvious solution. The cost of the war had completely drained the nation's coffers, and it was in debt to the United States, whose anti-communist President, Harry Truman, was in no mood to be lenient with the newly elected socialist government in the UK.

Britain had debts to pay, and the only way to raise money to do this was to tax the population, reduce imports, focus on exports and cease to import luxuries. Wristwatches were on the list of luxuries, meaning that Rolex could not sell watches in the country of its birth.

In 1947, things eased up enough, economically, that imported watches were permitted, but only manually wound steel ones; automatic and gold watches were still seen as an extravagant luxury. Nevertheless, Rolex decided to celebrate the return of the brand to its home country. It took the least-expensive Oyster watch, the boy's size manual-wind Speedking, reference 5056 and removed the classic 10½''' Hunter movement, replacing it with a very special movement that was completely hand built in Bienne. It was an ingenious concoction that used the base plate and the winding mechanism from the basic 10½''' Hunter and the balance and escapement from the movement used in the 4467 Mk1 Datejust, which was the first production free-sprung movement ever produced. The balance shaft was replaced with an extremely finely pivoted one, installed without shock protection, as it was believed that systems such as Kif or Incabloc precluded the perfect location of the pivots.

The plan was to produce 150 of these special movements and submit them for chronometer testing, not at Swiss observatories, but at the famed Kew Royal Observatory, where clocks and watches had been tested since the 1850s. The tests themselves were carried out at the National Physical Laboratory in Teddington, four miles away, but they bore the Kew name. In reality, only 145 movements made it to Teddington and all but nine obtained their A certificates.

The completed watches met the UK government's criteria for sale in the country as they were steel, manually wound and with no calendar or other complication. They looked identical to the basic watch, apart from the text "'Kew A' Certificate" around the subsidiary seconds. How they were allocated and sold, and at what price, is a mystery which may never be solved. But we know that not all were originally sold. In 1956, 24 of the movements were cased in 36mm 18-carat gold cases with the unique reference number 6210. Again, we have no idea how or when they were sold, but they remain – in my opinion – the rarest Rolexes of all.

→ This is one of only 24 versions of the 'Kew A' chronometer ever made in 18-carat gold. All the others were produced in a smaller-sized stainless-steel case. These were also unusual in that they were the only 'Kew A' watches with the supplementary dial text in red.

ROLEX
OYSTER
"KEW A" CERTIFICATE

1956

DATEJUST 6305

The Datejust lets its hair down, takes on a little bit of style and gains a Cyclops lens for the date. The Datejust as we know it is practically here.

- **Model number: 6305**
- **Date: 1956**
- **Dial: Brass**
- **Movement: A296**
- **Case material: 18ct gold**
- **Dimensions: 36mm**

→ Nowadays the Datejust is restrained, almost austere; if you want some frivolity you have to add precious stones to the dial or bezel. This was not so back in the 1950s, as the 6305 had wonderful arrowhead and double arrowhead hour markers, an intricately chiselled bezel and gorgeous leaf hands. The dial was also enhanced by the alternating black and red date numerals – known as the 'Roulette Date Wheel'.

The first changes to the Datejust (see page 82) happened in 1956 with the arrival of a new model, the 6305. Its Cyclops lens and new bezel design made it instantly recognizable. The movement was the same calibre 720 10½''' perpetual, but it no longer had a free-sprung movement, and the case was now a two-piece version with the bezel an integral part of the care centre. The coin-edge design of the bezel was replaced with much more widely spaced milling. It used the same movement as the original 4467, and so Italian collectors nicknamed these two models Ovettone (big egg) by virtue of their deep domed back which was needed to hold the extra-tall movement with its sweep seconds wheel and date mechanism. While the Italians were first to give it a nickname, French collectors soon followed, calling these models Bombé (named after the domed dessert). This name caused some confusion among Anglophone speakers as it is pronounced 'Bombay' in French, leading the British to believe that it was named after the city in India.

The Datejust was not the first Rolex to feature the new Cyclops crystal; it first appeared on the new Day-Date model, reference 6511 (see page 124), which had displaced the Datejust from the pinnacle of the Rolex. This had essentially freed the Datejust from its flagship role and it now became available in steel, steel and gold, and solid gold. Unusually, it was available in three different yellow gold carat weights; 9ct at 708CHF or 1,228CHF, depending on whether it was on a strap or a gold bracelet, 14ct at 792CHF or 1,447CHF, and 18ct at 891CHF or 1,661CHF. The white gold version was only available in 18ct and was priced at 1,188CHF, but if you wanted the white gold bracelet, it was only available with the diamond dial version at 1,866CHF on a strap and 2,113CHF on a bracelet.

The dials on these early watches are varied. The model name was sometimes printed in red, but usually in black. Others had their depth rating of 50m=165ft on the dial – also seen in both black and red print – but most did not. What all of them did have were the words 'Officially Certified Chronometer' on the lower half of the dial and the alternating red/black coloured Roulette date disc.

Launched at the same time as the 6605, the 6604 was an almost identical model with a simple polished bezel. It is much rarer than its milled bezel cousin and rarely appears on the market.

ROLEX
OYSTER PERPETUAL
DATEJUST
16
SUPERLATIVE CHRONOMETER
OFFICIALLY CERTIFIED
SWISS

1956

SUBMARINER 6536

The Submariner gets a new movement and starts to grow, but still looks the same externally.

- **Model number: 6536**
- **Date: 1956**
- **Dial: Brass, black galvanic paint, radium indices**
- **Movement: Calibre 1030**
- **Case material: Stainless steel**
- **Dimensions: 37mm**

If we have learned anything about Rolex during Wilsdorf's tenure, it is that development continued ceaselessly. This applied to sports watches too and, as one of the first to be introduced, the Submariner was the first to be revised. The 6204 (see page 102) was replaced by the 6205 (see page 104), which differed only in that the pencil hands were replaced by the Mercedes hands that had been introduced on the Explorer (see page 98). The change improved the low-light visibility of the watch immensely. At the same time as the introduction of the 6205, another version was launched – the 6200 had a much heavier case and much larger winding crown. It is important to note that, at this time, none of the Submariner models had a depth rating stated on their dial, so it is difficult to know if the 6200 was designed to go deeper than the 6204/5 watches, which were rated 182m (600ft) according to the promotional material. From this I assume that the first three Submariners had a 600-foot depth rating. The 6200 was fitted with the $10\frac{1}{2}$''' A296 Bubbleback movement, while the 6204/5 watches used the $9\frac{3}{4}$''' A260.

But, as we discussed earlier, the old Bubbleback movement was reaching the end of its life and was being replaced by the new 1030 self-winding movements. These were much slimmer and measured around $12\frac{1}{2}$''' in diameter. The 6204/5 was replaced with the 6536, which was slightly larger by 1mm – 37mm as opposed to 36mm – although the height of the watch on the wrist remained the same at 14mm. The 6200 was replaced by the 6538, which retained the thicker case and the big crown, but now the watches had their guaranteed depth ratings on their dials; the 6536 had 100m=330ft, while the dial on the 6538 bore the new legend 200m=660ft.

Both the new watches retained the high-gloss, galvanically printed black dials, but something new appeared on a few of them: the words 'Officially Certified Chronometer'. This meant that the watches were fitted with the free-sprung version of the 1030 (see page 122), which could be chronometer-rated. The early watches had bezel inserts with Arabic numerals for each ten-minute division and bars for the five-minute ones, but the new watches had individual minute dashes for each of the initial fifteen minutes.

→ Back on page 102 I discussed the first Submariners, the 6204 and the 6200; these could be called the little Sub and the big Sub, but there was no delineation between the abilities of the two models. Not so with the two which followed, the 6536 and the 6538. The 6536 now carried on its dial the depth at which it was certified to, in this case 100m/330ft whilst the 6538 was capable of descending to twice that depth.

ROLEX
OYSTER PERPETUAL
100/330
SUBMARINER

1956

SUBMARINER 6538

The original 'James Bond' Submariner, as worn by Sean Connery, but also – and more importantly – as worn by British Royal Navy mine clearance divers and the Special Boat Service.

- **Model number: 6538**
- **Date: 1956**
- **Dial: Brass, black galvanic paint, radium indices**
- **Movement: Calibre 1030**
- **Case material: Stainless steel**
- **Dimensions: 40mm**

A 1958 Rolex brochure for the 6536 Submariner has a note on page 3 in minuscule type. It reads, 'A heavy-duty version of the Submariner, guaranteed pressure proof to 660 feet, is available under the ref. 6538.' To me, this seems a rather mean introduction to one of the most iconic of all Rolex sports watches. The 6538 featured on the wrist of Sean Connery in the first James Bond film, *Dr. No* and was the first Submariner to establish the massive look we now all associate with the watch. Larger even than the 6200 (see page 102), it measured 40mm in diameter, 48mm lug to lug, and 15mm in height. It had wrist presence in spades.

The oft-repeated story is that Connery was loaned the watch by the film's co-producer, Albert 'Cubby' Broccoli. Obviously, I was not there, but my gut feeling is that the watch did not come from Broccoli. Rather, it came from the other major player on the film, its director, Terence Young. Young had a similar background to Ian Fleming: public school (Harrow), then Cambridge, before serving in intelligence during World War II. Fleming wore a Rolex Oyster Perpetual in real life, and he made sure that Bond did so in his novels. Young spent weeks with Connery before filming started, teaching him how to act and dress as if his background was Harrow, Cambridge and British Intelligence. He took the actor to his Savile Row tailor, wine merchant and the finest restaurants. He had lobbied to get Connery the role in the first place and built a close relationship with him. I think it is much more likely that it was Young, rather than Broccoli, who decided which watch Bond should wear, as Broccoli was concerned with the logistics, financing and selling of the film, not minor costume details like this.

There is also the matter of Young having exquisite taste in watches, in every photograph of him from the 1950s

↑ There seem to have been so many different dial layouts for the 6538; it was sold with both chronometer and non-chronometer dials, with the depth rating as '200m = 660ft' or just '200/660' and these ratings could be in gilt, silver or – in rare cases – red. Speaking of red, the triangle at 60 on the bezel could be in red too, or silver, or – like the watch shown here – replaced by Rolex during service with a tritium dot version.

and 1960s, he is seen wearing a Cartier London Tank Normale.

The 6538 was the first Rolex Submariner to be issued by the Royal Navy to their divers, although it was not the first Rolex they had been given. Divers had previously been supplied with the 6150 Explorer (see page 98). Evidently, the divers liked the Explorer dial layout and so when the Admiralty ordered Submariners for the Royal Navy, they were specified with Explorer dials. The story of these watches, the problems that the Navy divers encountered with them and how Rolex Geneva solved them will be told a little later.

1956

DAY-DATE

Rolex launches a new flagship watch with a new bracelet, and the 'Texas Timex' is born. And soon it will be the watch worn by the men who guide the destinies of the world.

- **Model number: 6511**
- **Date: 1956**
- **Dial: Brass**
- **Movement: 1055**
- **Case material: 18ct gold**
- **Dimensions: 36mm**

→ One of the things I love about these early Day-Dates is the dials (we know them now as 'Pie Pan' dials), where the perimeter with the minute track slopes downwards. It gives the dial a three-dimensional effect. The watch shown here doesn't have any luminous elements but it's easily readable because of the diamond-cut indices and faceted hands which catch the light no matter the angle it comes from.

Although the men's Datejust (see page 118) was now available in a variety of materials, it was still the most prestigious product in the Rolex line-up. But Wilsdorf decided that it was time for something a little bit more special, so along came the Day-Date. The 6511 Rolex Oyster Perpetual Day-Date was introduced at the Swiss Industries Fair Basel 1956. Reduced to its essentials, the 6511 was a simple evolution of the Datejust. A disc with the names of the week printed on its periphery was positioned above the date wheel, and as the date wheel moved, so did the disc. It appears to be simple, but it was not...

The Day-Date's status as a flagship product was signalled by the fact that it was only available in 18ct gold or, for the first time for an Oyster watch, platinum. It was also the first Rolex man's watch to be available with factory-fitted diamonds. Customers could choose to have two baguette diamonds at 6 and 9 with round stones at the remaining positions, or with ten baguettes, and, if desired, the bezel could also be set with an additional 46 round diamonds. The fully equipped platinum bracelet Day-Date was more than five times the price of the standard 18ct bracelet version. The bracelets for the Day-Date had a new configuration and were exclusive to this new model. Like the Oyster bracelet (see page 76), there were three links across, but like the Jubilee bracelet, the links were rounded. The watch was available on a leather strap or this new bracelet. If the client chose the strap option, a spare one was provided.

These early Day-Date watches were essentially prototypes, and the initial buyers were really beta testers for the watches. This can be seen in the number of variations known for the dials on these watches. Unlike the later versions, there is almost no consistency on the dials found on these early watches; some have the depth rating 50m=165ft on the dial, but most do not. Others have the model name below the centre post, while most have it above, and some even have it printed in red. Almost all of them have the legend 'Officially Certified Chronometer' above the 6, but on some watches, it is notable by its absence. If you see the legend 'Superlative Chronometer Officially Certified' on a dial, this means that the dial has been changed for a later one, as the 6511 never used this on its dials, I will explain later.

FRIDAY
ROLEX
OYSTER-PERPETUAL
DAY-DATE
7
SWISS

1957

THE FRENCH CONNECTION

Politics, economics and trust make strange bedfellows, but in this situation, they combined to produce some of the most exotic Rolex cases ever seen.

- **Model number: No model number**
- **Date: 1950s**
- **Dial: Brass, silvered, anodized gold indices**
- **Movement: Calibre HW**
- **Case material: 18ct gold**
- **Dimensions: 40mm long**

Following World War II, France was in economic and political turmoil. In the 12 years after 1946, there were 21 changes of government and, in essence, the country was the most unstable in Europe. The franc was frequently devalued and this posed a problem because the country's rulers were firm believers in the gold standard – that a country's currency should be backed by its gold reserves. During the 1930s and the Great Depression, both Britain and the US had abandoned the gold standard, but the French doggedly held on.

When French citizens saw their currency being devalued on an annual basis, they turned their savings into gold. This meant that the government did not have sufficient gold to meet its reserves, so it instituted a ban on private gold purchases. It could only be bought from the Bank of France by licensed jewellers or industrial users. Imports of finished gold products – an obvious way around the prohibition – were also banned.

Swiss watch brands faced a dilemma. Their French clients craved gold watches, but they were only allowed to purchase French-made watches, as these had French cases. The answer was to use cases that had been made in France. However, there were only a few industrial watch case makers in France, so the Swiss companies turned to France's pool of jewellery talent. The great French jewellers – such as Boucheron, Cartier, Chaumet, Clerc, Van Cleef & Arpels – were all based in Paris and had nearly a millennium of experience among them, making jewellery from simple wedding bands to imperial regalia and everything imaginable in between.

Every Swiss firm from Omega and IWC to Rolex and Patek followed this route. However, there is a huge difference between a factory-made case produced in the hundreds, if not thousands, and a handmade one built in a jeweller's atelier. A factory-made case needs to be easy to manufacture, suitable to be reproduced in volume and to use the minimum amount of gold because manufacturing costs are minimal once the mould has been made, but the cost of the gold is a significant part of the price. On the other hand, the major cost of a jeweller-made case is the wages of the skilled craftsman who constructs the case from scratch. This is why factory-made cases seem almost flimsy when compared with jeweller-made ones. The other factor worth taking into account is the design. The French jewellers were artists in precious metal – they were not particularly interested in making simple rectangles or circular cases with a little decoration in the lugs. They treated each watch case as a blank canvas and tried to outdo each other in the design before handing it over to the craftsman who would create the case itself.

The absolute scarcity of these pieces, and the lack of a manufacturer's stamp inside the case back when I do see one, means that there is almost no market for them. In my opinion this is nothing short of a tragedy.

→ The French didn't have a monopoly on making Rolex cases outside Switzerland, although theirs were, by far, the nicest. In the 1950s and as late as the early 1970s, gold cases were made in the UK and the US for non-Oyster Rolex watches in order to avoid high import duties. In Canada, because of high duties, they even made steel and gold-filled cases domestically.

1957

GMT-MASTER

One of the most iconic Rolex models finally makes an appearance. Rolex caught the zeitgeist and produced the watch nobody knew they needed, but the one which everybody wanted.

- **Model number: 6542**
- **Date: 1957**
- **Dial: Brass, galvanic gloss black paint, radium indices**
- **Movement: 1065**
- **Case material: Stainless steel**
- **Dimensions: 38mm**

The story of the GMT-Master begins in the early 1950s, when US airline Pan Am began regular transoceanic flights on the new Boeing Stratocruiser. On these flights over the oceans there were no visible landmarks to confirm that the planes were on the correct course. So the crew had to turn to celestial navigation, a technique used by mariners formerly where the navigator used a sextant to sight the moon, the sun or one of 57 known stars. In addition to the sextant, the system required a set of tables which allowed the user to read their location, as long as they knew the exact GMT time, accurate to the second.

As discussed on page 64, before World War II Rolex was known as the pilot's watch, as many of the pioneering long-distance flyers wore them. When war broke out, most British pilots discarded their RAF-issued timepieces and purchased Rolex Oysters with their own money. Later, when US pilots arrived in the UK in large numbers, they followed suit and Rolex became the pilots' watch of choice for the USAAF.

And so when Pan Am asked its senior navigator, the decorated World War II pilot Captain Frederick Libby, to nominate a watch company to work with on a special watch which would always show GMT and the local time, Libby instinctively thought of Rolex.

The knowledge that Libby had worn a Rolex during the war was not as significant as the fact that he was a navigator. On long-distance flights, particularly over oceans, the navigator was usually the senior officer in the cockpit and nominated as the captain of the flight, with the pilot following his orders.

Working with René-Paul Jeanneret of Rolex, together they came up with a watch which added a rotating bezel marked with the individual 24 hours and a fourth hand which was geared to rotate once every 24 hours. Using the newly introduced free-sprung version of the 1035 movement, the watch was accurate enough to be certified as a chronometer by the Swiss timing institutes and, therefore, accurate enough to fulfil Pan Am's navigation needs. It was issued to every pilot and navigator in the company and remained Pan Am's official watch until the airline went out of business in 1991.

As most airline pilots in the 1950s had been in the military, they were accustomed to using the 24-hour clock, and Libby and Rolex came up with the idea of a watch which would combine both the military (24-hour) and civil (12-hour) clock and somehow allow each to read a different time. And so the GMT-Master was born.

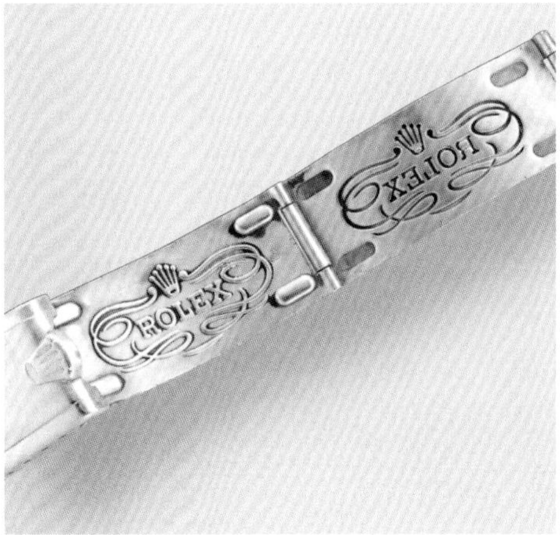

→ **We have always called the bezel insert on these early GMT-Masters 'Bakelite', but it isn't. Bakelite, which was the first industrially produced plastic, is opaque, while these bezel inserts are transparent. My belief is that the material used is some version of Perspex, also known as Lucite and Hesalite. In the 1950s Rolex was already using this material for watch glasses and so were familiar with it.**

ROLEX
GMT-MASTER
OFFICIALLY CERTIFIED
CHRONOMETER
SWISS

1957

MILITARY SUBMARINER A/6538

The first British-issued military Submariner, it has many claims to fame, but my favourite is that it is the only Rolex watch which left the Geneva factory twice.

- **Model number: A/6538**
- **Date: 1957**
- **Dial: Brass, matt black, tritium indices**
- **Movement: Rolex perpetual calibre 1030**
- **Case material: Stainless steel**
- **Dimensions: 38mm**

Like his creator Ian Fleming, James Bond was employed by the Admiralty in the 1940s, working in intelligence. Prior to the invasions of Italy and France, one of the roles of Naval Intelligence was to reconnoitre potential invasion sites at night using men in canoes launched from surfaced submarines. They were the progenitors of the famed Special Boat Service (SBS).

Bond's Royal Navy (RN) diving qualifications would have taken place at HMS Vernon near Southampton, UK. In 1956, the RN began to issue dive watches to all divers; these were Rolex 6538 Submariners and, if Bond maintained his diving qualifications, he too would have been issued with one.

The 6538 was chosen after lengthy tests. The RN divers appreciated the watch, but discovered two problems. When used for diving, the spring bars holding the strap were not strong enough under high levels of stress, and the rotating bezel was difficult to operate when wearing thick diving gloves. Some of the watches were sent back to Rolex for modification, and in Geneva it was realized that a newly designed and more easily gripped bezel would not fit the existing watches. To resolve this, a batch of cases for a new model, the 6540, was redesigned for the new bezel. The replacement bezels were made from German silver, an alloy of copper, nickel and zinc. They were not only twice as thick as the original bezels, but had much wider and deeper ridges, allowing for easy manipulation.

Rolex fitted the movements and dials from the original watches into the new cases. As they were modified reference 6538 models, they were given the new reference A/6538, and the engraved 6540 inside the case back was struck out and the new model number engraved alongside it.

What was most unusual about these watches was that, unlike other recent Rolex Oyster watches, they did not have the case (or serial) number engraved between the lugs at the 6 position. As these were replacement cases, they were given the same case number as the original watch that had the movement and dial they now carried.

The spring bar problem was solved by replacing them with much stronger solid steel bars, held in place by resin.

The dials on these watches had luminous hands and dials; the luminous element was activated by adding a small amount of radium to the paint used for the markings. In the early 1960s, the dangers of this material began to be understood, and the recent discovery of the isotope tritium meant that there was now a much safer option. Most manufacturers, including Rolex, switched to it. The dials were removed from the majority of the watches as part of their regular service, and sent to the Ministry of Defence's (MoD) supplier, Watch Dials (Burford) Ltd, which reprinted the dials in a reasonable facsimile of the original Swiss dials.

Neither Rolex nor the MoD have ever released the number of A/6538 watches ordered, but the generally accepted estimate is that around 50 were supplied. How many survived is even more difficult to calculate.

→ Because so few of these watches were ever made, and even fewer survive, very little is known about them. Nearly all the research on them has been done by one enthusiastic collector in Australia, known as Jedly1. Almost everything we know about the watches has been discovered by him. Guys like him, Ed Delgado, Niccoloy and David Boettcher are the reason we know so much about the history of Rolex.

ROLEX
OYSTER PERPETUAL
T
200/660
SUBMARINER

1958

LADY-DATEJUST

Though it is universally ignored, I feel this watch is more important to Rolex than all of the sport watches put together.

- **Model number: 6516**
- **Date: 1958**
- **Dial: Brass, gilt applied indices**
- **Movement: Calibre 1135**
- **Case material: 18ct gold**
- **Dimensions: 26mm**

The first Rolex lady's Perpetual watch did not appear until 1945, more than ten years after the Perpetual was launched. It was more than another decade before a women's Datejust arrived on the scene. Launched in 1957 as the 6516/17 (the only difference was a polished or milled bezel) it was an immediate success.

Although it was powered by the new 1135 calibre, its arrival was not delayed by the wait for the new movement. Rather it was the introduction of the Cyclops magnifying lens, two years previously, that made it possible. The date numerals on the Lady-Datejust were much too small to be viewed without the 2.5x magnification provided by the Cyclops.

The men's Datejust model was launched in yellow or red 18 carat gold, and less expensively cased versions were not available for another four years. Not so for the ladies' version – from day one, it was available in steel, steel and gold and all-gold with or without a gold bracelet. However, not all watches were the same. Only the all-gold ones bore the legend 'Officially Certified Chronometer' on the dials. If you wanted your lesser version to be sent for testing, there was an additional charge of 60CHF, which was around 20 per cent of the 305CHF price of the steel version. Speaking of costs, although the watch was diminutive at only 26mm, it carried a premium price – the 18 carat version on an Oyster bracelet was three-quarters of the price of a man's Datejust at 1212CHF compared with 1661CHF.

I believe Rolex decided to launch the watch in all materials because it had always focused heavily on watches for women. For example, the 1958 catalogue contained 47 models for men's watches—including five pocket watches—while there were 211 models for women. Almost all of these were dress watches, many with diamonds or other precious stones, and almost all on leather or silk straps. Two years later, the number of men's models had risen to 85, while there

↑ It's not just collectors and auction houses who rarely mention the Lady-Datejust, it's Rolex themselves who seemingly treat it like an afterthought. There are 14 different models listed on their website, 13 for men and only one for the 'fairer sex', the Lady-Datejust. It seems almost forgotten, yet spend some time looking at women's wrists and you will realize just how ubiquitous it is.

were slightly fewer for women at 192. Slowly but surely, these dress models vanished from the catalogues, and within a decade they had been reduced to a handful to be almost completely replaced by Oyster models.

Today, Rolex does not make dress watches for women; as with its men's watches, they are all Oysters of some kind or another. The Lady-Datejust may rarely feature in Geneva watch auctions or in discussions between collectors, but it is still – according to my sources – the most popular watch produced by Rolex today.

1958

ENAMEL DIALS

An almost forgotten side street on Rolex's path to horological domination, these are some of the most stunning dials ever sold by Rolex, and fitted to some of their simplest watches.

- **Model number: 6144**
- **Date: 1958**
- **Dial: Sterling silver, fired enamel**
- **Movement: Calibre 1210**
- **Case material: Stainless steel**
- **Dimensions: 34mm**

I already have discussed the cloisonné dials fitted to some of the more expensive Rolex models (see page 106). In the mid-1950s, Stern Frères introduced a simpler, single-coloured range of fired enamel dials and prominent among their clients was Rolex.

Cloisonné dials were extremely expensive to produce, and few clients were prepared to either pay for them or to wear such flamboyant creations. However, the new dials put an end to both these objections. While still more expensive than simple metal dials, the new enamel ones were sufficiently inexpensive to be fitted to steel watches, even manual-wind ones.

They were still grand feu dials, meaning that the enamel was applied to the dial in powder form then fired in an oven at temperatures reaching 1,200°C (2,192°F). Next it was polished to produce an absolutely flat surface, any text was printed on the dial, and then a coat of clear lacquer was applied to protect it. Finally, the dial was drilled to accept the hour indices.

These dials were less expensive because there was no elaborate creative work and, unlike the multiple firings needed for the polychromatic cloisonné dials, they required only one firing. Each firing in the oven increased the risk of the dial cracking and destroying days of complicated work.

These watches appear to have used a limited palette of colours: a Havana brown, a very bright green and an almost ultramarine blue. I have owned both blue and green examples and always preferred the blue. It has a depth that the other colours lack, and almost looks three-dimensional.

Unlike the cloisonné dials, which were only available in solid gold Oyster Perpetual watches, almost all 34 or 36mm in size, the monochrome ones came in a variety of sizes. The smallest I have encountered were 32mm Bubbleback watches, and the largest a 38mm non-Oyster manual-wind dress watch. But the majority appear to be 34mm manual-wind watches, in both steel and solid gold. I have not encountered enamel dial watches in two-tone cases. This does not mean that they were never made – rather that I have never seen one.

To me, the most interesting thing about these dials is that, unlike the cloisonné ones, the enamel never covered the entire dial – there was always a plain border where the minute markers would be placed. The applied hour indices could also be positioned here, meaning that the enamel would not need to be drilled, reducing the risk of cracks. In fact, one of the most interesting monochrome enamel dials had the numerals outside the green enamel area. These numerals were Indian Arabic style, and this very exotic dial was fitted to a steel manual-wind chronometer. In other words, one of the most exotic Rolex dials I have seen was fitted to one of the least expensive models that they ever made.

↔ **The cloisonné dials are the really desirable ones, which fetch spectacular prices at auction, but I prefer these one-colour dials. They are still handmade and sensational-looking, but they are nowhere near as flamboyant as their more expensive cousins. However, there is no way that anyone could describe either of the dials shown here as 'discreet'.**

ROLEX
OYSTER
SHOCK-RESISTING
SWISS

1958

VERIFLAT

A very technically and aesthetically interesting watch which never found its intended market and is equally ignored nowadays – unfairly, in my opinion.

- **Model number: 6512**
- **Date: 1958**
- **Dial: Brass, gilt finish, sunken gold indices**
- **Movement: Calibre 1000**
- **Case material: 18ct gold**
- **Dimensions: 34mm**

→ I almost feel sorry for the Veriflat, so much effort was put into making this watch a reality. A special case with a unique back, a movement stripped of every component above and below the main plate and a special dial with carved indices. Yet despite all of these procedures, essentially, nobody bought the watch. So, I suppose I really feel sorry for the watchmakers and designers behind the project.

The reference 6512 Veriflat is one of the most unusual watches Rolex made during the 1950s – which was definitely their strangest period. It is, essentially, the answer to a question that nobody had ever asked: was there a market for a waterproof watch that was as slim as a Cartier Tank? In the mid-1950s, was anyone looking for a watch they could wear while washing the car and while wearing a dinner jacket?

In November 1954, Rolex registered the name Veriflat. It evidently saw slimness as a selling point, because 18 months later it also registered the names Verislim, Verifine and – bizarrely – Leaf-Thin as potential model names. It is worth remembering the nicknames we have given to the other Rolex Oysters from this period: Bubbleback (see page 56), Bombée (see page 118) and Ovettone (see page 118). Rolex Oyster watches from this time were substantial, but this was probably the only criticism that could be thrown at them. So, it is as though someone at Rolex said, 'You want a thin Oyster; we will give you a thin Oyster'.

Rolex used every trick in the book to reduce the height of the Veriflat to a scant 9mm. The first thing the company worked on was the movement. The 6512 Veriflat was the first watch to use a calibre 1000, it was the same as the one used in the Datejust but it had been stripped of everything which stood in the way of being slim. The date mechanism was ditched, saving 0.81mm, and then the sweep seconds pinion and its associated gears were removed, saving around 0.4mm. But the biggest savings came from abandoning the self-winding apparatus, losing a full 2mm. Now the movement was only 3.45mm in height, by far the slimmest movement ever to sit in an Oyster case.

But Rolex was not finished yet – the case came in for some treatment too. Oyster case backs were normally raised from the case body with the teeth for the Oyster opening tool milled into the perimeter of the case. Here, the milling was sunk into a recess inside the periphery of the case back, enabling a perfectly flat back. There was still one more area to work on, and so the dial was slimmed down; the Veriflat was only available in solid gold, every other gold Oyster in the catalogue has these words in the description: 'solid gold dial figures' but not the Veriflat. When applied gold dial indices are used, they add between 0.3 and 0.5mm to the height of the dial, meaning that the hands have to be raised even more to clear the figures. For the Veriflat, the indices were carved into the dial, leaving recesses which were then plated with gold. At first glance the dial looks identical to ones with applied indices, but a closer inspection reveals the truth.

Rolex put so much effort into developing the watch, yet – despite being in production for seven years – it must be counted as a noble failure. The technical skill and the craftsmanship were there, but the market was not.

ROLEX
OYSTER
VERIFLAT
OFFICIALLY CERTIFIED CHRONOMETER
SWISS

1958

DAY-DATE

The Day-Date gets a new movement, which improves both the accuracy and the day and date changeover, and also gains a lot more style.

- **Model number: 6611**
- **Date: 1958**
- **Dial: Brass, gold-plated applied Indo-Arabic numerals**
- **Movement: 1056**
- **Case material: 18ct gold**
- **Dimensions: 36mm**

As I mentioned, the only real difference between the Datejust (see page 118) and the Day-Date (see page 124) was the addition of the disc bearing the days of the week and the mechanism to drive it. However, while the date wheel was only 3mm wide, the day disc was made from solid aluminium and extended all the way to the centre post of the dial. Because Rolex had chosen to spell out the days in full (and some days have eight or nine letters), and as there was no magnifying lens over the day window, they had to be printed large enough to be read. This meant there was only room to print the days once on the disc. It required a much heavier disc which had to be rotated through 50+° at midnight, while the much lighter date wheel only needed to move 11+°. The energy required to move both the day disc and the date wheel had to come from the mainspring, which also had to drive the balance wheel. But as midnight approached, so much energy was needed that the isochronism of the balance was affected, and accuracy around this time went down the proverbial toilet.

Accuracy mattered more than anything to Hans Wilsdorf, so only a few months after the watch was launched, a completely revised movement was introduced. The new movement was called the 1055B and replaced the initial model, 1055. The principal differences were a reprofiling of the cam, which enabled the day jumper spring to build up energy throughout the day rather than taking it all just before midnight. Two table jewels were added to the top of the movement, enabling the day disc to float on top of them, reducing the friction and so lowering the amount of energy needed to move the disc. The only downside was that now the movement was 7.1mm high, rather than the 7.0mm of the 1055. This small height difference meant that it was not advisable to fit the new movement into the original 6511 cases (see page 124), so a new model – the 6611 – was introduced with the new movement.

→ By the end of the 1950s, the Day-Date began to find its feet, as the world's economies were improving and austerity slowly faded into the background. Rolex began to experiment with different case-finishing techniques – this tight cross-hatching is known as a Florentine finish and can only be done by hand, using incredibly fine-pointed miniature steel tools.

As the movement was being replaced, Rolex took the opportunity to change one other part of the calibre: the simple index regulator on the balance cock was discarded, and the balance changed to a free-sprung one using timing screws on the wheel. This was the first mass-production free-sprung movement from Rolex, and predated the use of the Rolex patented Micro-Stella adjustments, which did not arrive until the 15XX movements several years later.

These free-sprung movements were used in the Datejust, Milgauss (see page 140) and GMT-Master (see page 148) watches, as the 1035, 1080 and 1065 calibres, respectively, and the thing which unites all of them and the 6611 Day-Date is the new 'Superlative Chronometer Officially Certified' text on the dial.

الثلاثاء
ROLEX
OYSTER PERPETUAL
DAY-DATE
٢٨
SUPERLATIVE CHRONOMETER
OFFICIALLY CERTIFIED
T SWISS T

1958

MILGAUSS 6541

By far the most exotically styled of all the 'tool' watches, the Milgauss was a tremendous technical achievement and a commercial disaster.

- **Model number: 6541**
- **Date: 1958**
- **Dial: Soft iron, honeycomb effect black gloss paint, applied and luminous indices**
- **Movement: 1080**
- **Case material: Stainless steel**
- **Dimensions: 40mm**

In 1957, CERN – the European Organization for Nuclear Research – switched on its first accelerator that was powered by huge electromagnets. It is based in Geneva, on the border of France and Switzerland and is just 25 minutes away from Rolex's headquarters on Rue François-Dussaud on the outskirts of the city. Even before the machine was turned on, the accelerator's scientists and technicians noticed that their supposedly anti-magnetic watches were massively affected by the magnetic fields produced by the new equipment.

Historically, the effects of magnetism in watches had been ameliorated by the use of materials such as Nivarox for the hairsprings. These work well when confronted by domestic levels of magnetism, but failed completely when exposed to the ferocious output of CERN's new machines. When a watch is bombarded by magnetism, the hairspring itself becomes magnetized, causing the coils to attach to each other. This effectively shortens the length of the spring, causing the watch to lose time, or, if the magnetism is strong enough, causing the coils all to stick to each other. If that happens, the watch will stop completely.

There are two ways to solve this problem: build a shield around the movement so that the magnetism will pass by it, or construct the entire movement from non-ferrous materials so that magnetism will have no effect. Rolex launched the Milgauss, reference 6541, towards the end of 1956. It was the last of its 'tool' watches and arrived not long after its numeric predecessor, the 6542 GMT-Master. Rolex chose to shield its movement, using what is commonly known as a Faraday cage – a soft iron frame that surrounds the movement. 'Soft iron' may sound like a contradiction, but it refers to a form of the metal which is easily magnetized and demagnetized. When magnetic waves hit the watch, they are captured by the frame and never reach the movement. The frame is formed from a soft iron dust cap which sits between the movement and the case back, a movement ring surrounds its perimeter and an extra thick dial is made from the same material.

The dial was unlike any of the sports watches that had preceded it. They were austere, functional pieces and the only embellishment was the red/blue bezel of the GMT-Master. The Milgauss contained a black galvanic dial with an unusual textured finish, the quarter-hour indices were multi-faceted arrowheads, and the hour and minute hands were a highly polished and faceted dauphine style. It also had an unusual lightning-bolt sweep seconds hand. Even the bezel insert was different, rather than the usual 0 to 60 markings, the Milgauss had 0 to 6 markings, but with 60 divisions.

Unfortunately, the market for watches designed to be used by people who work in highly magnetic environments was extremely limited, particularly when IWC, Jaeger-LeCoultre, Omega and even Patek Philippe also produced watches to meet this microscopic market. The Milgauss struggled on until 1960/61, when it was replaced by the much more austere and conventional reference 1019. However, the 6543 remained in stock with both Rolex USA and Rolex UK until the late 1960s.

→ The 6541 was such a failure that for over a decade following it being discontinued, Rolex USA still had lots of them in stock. So, they were used as prizes for Rolex-sponsored motoring events in the US. Look at any photograph of a winner at Daytona or other US tracks and if Rolex are awarding a watch, it will be a 6541 Milgauss.

ROLEX
OYSTER-PERPETUAL
SWISS

1959

DATEJUST 1601

In its third incarnation, the Datejust lost a lot of its flamboyance but became the archetype for all the Datejusts which were to follow in its wake.

- **Model number: 1601**
- **Date: 1959**
- **Dial: Brass, silvered, white gold indices**
- **Movement: 1535**
- **Case material: Steel, white gold**
- **Dimensions: 36mm**

→ This is the archetypal Datejust, it's what we envisage in our minds when we hear the name 'Datejust'. The playfulness of the earlier versions has gone, replaced by a much more austere, almost brutalist design. The indices are straight bars, sliced vertically by a stripe of black enamel, and the rest of the dial is devoid of any ornamentation. It is reduced to its elements, a pure object.

Now that the Day-Date was the Rolex flagship, the Datejust was liberated. It was by far the company's most popular men's watch, and Rolex chose to exploit this. Not only was it available in a variety of materials – stainless steel, steel with pink, yellow or white gold bezels, and solid gold in all three colours – it came with four different bezel configurations as well as four case finishes.

The reference 1600 was available in all materials and had the most restrained look with a simple flat, polished bezel. The 1601 was the most common version of the Datejust, and had the classic Rolex diamond-cut fluted bezel in one of the three colours of gold.

To the best of my knowledge, the 1602 was only available in 18 carat yellow gold and had a Florentine finish with micro cross-hatched engraving on all the visible portions of the case and the bracelet, if fitted. The 1603 was a much less common watch, with a steel bezel machined with bars at each minute and thin engraved lines between each bar. It was priced between the 1600 and the 1601.

The 1604 is a bit of an enigma; it appears in all the parts catalogues from the era, but in none of the sales or master catalogues. This is probably explained by the fact that in the parts catalogues, both the case body and the bezel are listed as serti (jewel set). I assume that it was a jewel-set gold or platinum version that was only available as a special order.

The 1605 is probably even more rare than the 1604; it has a bezel with unusual machining: rather than the conventional fluted bezel, the cuts form triangles. It has been described as the Piranha-tooth bezel, but the parts catalogue lists it as Guilloche Pyramid, which is a rather more peaceful description.

There does not seem to be a 1606, but the 1607 was weird enough for both numbers. Only available in 18 carat yellow gold, the bezel was finished in a random machined effect that Rolex called Bark. If the watch came on an 18 carat Jubilee bracelet, the surface of the three smaller central links also had this finish.

The 1611 was pretty much identical to the 1607, except that rather than a Bark finish to the bezel (and bracelet, if fitted), it had what Rolex called a Tsoca surface. This looked as if the surface has been hit thousands of times with the world's smallest hammer. It is rare and – in my opinion – not very attractive.

If you think that this is a phenomenal number of variations for one model, you are not wrong. But Rolex was not finished with Datejust options.

ROLEX
OYSTER PERPETUAL
DATEJUST
7
SUPERLATIVE CHRONOMETER
OFFICIALLY CERTIFIED
T SWISS T

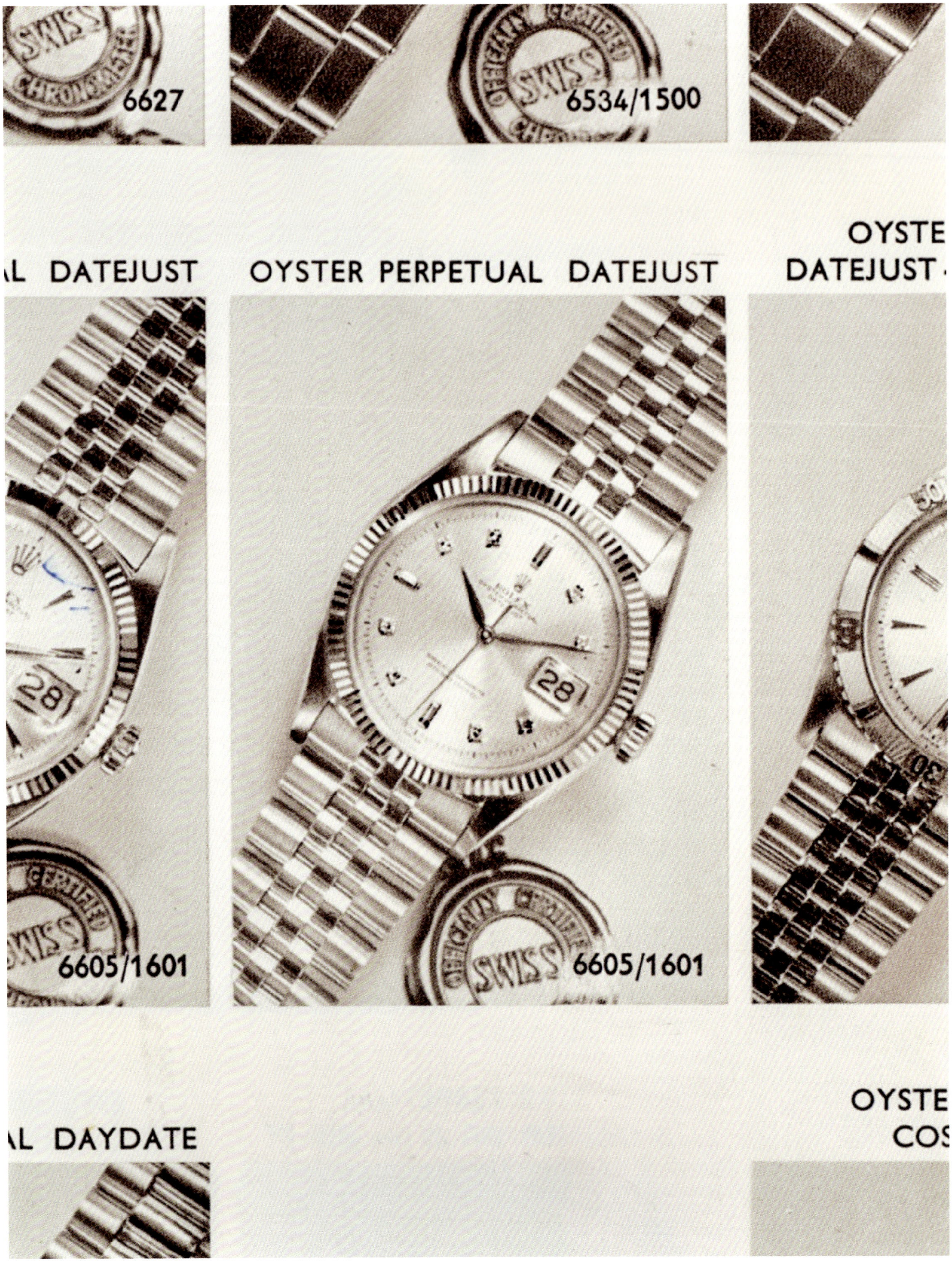
6627
6534/1500
L DATEJUST
OYSTER PERPETUAL DATEJUST
OYSTE
DATEJUST
6605/1601
6605/1601
OYSTE
COS
L DAYDATE

↑ The image above shows an early Datejust 1601 next to its image in a 1960s training booklet for Rolex US retailers.

← This 1960s catalogue demonstrates how little difference there was between the Datejust 6605 and 1601. Only the movement changed between these models.

1959

SUBMARINER 5508

The last of the 'James Bond'-style Submariners, the 5508 was the bridge to the modern Submariner: it used the old-style case but the modern 1530 movement.

- **Model number: 5508**
- **Date: 1959**
- **Dial: Brass, black galvanic paint, radium indices**
- **Movement: 1530**
- **Case material: Stainless steel**
- **Dimensions: 37mm**

There is a strange listing in the autumn 1958 Rolex master catalogue. Most entries state the model number, the model name, whether a watch is automatic or not, the number of jewels in the movement, the case material and if it has a bracelet or strap. But the watch listed on page 3 had two model numbers, 6536 and 5508. In other words, this was the point at which Rolex switched between two models. Actually, it was switching between two movements – otherwise the watches were identical.

The only difference between the 6536 and the 5508 was the replacement of the 1030 movement with the new 1530, the first version of the 15XX movement which would power Rolex watches for two decades. I think the 5508 was the first Rolex model powered by the new movement: at this time, the Submariner was still in its adolescent phase and this low-production, niche model made an ideal test bed for the new calibre. The 6204/6205 models (see page 120) powered by the venerable A260 had been in production for just over a year, from the end of 1953 until the early part of 1955. They were replaced by the 6536 which was identical except for the new flatter case back which reduced the height from 13mm to 12mm. The 6536 lasted for just over three years, until the 5508 appeared in late 1958. It would be foolish to assume that production of the 6536 ceased on one day and production of the 5508 started on the next day. There was an overlap from the end of 1958 to mid-1959 when you can see similar production dates, which explains why two model numbers were listed in the catalogue. In many ways, the 5508 represented the end of an era. It was the last of the thin-case, 100m depth-rated and Galvanic dial Submariners.

Galvanic dials are often referred to as 'Gilt' dials, where the text and minute track appear to be printed in gold. In fact, the gold elements aren't printed on the dial. These elements are the original brass dial colour revealed from beneath. This was achieved by first printing the desired markings with clear lacquer. The entire dial was then submerged in an electrolytic black paint solution. An electrical current ensured a perfectly even black coating everywhere except where the clear lacquer protected the brass.

This galvanizing process offered a significant advantage over conventional printing: the text wouldn't rub off over time. After emerging from this galvanic treatment, a further coat of clear lacquer sealed the paint, prevented oxidization, and provided the high-gloss finish prized by collectors. However, these dials weren't without their issues. One problem was that the lacquer used was organic, most likely made from tree sap, and tended to attract moisture, resulting in bubbles forming on the surface of the dial under the lacquer.

→ Almost the 'lost' Submariner, the 5508 was only produced for less than three years, and during the period it was on sale it was overshadowed by the newly introduced 5512. That's a shame, because in many ways it was the best of the vintage Submariners, still using the slimmer non crown-guard case but fitted with the reliable and accurate 1530 movement.

100m = 330ft
SUBMARINER

1959

GMT-MASTER

The first solid gold 'tool' watch. But the case material was not the only difference; the dial, hands and colour of the bezel insert were considerably different from the steel version.

- **Model number: 6542**
- **Date: 1959**
- **Dial: Brass, galvanic black paint, applied gold indices**
- **Movement: Calibre 1065**
- **Case material: 18ct gold**
- **Dimensions: 38mm**

→ The first solid-gold sports watch from Rolex, the gold GMT-Master showed how well Rolex understood the market. The Submariner had to go through four iterations before Rolex produced a gold version, but the GMT-Master was there from the beginning. Quite simply anyone who could afford the early international jet flights could afford a gold watch. The steel GMT-Masters were worn in the cockpit, the gold ones in first class.

The newly launched GMT-Master was unlike any previous Rolex – the two-tone bezel and red 24-hour hand made it almost flamboyant. The bezel insert was made of plastic; it is usually referred to as Bakelite but it is almost certainly some form of Perspex as it is translucent and Bakelite is opaque. The insert was engraved with the even numbers between 2 and 22, with engraved dots between and the engravings were filled with luminescence. The rear half of the insert was painted blue between 18 and 6, and red on the other half.

But there was a problem with the insert or – at least – some of the inserts. In 1959 and 1960 various organizations noticed that their employees' radiation monitoring badges were showing high levels of Strontium-90 (Sr-90) exposure. Sr-90 is a radioactive silver metal that can be found in nuclear waste.

The assumption had always been that the radium used on the bezel hour numbers was somehow contaminated with atmospheric Sr-90 from nuclear weapons tests. The truth was that between 1957 and early 1958, Sr-90 from a wholly owned entity of the British government – UK Atomic Energy Authority (UKAEA) – was used as a replacement for radium by Swiss dial and bezel makers.

In a House of Lords debate on 29 March 1962, Lord Hailsham stated that the UKAEA had sold supplies of Sr-90 to a Swiss company for dial luminizing, but that these sales ceased at the start of 1958.

The dial firms wanted to use Sr-90 because at the time it was considered to be safer than radium as it emitted far fewer dangerous gamma rays. It was soon realized that Sr-90 was attracted to calcium and so remained in the bones and bone marrow of people exposed to it. At the end of 1959, the US Atomic Energy Commission issued a notice to 15 Swiss watch firms that they must recall any watches that used Sr-90. This was eight months after Rolex had ceased production of the 6542 and its potentially dangerous bezel.

The 6542 was introduced at the 1956 Swiss Industries Fair in Basel. Its replacement, the 1675, came along three years later at the 1959 fair. So, if we conclude that the 6542 was in production for 36 months and Sr-90 was used for around 12 of those months, it stands to reason that up to 33 per cent of the production may have been fitted with the contaminated bezel inserts.

Not all of the early bezels suffered this contamination. Both of the watches I have seen had been tested for Sr-90 and the results were negative, meaning that they were probably produced before the switch to Sr-90.

ROLEX
GMT-MASTER
SWISS

1960

TRU-BEAT

One of the most obscure models from a time when Rolex was at its most inventive. The name has a perfectly 1950s space-age sound to it, although, in the US, it was named the 'Metropolitan'.

- **Model number: 6565**
- **Date: 1960**
- **Dial: Brass, silvered, applied steel indices**
- **Movement: 1040**
- **Case material: Stainless steel**
- **Dimensions: 34mm**

Rolex has a history of taking an existing concept, improving it and successfully marketing it. It was not the first to make a wristwatch, make a waterproof case or manufacture an automatic wristwatch. But it succeeded where the original inventors are all, now, pretty much forgotten.

The one thing that Rolex can claim as its own was the industrialization of movements capable of chronometer certification. By the mid-1950s, it was producing well over half of all Swiss-certified chronometers. Pilots and navigators used the GMT-Master (see page 148) to help plot flight paths, divers used the Submariner (see page 146) to time decompression times, and doctors used the Datejust (see page 142) to time patients' pulse rates. But there was a slight problem with the last one; the doctor would mentally log the number of pulses while keeping an eye on the watch. When they had counted the desired number of pulses, they had to decide exactly which seconds the hand was registering. Because the seconds hand was always in motion and normally somewhere between two indices, the doctor had to know if it was at one point or the other before they could make their calculation. Historically, any timepiece used for time-critical measurements would feature a dead-beat seconds hand, where it would sit on the current second's index for one second before jumping to the next one, where it would pause again. This made reading the exact time foolproof. If you think that this sounds like the action of a quartz watch, you are correct.

Sometimes it seems as if there is a collective mentality in the Swiss watch industry. In the mid-1950s, two of the biggest manufacturers, Rolex and Omega, along with a large movement manufacturer, Chézard, all introduced dead-beat seconds movements.

The 6565 Tru-Beat is one of the most obscure watches ever made by the house that Hans Wilsdorf (see page 12) built. The Rolex Bienne factory took the basic 1030 chronometer movement (see page 120) and added or replaced 30 components including a complete secondary escapement to produce the calibre 1040, first launched towards the end of 1954. However, because it was a development of the 1030 rather than a brand-new movement, the basic design was compromised and prone to failure. Because of this, many less than well-qualified watchmakers removed the jump-seconds mechanism when servicing the watch. This has resulted in an unmodified Tru-Beat being a very rare watch.

Despite these problems, or maybe because of them, Rolex ploughed considerable resources into the continued development of the 1040 movement; it is difficult to believe now, but there are actually three variants of it. The differences are in the design of the small pallets that operate the stop/start mechanism of the seconds hand.

→ **The 1950s was a time of unprecedented experimentation for Rolex, and probably no watch exemplifies this more than the Tru-Beat. Dead-beat seconds movements already existed, using a star wheel and an additional hairspring, but that wasn't good enough for Rolex. Wanting a no-compromise solution, they devised a complete additional escapement which sat immediately under the dial.**

The final development (and the only successful one) has straight but almost razor-thin pallets. But although they enable accurate operation of the seconds hand, they do make the watch quite susceptible to shocks.

It is an interesting watch aesthetically as well as technically. The case is the simple polished-bezel Oyster one, but the face of the watch is very attractive, with cross hairs and a bright red sweep seconds hand. Over 25 years ago, I took a rare 18-carat version into Rolex London to be serviced and when it was returned to me, the staff confirmed that the 18-carat versions were produced in 'single digits'. In my opinion the Tru-Beat is the penultimate 'If you know, you know' Rolex, second only to the 'Kew A' (see page 116).

1960

EXPLORER 5500

I suppose this was intended as the Rolex Explorer for the 'working man': no chronometer certification, 2mm smaller than the 1016 and around 40 per cent cheaper.

- **Model number: 5500**
- **Date: 1960**
- **Dial: Brass, gloss black galvanic paint, tritium indices**
- **Movement: 1530**
- **Case material: Stainless steel**
- **Dimensions: 34mm**

→ As these watches were essentially Air-Kings with different dial and hands, none of them were ever chronometer tested. This means that instead of the SCOC text, the word 'Precision' was printed below the centre post. However, some watches – like the one shown here – had the designation 'Super Precision' instead. Is this a halfway house between SCOC and Precision or just a marketing gesture?

I have already described how Rolex used testimonials from pilots in their Rolex Oyster advertisements in the 1930s (see page 44). Record-breaking airmen such as Owen Cathcart-Jones, Arthur Clouston and Alex Henshaw were prominently featured as at the time they occupied the same place in the public eye as astronauts did in the 1960s. In the minds of many people, the Rolex Oyster was the pilot's watch. And so, during World War II, as many pilots as were able to – particularly fighter pilots – purchased Oysters for themselves. When the war ended, Rolex repaid the compliment by naming an entire range of watches for them, including the Air-Giant, Air-Tiger, Air-Lion and Air-King. These were all manual-wind steel Oysters and were between 32mm and 36mm in size. As the Perpetual became more accepted, the manual watches were slowly dropped from the catalogue, and the last remaining Air watch, the Air-King, was equipped with the automatic calibre 1030. This was the 6552, a 34mm polished-bezel watch with applied arrowhead indices and leaf hands. Despite being fitted with the 1030 Perpetual movement, it was not a chronometer and the lack of certification – and the costs involved – meant that the new Air-King became the entry-level Rolex Oyster Perpetual in 1959.

Within two years, things had changed. The 1030 calibre was replaced by the recently introduced 1530, and while the model name stayed the same, the model number became 5500 and the dial and hands changed to the simple batons and stick hands of the contemporary Datejusts.

However, not all of the 5500 watches had this dial. With the success of the recently launched 1016 Explorer, there was a demand for a less expensive version. Initially, the watches seemed to have been sold exclusively by the NAAFI (Navy, Army and Air Force Institutes), the British equivalent of the American PX stores. Like the early 1016 watches, they featured a high gloss dial, inverted triangle 12 index, large luminous Arabic numerals at the quarter hours and luminous batons for the remainder. The watch also had the Mercedes hour hand, the oversized minute hand and the large luminous dot near the tip of the seconds hand, and – rather than Air-King – it bore the model name Explorer. While the early ones came from the NAAFI, by 1962 the watch was in the general catalogue (the UK one at least), where it sold for £51.3.0 as distinct from the regular 5500 Air-King, which was priced at £49.2.0. But when the 1016 switched from the gloss black galvanic dials to the much less expensive matt printed ones, the 5500 Explorer disappeared.

ROLEX
OYSTER PERPETUAL
EXPLORER
SUPER PRECISION
SWISS

1960

DAYTONA

The first modern chronograph from Rolex, which occasionally carried the Paul Newman dial.

- **Model number: 6239**
- **Date: 1960**
- **Dial: Brass, gloss black paint, gilt indices**
- **Movement: Calibre 722**
- **Case material: 18ct gold**
- **Dimensions: 36mm**

The history of the chronograph is inextricably bound to that of the motor car; both were invented in the 19th century but came into their own in the 20th. Once cars began to compete against each other it became vital to time their performance, and the chronograph was the only tool available. By the 1920s, it had become small enough to move from being a pocket watch to a wristwatch. This enabled it to be worn and used by a driver on the move, as one hand could remain on the wheel while the other activated the timing pushers.

Chronograph makers chose race names for their pieces. Heuer chose Carrera after the famed Mexican road race and Autavia (from AUT-omobile and AVIA-tion), to say nothing of an entire series named after F1 tracks including Monaco, Silverstone and Montreal. Tudor called one of its watches the Monte Carlo, and the firm's sister brand, Rolex, used the name Daytona.

However, it almost was not called the Daytona at all. Nowadays we tend to think of Rolex as a decisive firm. This was not the case in the 1950s and 1960s, when there was often indecision about model names. The Submariner was almost called the Rolex Skin Diver, and some watches found their way to market with dials marked as such. Similarly, the Daytona was originally planned to be called the Le Mans. The reason for the last-minute change was, most likely, pressure from the US branch of the firm.

Like most Rolex introductions, the Daytona evolved from an existing watch,

→ The Paul Newman dial is, by far, the most desirable of dials for the Daytona. But it was never an option – as far as Rolex was concerned it was simply one of their normal dials. If you ordered a Daytona, you might get this dial configuration – but you probably wouldn't. It came in three colours for the steel watch (black, white and red) and just two for the gold version (black and gold).

the 6238 chronograph. Rolex had given the most recent versions of the 6238 a more modern and cleaner look than its predecessor – the 6234 (see page 114) – by removing the tachometer and telemeter scales from the periphery of the dial. The new look was good, but it meant that one of the basic functions of a chronograph – calculating average speed or rates – was no longer possible. The ability to do this was re-introduced on the new 6239 by replacing the smooth polished bezel on the 6238 with a flat steel one with the tachometer markings engraved into the surface and filled with black lacquer. The other big change was the dial. It was no longer monochromatic and the three registers – in clockwise rotation they were the 30-minute register, the 12-hour one and the constant running seconds – were now in a contrasting colour to the dial: silver on a black dial or vice versa.

The movements for the early Daytonas were carried over from the 6238, the Valjoux 72B (later renamed the 722). This was a classic Valjoux three-register, 17-jewel movement, produced to the highest of Valjoux's optional finishes. It was equipped with the free-sprung Rolex patented Micro-Stella regulated balance and Kif-flector shock protection in place of the usual Valjoux Incabloc. Like all Rolex movements of this period, these movements were devoid of decoration but well-finished and robust.

1962

EXPLORER 1016

By far the nicest of all the Explorer 1016 watches, the early versions with the high gloss dial and tritium indices are eagerly sought after.

- Model number: 1016
- Date: 1962
- Dial: Brass, gloss black paint, tritium indices
- Movement: 1560
- Case material: Stainless steel
- Dimensions: 36mm

→ I don't know how much time, money and effort Rolex put into developing the Veriflat (see page 136), as a 'dress' Oyster. They needn't have bothered, the 1016 – to me, at least – is it, particularly with the gloss dial and gilt print. It would slide under the French cuffs of a pleated dress shirt just as easily as it would under a denim shirt worn with Levi's.

Only two years after the launch of the 6350/6150 Explorer models, Rolex introduced a new version of the watch, the 6610. It was the first to use the firm's new 1030 movement, which Rolex designed from scratch as a self-winding movement. It was much slimmer than the A260, and so the 6350's heavily domed case was replaced with a new, thinner one with a flatter back. The Explorer was Rolex's first 'tool' watch, but when the 6610 was launched in 1956, it was priced between the other two tool watches – the Submariner 6536, which cost 245CHF, and the GMT-Master 6542 at 358CHF. At 295CHF, the 6610 Explorer was more expensive than the Submariner because, like the GMT-Master, it was now only sold as a chronometer.

The case and movement may have changed, but the layout of the dial remained constant – gloss black on a polished brass dial base. On the early 6610s, the only change was the addition of the depth text '50m=165ft'. What is interesting is that the outer minute track and the text were not printed on the dial – the colour of the brass dial was allowed to show through. The track was printed on the dial using clear lacquer and then the whole dial was immersed in an electrolytic black paint solution, an electric current was passed through it and a perfectly even coat of black paint coated the dial except where the lacquer had been applied. The great advantage of galvanizing the dial over conventional dial printing was that the text could not be rubbed off over time. When the dials emerged from the galvanic process they were then given a coat of clear lacquer to seal in the paint, prevent oxidization and give the high gloss effect loved by collectors. The only problem with these dials was that the lacquer was a natural one, made from tree sap, and offered no ultraviolet protection. Consequently dials subject to this kind of exposure were prone to discolouration and have been known to fade to different shades of brown. There were also problems when the dials were exposed to variations in temperature as the rates of expansion of the brass dial and the lacquer were different. This resulted in spiderweb-like cracks in the lacquer.

The 6610 had a slightly longer life than the 6350, but it was still only available for three years as, in 1959, the longest-lived Rolex model, the 1016, arrived. Fitted with gloss galvanic printed black dials, the 1016 can be distinguished from its predecessors by the 'Superlative Chronometer Officially Certified' text below the centre post.

ROLEX
OYSTER PERPETUAL
EXPLORER
9
3
SUPERLATIVE CHRONOMETER
OFFICIALLY CERTIFIED
6
SWISS – T < 25

1962

TRIPLE CALENDAR

The 6236 Jean-Claude Killy is one of the most sought-after watches from the early 1960s, particularly when in exceptionally clean condition, like this example.

- **Model number: 6236**
- **Date: 1962**
- **Dial: Brass, silvered, applied steel indices**
- **Movement: Valjoux 72C**
- **Case material: Stainless steel**
- **Dimensions: 36mm**

→ The 6236 was the last hurrah for complicated watches at Rolex until the Sky-Dweller came along exactly 50 years after the 6236 ended production in 1962. I love the fact that the hour indices at the 1 and 11 positions are cut short, so as to give space for the day and month windows – it's always the details which grab my eye.

The Rolex Oyster Triple Calendar Chronograph reference 6236 is too much of a mouthful for anyone outside of an auction house, so everyone else refers to these watches as the Rolex Dato-Compax or the Jean-Claude Killy.

This is ironic as neither of those nicknames has anything to do with the watch. Universal Genève did make a watch called the Dato Compax at around the same time that Rolex launched the 4767 and 4768. The name Dato Compax has come to mean a full calendar chronograph with windows for the month and day and a peripheral calendar, and these watches are almost always powered by the venerable Valjoux 72C (see page 96). The Universal Genève Dato Compax fits none of these criteria. It is a three-register chronograph with a fourth register at the 12 position which indicates the date only. It does not have any windows in the dial and there is no method to indicate the day or the month.

As for Jean-Claude Killy, his connection with Rolex is that he was one of the first to give them a testimonial, lives down the street from Rolex in Geneva and was a board member for around 40 years. As far as I can tell, Killy never wore any of the models which bore his name. He became a Rolex ambassador in 1969, half a decade after the last 6236 watches disappeared from the catalogue.

Killy signed up with Mark McCormack's International Management Group (IMG), in May 1968 after winning the triple crown of Olympic skiing at the Grenoble Winter Olympics. McCormack was famed for representing sports players and linking them with the international brands he also represented; Rolex was among them. Arnold Palmer, Jack Nicklaus and Jackie Stewart are just a few of the stars who became Rolex ambassadors, but none nurtured the relationship better than Killy. Rolex picked him because of his sporting prowess, but once they saw how driven he was it became obvious that he could be more than just a face in an advertisement. He retired from skiing following his Olympic triumph, and over the next few years he bought a sportswear firm, raced at Le Mans and the Nürburgring, learned to fly a helicopter and became chairman of the committee for the Winter Olympics at Turin and Sochi.

Perhaps it is surprising to learn that Killy knew nothing about Rolex until he became an ambassador. During his skiing years he wore a Breitling Co-Pilot, reference 765CP, one of the most oversized and masculine of the firm's chronographs. He was also a watch collector, so he may have owned a 6036 (see page 97) or a 6236, but he was always photographed wearing a Rolex from the current collection, usually a Day-Date. However, the watch he wore most often in the Rolex advertisements was the Explorer II (see page 204), the 1655, the watch which should have been named the Jean-Claude Killy.

FRI
APR
ROLEX
OYSTER CHRONOGRAPH
ANTIMAGNETIC
SWISS

1964

MILGAUSS 1019

After the dismal failure of the first model, Milgauss 6541, Rolex persevered with the model and brought out a completely redesigned version. It had a similar level of success.

- **Model number: 1019**
- **Date: 1964**
- **Dial: Soft iron, black paint, applied white gold indices**
- **Movement: 1580**
- **Case material: Stainless steel**
- **Dimensions: 37mm**

→ I am always amazed that the Milgauss 1019 isn't more popular than it currently is. It has a unique case, larger than its contemporaries, a unique movement, a unique dial – the only one with red print throughout its life, unique hands and a great back story. And the watch is perfectly wearable as an everyday watch, but for some reason it has never 'taken off' with collectors.

Samuel Johnson, the 18th-century diarist and dictionary compiler, famously said that 'a second marriage is the triumph of hope over experience'. At the end of the 1950s, Rolex was definitely hopeful. In 1960, despite the commercial failure of the 6541 and 6543 versions of the original Milgauss (see page 140), it introduced a completely new version, the 1019.

Rolex was known for incremental, evolutionary changes – not radical ones – yet the 1019 was certainly radical. Nothing had been carried over from the previous versions – no rotating bezel, no lightning strike seconds hand and no textured dial. It was as if Rolex had decided to produce a watch which was the opposite of its original watch.

However, one thing remained: the raison d'être of the watch, its ability to ignore magnetic fields, was unchanged. The system it used also remained – a soft iron cup shielded the bottom and sides of the movement, while an extra-thick dial of the same material protected the top.

It was as if the new version had thrown away Superman's uniform and donned Clark Kent's business suit but – like the mild-mannered reporter – it retained his impressive but well-concealed abilities. The new Milgauss was a more sober, restrained watch. It was the perfect engineer's watch – the very market that it was designed for. Its utility is best demonstrated by the fact that it was the only Rolex which could be ordered with or without a luminous dial. The non-luminous dial was important because machines producing very high magnetic fields, like cyclotrons, are often used to produce radioactive isotopes. In situations like these, very sensitive radiation detectors are installed to ensure that none of the radiation escapes the machine. The detectors are sensitive enough to be triggered by the tritium on a watch dial, so the non-luminous dial was an option. The 1019 was available with a silver or black dial; luminous indices and hands are much more readable against a black dial, so the non-luminous dial was never available on the black dial, only the silver one.

Despite all these choices, the 1019 never really found a market, it was 12 to 15 per cent more expensive than the 1016 Explorer, while its anti-magnetic benefits were of no use to 99.5 per cent of possible purchasers. I was intrigued by the watch in the mid-1980s and went to the Watches of Switzerland store on Bond Street, London, to buy one, only to be told that they were only produced by Rolex when there was sufficient demand for them to produce a batch, so I left empty-handed. In 1988, Rolex threw in the towel and dropped the watch from the catalogue, although I think production had ended considerably earlier. The 1019, along with the 1016 Explorer (see page 152) and the 5513 Submariner (see page 174) were among the last watches still using 15XX movements, but both the 1016 and 5513 were replaced by new models using the new 30XX movement, not the 1019. It just slipped away.

ROLEX
OYSTER PERPETUAL
MILGAUSS
SUPERLATIVE CHRONOMETER
OFFICIALLY CERTIFIED
T SWISS T

1964

SUBMARINER 5512

Launched in 1959, the model 5512 Submariner must have seemed a radical change for fans of the watch, but it was a classic example of Rolex doing what it does best... evolving.

- **Model number: 5512**
- **Date: 1964**
- **Dial: Brass, galvanic black paint, tritium indices**
- **Movement: 1530**
- **Case material: Stainless steel**
- **Dimensions: 40mm**

→ The 5512 seems to be overshadowed by its more popular and populous cousin, the 5513. But it's worth remembering that the 5512 always had the better movement and also that the 5512 was there three years before the 5513 saw the light of day. There are probably twenty 5513 Submariners for every 5512, yet the prices don't reflect this disparity; in other words, the 5512 is a hidden bargain now.

The experience of Royal Navy (RN) divers with the original 6538 Submariners (see page 122) had shown that there was a problem with the bezel design. All the testing for the first Submariners had been done in the warm waters of the Mediterranean, off the Côte d'Azure, where the divers wore only swimming trunks, flippers and a mask. But when the RN used the watch in the cold waters of the North Sea or the English Channel, they had to do so wearing a full diving suit and neoprene gloves. Dressed like this, it was almost impossible to use the bezel. Thus, a new bezel was designed with much deeper and angled indentations on its perimeter. The design of this new bezel was one of the two things which made the 5512 stand out from any preceding Submariner model; the other was the shoulders which surrounded much of the winding crown.

Rolex had always known that the Oyster winding crown, and the tube that it screwed into, were the weakest link in the ability of the case to remain watertight in any situation. Because the crown projected from the side of a watch, it was always going to be the first part to be hit or snagged; if it was displaced by as little as half a millimetre, the impermeability of the watch was fatally compromised. The new shoulders made this much less likely, as the first redesign enclosed almost 50 per cent of the area of the winding crown. This was the so-called Square Shoulder design. Rolex made a great deal out of the new design, but much of the crown was not only protected but also inaccessible to gloved fingers. So, within six months of the launch of the 5512, the cases were modified in-house by machining away a large portion of the shoulders, producing a pointed but angular silhouette nicknamed the eagle beak. This still provided plenty of protection for the crown while making it easier to adjust. This silhouette – the so-called pointed crown guards – was adopted for the remainder of the early production of the 5512.

The difference between the 5512 and the 5513 is that the former is a chronometer, and the latter is not. But that was not always the case. Throughout the history of the Submariner there have always been two versions: one with a thin case and one with a thick one. They were the 6204/5 and 6200, the 6536 and 6538, and the 5508 and 5510 (see pages 120 and 146). When the 5512 was introduced, the 5508 was kept in production for another three years as the thin case version of the Submariner. During this period, the dials of most 5512s were not signed as chronometers.

ROLEX
OYSTER PERPETUAL
200m=660ft
SUBMARINER
SUPERLATIVE CHRONOMETER
OFFICIALLY CERTIFIED
SWISS - T < 25
10
20
30
40
50

CHAPTER SEVEN

1966–1975

ROLEX
OYSTER
COSMOGRAPH
DAYTONA
SWISS
UNITS PER
HOUR

1966–1975

ROLEX TAKES OFF

André Heiniger, J Walter-Thompson and Mark McCormack join forces to make Rolex a marketing powerhouse.

In the introduction to the previous chapter (see page 111), I said that I would discuss the second important relationship that René-Paul Jeanneret established at a later point. This is the time. In early 1968, the sports agent Mark McCormack wrote to André Heiniger suggesting a meeting, Heiniger – who, by this time had taken on the role of CEO – was too busy and suggested that Jeanneret meet him instead. This first encounter took place in Geneva and seems to have gone well enough for the two to continue meeting and discussing the potential of a commercial relationship. The introduction between the two was initially arranged by John Read, head of Rolex Tokyo, who had previously worked with McCormack on a Rolex-sponsored golf tournament in Japan.

But McCormack started the relationship on the wrong foot. He thought that Rolex was leaving a lot of money on the table by not licensing its name to other manufacturers, such as cameras. He did not yet understand that the firm's most valuable asset was its name and reputation; licensing it to others would mean diluting it, and Rolex had no intention of doing that. He soon saw this was going nowhere and switched to Rolex-sponsored golf events. This proved to be a much more fruitful path and an initial agreement was made for a major Tokyo event. My assumption as to why it wanted another Tokyo event was that the Japanese were golf crazy, but – more importantly – if the Japan event was a failure, it would not reflect too badly on Rolex Geneva as at the time Rolex Japan was operated by an independent company. At the end of 1971, Heiniger took over the relationship with McCormack, who in March 1972 suggested that Rolex might like to get involved with some of his clients. He mentioned American golfer Arnold Palmer (who had been his first client) and English golfer Tony Jacklin, and also proposed that French alpine ski racer Jean-Claude Killy might be a good ambassador for the firm.

The deal was done. Palmer and Killy became official faces of Rolex, and the long-term marketing strategy of the firm changed. As it does today, IMG, the company McCormack founded, represented other prominent figures and so now Rolex advertisements featured classical musicians Dame Kiri Te Kanawa and Plácido Domingo who were both its clients.

But McCormack's greatest coup was when he put Rolex together with another one of his clients – the All England Lawn Tennis & Croquet Club – or, as it is more commonly known, Wimbledon. The first tentative step was to get a Rolex-branded clock on the scoreboard and, once this was done, the involvement gradually increased.

Apart from advertising featuring the brand ambassadors – although Rolex calls them testimonees – there was an evolution of the 'Men who guide

← Daytona, 1972 (see page 188).

The advertisements implied that no matter how tough or stressful the situation, you – and your Rolex – could handle it.

the destinies of the world' campaign. Once again, no people were shown, just locations such as a racing yacht or the cockpit of an airliner, with the tag line 'If you were here…' along with a photograph of a Rolex. The advertisements implied that no matter how tough or stressful the situation, you – and your Rolex – could handle it.

What I find really interesting is that while all this was happening, the majority of the Swiss watch industry was crumbling around Rolex. The so-called quartz crisis, which ran pretty much through the entire 1970s, was decimating the entire industry – apart from Rolex. I say so-called because the crisis which hit Swiss watchmaking had absolutely nothing to do with Japanese quartz watches. If the finger of blame can be pointed anywhere, it should be towards Richard Nixon, not towards Seiko. On 15 August, 1971, Nixon took the first steps in changing the world's monetary order. Until that day all exchange rates were fixed and gold had an official price of 35 US dollars per ounce. When the markets finally settled down, the Swiss Franc was worth 40 per cent more than it was before Nixon spoke, and by December 1973 gold had gone from 35 US dollars per ounce to 85 US dollars. So, the price of a Swiss watch in the US rose by 40 per cent, simply due to currency fluctuations; and if there was any gold in it, that percentage rose by almost three times. This massively impacted the Swiss watch industry because watches are a discretionary purchase – very few people actually need a watch, and almost everyone buys one because they want to. But when prices rise by this amount during a time of economic uncertainty, most potential clients stop and think about the purchase. This had a devastating effect in Switzerland, and not just in the watch business. The total proportion of the population working in all manufacturing was over 40 per cent in 1970, at the end of the decade it was down to 32 per cent.

So how did Rolex come through this comparatively unscathed? To return to McCormack, in his book *What They Don't Teach You at Harvard Business School* he tells his story of having dinner with André Heiniger, the Chairman of Rolex. On being asked by a passing friend, 'How's the watch business?', Heiniger responded, 'I have no idea'. This was met with a laugh – the man at the helm of the world's most prestigious watch company didn't know what was going on in the watch industry. But, in McCormack's words, 'Heiniger was deadly serious. "Rolex is not in the watch business," he continued. "We are in the luxury business."'

Rolex survived because it was not in competition with Omega or Jaeger-LeCoultre. The advertising and promotional train that it had started over a decade before had moved it from merely a watch brand to an icon, and a very desirable one at that.

→ On the back cover of this US promotional booklet we see the logos of Pan-American Airlines, Daytona Speedway and the US Air Force Thunderbirds. Each of these organizations was responsible for a Rolex model: Pan-Am for the GMT-Master, Daytona Speedway for the Daytona and the Thunderbirds for the Datejust Turn-O-Graph.

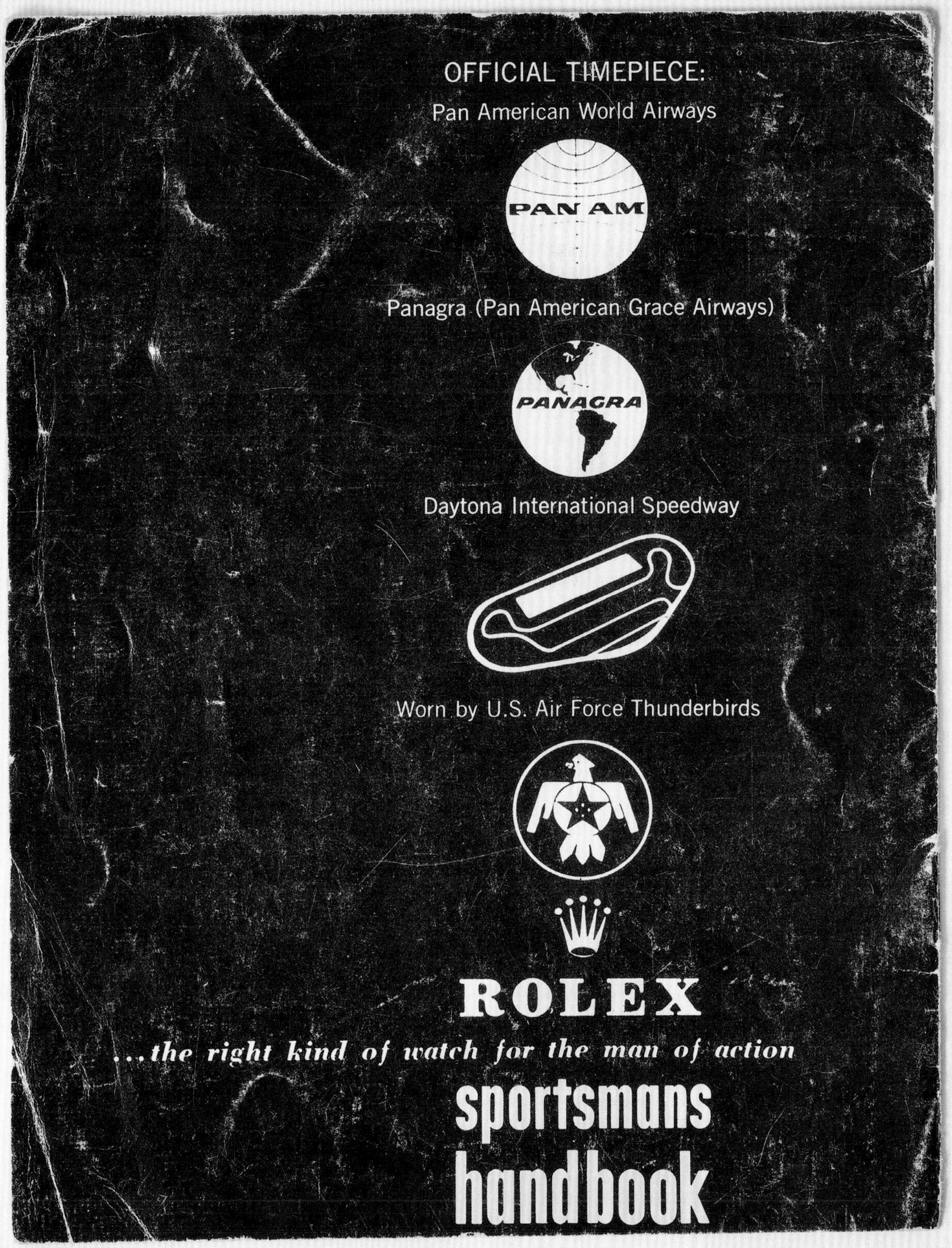
OFFICIAL TIMEPIECE:
Pan American World Airways
PAN AM
Panagra (Pan American Grace Airways)
PANAGRA
Daytona International Speedway
Worn by U.S. Air Force Thunderbirds
ROLEX
...the right kind of watch for the man of action
sportsmans
handbook

1966
OYSTERDATE

You could call this a very restrained, austere watch if you wanted to be complimentary, or say that it's a bargain basement Rolex for someone who can't afford a better one. I pick the first choice.

- **Model number: 6694**
- **Date: 1966**
- **Dial: Brass, silvered, applied gilt indices**
- **Movement: 1245**
- **Case material: Stainless steel**
- **Dimensions: 34mm**

There are no two ways about it: the Rolex Oysterdate is a weird watch. This is not just down to its diminutive size, 34mm, but the fact that it is missing two of the attributes everyone expects from a Rolex: an automatic movement that is also chronometer rated.

Introduced in 1953 as reference 6094, it remained in the catalogue until 1989 – a run of over 35 years. This is remarkable for a watch that almost nobody in the collecting world ever talks about. Yet it must have been popular. Just like the Datejust (see page 142), in the 1958 catalogue Rolex made the model in three different sizes: the 26mm reference 6406, the 31mm 6466 and the 34mm 6494.

The first Oysterdate was the reference 6094. Launched in 1953, it came with a silvered dial, applied triangle and arrowhead indices, and was fitted with dauphine hands. It predated the Cyclops lens, but the date disc did have red-coloured even numbers and black for the odd-numbered dates – the so-called Roulette date disc. The 1950s were a time of constant change for Rolex, and within two years a new reference was launched, the 6294. It kept the same 745 calibres, with 17 jewels, two adjustments and the early Parachoc shock protection. The only real difference was that the new watch had much more interesting dials – both linen and honeycomb textures have been found on silvered and lacquered black finishes.

In 1958, it was replaced by the 6494. Now, the textured dials had gone, and even the movement was changed to the 1215 calibre. Like the 745, this was still a descendant of the 10½''' Hunter, with indirect drive centre seconds and the updated Kif shock protection. Finally the watch was blessed with a Cyclops on the crystal.

In 1959–60, Rolex made the final changes to the Oysterdate, with the arrival of the 6694. The calibre 1215 was replaced with an updated version, the 1245. It was essentially the same but had a slightly faster beating balance of 21,600 instead of the old 18,000 bph. The other change was that a leather strap was no longer an option; the three-link folded-steel Oyster bracelet was obligatory.

This was the specification in which the Oysterdate soldiered on for almost another three decades. Just before it left the catalogue in 1988, it was unique in several ways:

- it was the last Rolex Oyster fitted with plastic glass,
- it was the last manual-wind Rolex Oyster, and
- it was the last watch in the catalogue to be fitted with a movement derived from the venerable 10½''' Hunter.

I believe that much of the Oysterdate's popularity derived from the fact that it was, for most of its production run, the slimmest Oyster you could buy – it was 2mm slimmer than its automatic cousin the Oyster Perpetual Date. Also, the lack of the 'Superlative Chronometer Officially Certified' text on the dial gave it a much more restrained, almost austere, look that appealed to a very low-key clientele.

→ The 6694 Oysterdate was the least expensive Oyster when it finally went out of production, but it wasn't a cheap watch in the derogatory sense – it was capable of surviving under 50m of pressure, just like the Datejust. Others like it because it was one of the most stripped back, pure iterations of the Rolex Oyster, with the cleanest dial in the catalogue.

ROLEX
OYSTERDATE
13
PRECISION
T SWISS T

1966

DATEJUST TURN-O-GRAPH

The 1625 and its predecessors had the class and elegance of the Datejust with the convenience of a rotating timing bezel like that of the Submariner.

- **Model number: 1625**
- **Date: 1966**
- **Dial: Brass, gilt finish, applied gold indices**
- **Movement: Calibre 1575**
- **Case material: Stainless steel, 18ct gold bezel**
- **Dimensions: 36mm**

The 6202 Turn-O-Graph (see page 100), the first mainstream Rolex with a timing bezel, was not much of a success, but it paved the way for the Submariner (see page 102) and most of the sportswatches which followed. While there was no direct replacement for the 6202, its name lived on in the bezel attached to the reference 6309 Datejust, released only two years after the 6202. The earlier watch was powered by the early automatic A260, the $9\frac{3}{4}$''' version of the Bubbleback, while the 6309 used the larger A296 $10\frac{1}{2}$''' version which is found in all second generation Datejusts.

Because the 6309 was a Datejust – and the first with a rotating bezel – the watch was available in steel, mixed metal or solid gold, but the bezel only came in 18-carat gold, white, yellow or pink, depending on the case material. The bezel was unlike any other from Rolex: the ten-minute divisions featured full-size cast Arabic numerals, the five-minute divisions were cast single bars and the remainder of the bezel had a hobnail finish. The dials came in all colours, but almost all had the name Datejust printed in red, and the date wheel was always printed in red; some even had the depth rating 50m = 150ft in red on the dial.

The 6309 featured in the catalogues for just about as long as the 6202. It was history in just over two years, replaced by an almost identical-looking 6609 Datejust, powered by the latest 1065 calibre. In 1960, the 6609 was adopted as the team watch by the US Air Force (USAF) Demonstration Squadron, known as The Thunderbirds. The name comes from both the mythical Indigenous American beast, and also from the fact that all early USAF jets had names starting with Thunder.

The watch was officially known as the Datejust Oyster Perpetual with Turn-O-Graph bezel. But the Thunderbird nickname, which was only used in US advertising material, has stuck and seems to be the name most people use. The 6609 lasted not much longer than the 6309, as by the end of 1960 it was gone. Most people would have great difficulty in telling the difference between the old watch and its reference 1625 replacement. As with the previous two watches, all that changed was the movement; now it was powered by the more modern and robust calibre 1575.

→ I have always loved the 1625 Datejust with the 'Thunderbird' rotating bezel. To me, it's a more usable everyday watch than the Submariner Date. It does everything that the Submariner does – except dive to 200m – but the 1625's 50m is perfectly sufficient for me. It's also a lot more discreet and slides under a shirt cuff without a problem.

OYSTER PERPETUAL
SUPERLATIVE CHRO
OFFICIALLY CERT
5
50
10
20
30
40

1967

SUBMARINER 5513

The longest-lived Submariner of all was produced from 1962 until the turn of the century.

- **Model number: 5513**
- **Date: 1967**
- **Dial: Brass, black pad printed, tritium indices**
- **Movement: 1520**
- **Case material: Stainless steel**
- **Dimensions: 40mm**

In 1962, a full three years after the launch of the 5512 (see page 160), the 5513 usurped the 5508 (see page 146) as the more affordable version of the Submariner. At first glance there was no difference between the 5513 and the first generation 5512. Both had high gloss dials with '200m=660ft' printed below the model name, cases with pointed crown guards and boldly numbered rotating bezels. Even the movements were the same – the calibre 1530 (see page 146), the first iteration of the 15XX movements.

But the birth of the 5513 saw the movement in the 5512 upgraded to the free-sprung chronometer certified version of the 1520, and it proudly bore its new chronometer qualifications on its dial. The dials were printed using a galvanic process which left the brass colour of the dial to show through as the text (see page 146). During this period the dials for the two models were identical – the only difference was that the 5512 had the chronometer text printed on top of the dial lacquer. This printing was done in a different typeface to all the other text and in a different silver colour.

The movements in the 5512 and 5513 were both self-winding 26-jewel movements, except for the 5513 watches sold to the US. Because of outdated regulations designed to protect the US watchmaking industry, models with 18 jewels or more were taxed at a higher rate. So, Rolex made specific 17-jewel movements for the US market. The majority of the jewels were removed from the automatic winding system, so they did not have any effect on the performance of the watch. These less expensive movements can also be recognized by the ROW engraving on the mainplate or the balance bridge which identified the recognized US importer of the watch.

The 5513 became one of the longest-lived Rolex watches, so it stands to reason that it will have gone through many variations over its 27-year production run. Some of the most desirable are the late gloss dials with large luminous 3, 6 and 9 numerals and slim bars for the remainder. Known as Explorer dials, for some bizarre reason they seem mostly to have been sold in the UK. They are rare and very desirable.

Only a year after it was launched, the 5513 underwent a major redesign. The pointed crown guard case disappeared and a new thicker case with rounded shoulders was introduced. It was less than 1mm thicker, bringing the height up to 14.5mm, but it made the whole watch feel substantially more robust.

In 1967, the aesthetics of the watch changed again as Rolex bade farewell to its Galvanic dials. The new matt black dials were much less expensive to produce, less likely to deteriorate and were a better contrast for the luminous indices at night. The matt dial, round-shoulder 5513 continued in production for an unprecedented 15 years and became – in most people's eyes – the archetypal Submariner.

→ **The Submariner had been in production for eight years before the 5513 was launched, and there had been eight previous models during that period, but it was the 5513 which really took off and became everybody's idea of what a Submariner looked like. The 5513 was the basis for the two most desirable Submariners of all, the COMEX 5514 and the Royal Navy 5517.**

ROLEX
200m=660ft
SUBMARINER
SWISS – T<25
10
20
30
40
50

1967

NON-CATALOGUE WATCHES

These were special-order watches for select individuals who had influence, either with one of the more important Rolex dealers or directly with the factory itself.

- **Model number: 1804**
- **Date: 1967**
- **Dial: Silvered brass, applied white gold Arabic numerals**
- **Movement: 1555**
- **Case material: Platinum**
- **Dimensions: 36mm**

When talking about off-catalogue watches, most people think about the watches produced for Middle Eastern royalty and governments. But the option returned at the start of this century, and the impetus behind it, seems to have been the firm's CEO, Patrick Heiniger. He took over as CEO of Rolex in 1992 when his father André moved up to become Chairman and then took on that role too when his father resigned in June 1997. The watches made for the Middle East tended to be regular models with special dials, while the watches produced during Patrick's tenure were more flamboyant. He is best remembered as the driving force behind the consolidation of around 30 production sites into four enormous ones, the purchase of Rolex Bienne from the Aegler and Borer families and the introduction of the in-house Daytona movement. These actions changed Rolex for ever and were the foundations of the company as we know it today. But, under his leadership, the firm introduced the Daytona 'Beach' models (see page 234), the Yacht-Master (see page 246) and, let us not forget, the 'Leopard' Daytona (see page 268), three of the most flamboyant models ever to come from one of the most austere of the Swiss watch firms.

Like his father, Patrick had trained as a lawyer – specifically an intellectual rights one – and had run his own practice in New York before joining Rolex as Marketing Director at the age of 35. What was really interesting to me is that although both Heinigers trained as lawyers, neither of them looked or acted in the way you would expect from a Swiss lawyer. André wore a dark suit on the two occasions that I met him, but the belt around his waist was held in place by a giant gold cowboy-style buckle. I only met him on social occasions, but I never saw him without a cigarette in one hand and a drink in the other. I would like to have known him better, he seemed like a fun guy. Patrick, on the other hand, always reminded me of the younger son of minor European royalty. He was incredibly gracious, but slightly aloof and always immaculately dressed. One Saturday, at around 7am, I was wandering around the Portobello Road Market in London, when I saw him – which was easy, as he was several inches taller than anyone else – and even this early in the morning he was immaculately attired. His blazer was impeccably tailored, the crease in his flannels razor sharp and his shoes gleamed. This was how I had seen him on the couple of occasions we had met at the factory, but to see him identically dressed at this god-forsaken hour in a location where he had no need to impress anyone gave me an insight into the man he was.

→ Rolex have always made watches which aren't listed in their catalogues. Almost forty years ago I bought a cushion Oyster in 14 carat white gold. The serial number dated it to 1926/27, but Rolex had never catalogued an Oyster cushion in white gold or in 14 carat in any colour gold – yet, there it was. Another one of the watches I wish I had kept.

الخميس
ROLEX
OYSTER PERPETUAL
DAY-DATE
SUPERLATIVE CHRONOMETER
OFFICIALLY CERTIFIED
T SWISS T

1967

SEA-DWELLER PROTOTYPE

The Sea-Dweller didn't spring fully formed from Rolex's drawing board – there were several intermediate steps on the way, and this is just one of them.

- **Model number: 1665**
- **Date: 1967**
- **Dial: Brass, matt black paint, tritium indices**
- **Movement: 1535**
- **Case material: Stainless steel**
- **Dimensions: 40mm**

Late in 2011, a friend on the west coast of Canada told me about a watch that he had been offered, an early Rolex Sea-Dweller with some interesting differences from the norm. It did not have the expected engravings on the case back, and it lacked the gas escape valve which was a signature of the model.

A few weeks later, following a meeting in California, I took a flight up to Vancouver. I arrived late one afternoon to weather which made London seem welcoming – a torrential downpour which did not let up for my entire 36-hour visit. The following morning reception called up to let me know that my guests had arrived. My friend Steve introduced me to Doug, the owner of the watch, and we sat down to examine it. Steve had brought some tools and opened the back of the watch. It lacked the gas escape valve, the dial had been replaced by a later version and I subsequently discovered the movement had been changed too. But the serial number and the date inside the case back were proof that this was one of the original Sea-Dweller prototypes.

Doug told me his story. In 1971 he was working in Vancouver for an American named Don, who had a small diving school. As the city became the world centre for the construction of commercial submersibles, more divers were required. So Don turned his school into a business where divers could be hired on a short-term basis. When Doug was given a new assignment, which involved him working at considerable depth, he told Don that he would need a watch. Don rifled through his drawers and eventually brought out a large cardboard box which rattled as he moved it to his desk. He turned out the box on to the desk and an assortment of tools, diving regulators and sundry junk tumbled out. He sorted through the pile and came out with this watch, which he shook a couple of times, noted that it was running and gave it to Doug, saying, 'I got this when I worked for the government'.

Don's firm was forced out of business by larger businesses which came into the market, and two years later he was lost at sea when his boat was found overturned... his body was never found.

Doug remained a diver until retirement, and his next employer was Vickers Oceanics, who built, operated and leased manned submersibles. He was on board the mother ship when the submersible Pisces III sank to a depth of 480m (1,575ft) in the Irish Sea. When it was finally rescued from the greatest depth at which a rescue had ever been attempted, he attached the hook to the submersible and opened the hatch so the divers could see sunlight for the first time in 84 hours.

→ Sea-Dweller development started with Rolex producing a 'Super Submariner' with a depth rating of '1660=500m', which was made for the US Navy's Sealab programme. These watches didn't have gas escape valves (see left), as the need for them was not discovered until after the watches were delivered. The only book about the programme written by one of the participants is *Sea Dwellers* by Bob Barth.

1969

RED SUBMARINER

The first Submariner with a date window and Cyclops lens, and also the first to have the model name 'Submariner' printed in red on the face of the watch.

- **Model number: 1680**
- **Date: 1969**
- **Dial: Brass, black paint, tritium indices**
- **Movement: 1575**
- **Case material: Stainless steel**
- **Dimensions: 40mm**

→ The watch shown opposite is a classic example of what collectors call a 'Tropical' dial. This happens when the lacquer on the dial discolours due to exposure to sunlight, or other ultraviolet, and begins to turn brown. The bezel insert has also been subject to too much ultraviolet light and has begun to fade. If this effect continues, it produces what are known as 'ghost' inserts where the numbers are only faintly visible.

When we talk about the Red Submariner, it is assumed that we are talking about the reference 1680, introduced in 1969. But the 1680 was not the first Submariner to use red text on the dial. There are examples of both the 6536 (see page 120) and the 6538 (see page 122) where the depth rating is printed in red on the dial, but I am going to ignore them and concentrate on the 1680.

When it launched the 1680, Rolex acknowledged that the Submariner was no longer a dive watch, but rather an everyday watch for occasional diving use. Because, to be honest, of all the features which might be useful to a diver, a date display has to come at the bottom of the list. But, for someone who signs cheques and makes appointments, a date is a useful feature. The 'civilian' status of the Submariner was reinforced when Rolex released an all-18-carat version at the same time as the steel version.

These first-generation Submariner Date watches can easily be identified by the depth rating on their dials, which reads '200m=660ft', so they are known as 'metres first' watches, differentiating them from the later versions, introduced in 1972, where the depths were reversed and read '660ft=200m'. There are conflicting accounts of why the change was made; some say it was because of the importance of the US market, others that it was simply for marketing reasons – 660 is a much bigger number than 200.

Around the same time that the switch was made to 'feet first' dials, Rolex introduced a new variant of the gold 1680, an all-blue dial and bezel version. It was as if the solid 18-carat black dial version was not flamboyant enough. The blue dial 1680 became the preferred watch of the 1970s Mediterranean playboy, preferably worn low and loose on the wrist.

While the gold versions were the most flamboyant, the red text on the dial of the steel version has always been an eye-catcher and is probably the reason it has always been a favourite with collectors. And it was collectors who noticed small differences between the dials and catalogued them. For example, in the very first versions the red text is printed on top of white text, making the red stand out when compared to later models where the red is printed directly onto the matt black dial. The Red Submariner and the Red Sea-Dweller were the first watches where this level of detail became important to collectors, and much research was conducted. Edward Delgado of Florida was instrumental in investigating to this forensic level of detail and making it widely available.

ROLEX
OYSTER PERPETUAL DATE
SUBMARINER
200m=660ft
SUPERLATIVE CHRONOMETER
OFFICIALLY CERTIFIED
SWISS-T<25
50
10
20
30
40

1970

GMT-MASTER 1675

The GMT-Master 1675 was the breakout model for Rolex. It became their most popular 'tool' watch, it was easier to wear than the Submariner and it was much more useful for the majority of the population.

- **Model number: 1675**
- **Date: 1970**
- **Dial: Brass, galvanic black paint, tritium indices**
- **Movement: 1565**
- **Case material: Stainless steel**
- **Dimensions: 40mm**

It is difficult to argue with the proposition that the reference 1675 is the model which made the GMT-Master. The original GMT-Master, reference 6542, was produced for only two years, and the new version was introduced in early 1959. The 1675 was 40mm in diameter – 2mm larger than the original GMT-Master— but there were much more important changes, both internally and externally. The distinctive plastic bezel insert was replaced by a silkscreened aluminium one, but the most obvious change was the crown guards on the right side of the case. It has been assumed that crown guards first appeared on the 5512 Submariner, but this is not so – the 1675 and 5512 were launched together.

The movement was an adaptation of the new 1535 calibre – called the 1565. It was the first movement Rolex made with bi-directional winding for the automatic movement, meaning that no matter how the wearer moved their wrist, the rotor would spin and wind the mainspring. The new 15XX calibres were more efficient than their predecessors, the 10XX calibres, and considerably more robust. In fact, they are referred to in the Swiss watchmaking community as *tracteurs* (tractors) as they are robust and able to get the job done under all conditions. The 15XX calibres powered all of Rolex's most iconic models and were produced for more than 30 years.

The first 1675 watches can be considered to be transitional models; the dial on the steel versions was slightly bigger, and the dial feet in different locations to those on the previous model. Yet the dial bore the same text as the old ones, 'Officially Certified Chronometer', rather than 'Superlative Chronometer Officially Certified' which the 1565 certainly justified. The gold version was even more of an adulterated form in that, while it had the new movement and reference number, it still used the original 6542 case without crown guards.

The first major change in the appearance of the 1675 came in 1964 when the case grew by almost half a millimetre in height. This heavier, more robust case saw a change in the profile of the crown guards; no longer pointed, they now had a rounded appearance. Two years later, the iconic galvanic dial was replaced by the matt-finish version, which the 1675 wore until it vanished from the catalogue.

In forty years of collecting, I have only ever owned two 6542 GMT-Masters that were bought from the original owners. One was a navigator in the Royal Canadian Air Force and the other a pilot for Air France. This is hardly a large sample to draw conclusions from – but I am going to. I believe that the 6542 was very much the flying professional's watch, while the 1675 appealed to a broader spectrum of clients.

The 1675 was launched at the right time. When transatlantic jet flights began in 1958, and international direct dialling became feasible in 1963, the market for watches that show more than one time zone expanded rapidly. For example, in the late 1970s I was a partner in a business in Southern California and the only way to communicate was by telephone. That is when I bought my first Rolex, a 1675 GMT-Master, and I was not the only one. The majority of users may have been civilians like myself, but the GMT-Master was still the pilot's watch, and there were no more-daring pilots then than the pre-astronaut era NASA test pilots. The astronauts may have gone down in horological history as Speedmaster wearers, but the test pilots were GMT wearers to a man.

→ These early 1675 GMT-Masters are my favourite version. I love the high-gloss dial, the gilt text and logo, the red 24-hour hand with small triangle at the tip and the tritium luminosity which has aged to a lovely café au lait colour. The way the red and blue colours on the bezel insert have faded adds the finishing touch to a gorgeous vintage piece.

ROLEX
GMT-MASTER
SUPERLATIVE CHRONOMETER
OFFICIALLY CERTIFIED
SWISS – T < 25

1970

BETA 21 'TEXANO'

Rolex were a founding firm of the consortium formed to build Switzerland's first quartz watch. Unfortunately, it proved to be a technological dead end and Rolex went on to develop their in-house Oysterquartz movement.

- **Model number: 5100**
- **Date: 1970**
- **Dial: White gold**
- **Movement: Beta 21**
- **Case material: 18ct gold**
- **Dimensions: 40mm**

I believe quartz technology is the most important horological invention of the 20th century.

Now that I have got that out of the way, I will discuss Rolex's brief dalliance with it.

The horological world was amazed when Seiko introduced its QC-951 quartz chronometer in late 1963 in readiness for the 1964 Tokyo Olympic Games. Most previous quartz clocks were used in laboratories and were the size of a domestic refrigerator. The QC-951, in contrast, was smaller than a shoebox and ran for a year on two D-cell batteries.

If this technology could be shrunk so dramatically, then it must be possible to reduce it even further to fit a wristwatch. The race was on between Japan and Switzerland to accomplish this task. The Japanese took the lead thanks to their expertise in electronics, but a group of researchers at the Centre Electronique Horloger in Neuchâtel, Switzerland, were first out of the gate with a functioning wristwatch, the Beta 1, in 1967. It subsequently proved to be the most accurate wristwatch ever tested by the Neuchâtel Observatory.

However, the consortium brought together to build the quartz watch was divided. On one side was the young and unburdened electronics team, and on the other the representatives of the manufacturers who wanted an electronic watch that would be more accurate than tuning fork watches and which – importantly for them – could be built using existing watchmaking machinery.

Eventually the electronics team won, but this had two unfortunate effects. First, its movement, the Beta-21, was introduced four months after Seiko's Quartz-Astron 35SQ, meaning that it lost its lead in the race. Secondly, none of the manufacturers involved were able to make the new movements. This meant that construction was divided between three sites, with final assembly at a fourth. The result was that both the movements and the watches themselves were extremely expensive. For example, when the watch shown here, the model 5100 Texano, was launched in 1970 it was about the same price as the contemporary Porsche 912.

→ There has recently been some question as to whether the 5100 was designed by Gérald Genta. It certainly bears many of the hallmarks of his designs from this period, but there are no records to confirm the matter one way or another. My thought is that it is possible, but I believe that the inspiration for the design of the case body goes back to the 1930s Rolex Viceroy. Both cases have a flat-top, tonneau-shaped body with a decorated circular bezel perched on top. Whoever designed the 5100, one thing is absolutely certain, its design was the inspiration for the next quartz watches from Rolex, the 17000, the 17013/4 and the 19018/9.

ROLEX
QUARTZ
29
SWISS MADE

1971

STELLA DIALS

The colourful Stella dials were popular when introduced in the 1970s, but only among a small section of the Rolex clientele. They fell out of fashion along with bell-bottomed jeans, but returned to favour a few years ago.

- **Model number: 1803**
- **Date: 1971**
- **Dial: Brass, multi-coat enamel, diamond indices**
- **Movement: 1555**
- **Case material: 18ct white gold**
- **Dimensions: 36mm**

→ For a long time Stella dial Day-Dates didn't fetch much in the used market. This all changed when the Italian collectors discovered them, first worn on leather straps by women and then on the original bracelets by men. They reached their peak in about 2015, when Pucci Papaleo's *Rolex Day-Date* was published, and when Phillips had a special auction for Day-Dates, in which several Stella dial watches reached record prices.

In the 1950s and 1960s, Rolex used the slogan 'Men who guide the destinies of the world wear Rolex watches'. It could – just as easily – have said, 'We are a serious watch company, making serious watches for men with serious jobs'. Yet this was the moment when Rolex decided to adorn its flagship watch with a veritable rainbow of coloured dials.

They were known as the 'Stella' dial watches, were produced in a range of bright (and a few subdued) colours and fitted the flagship of the Rolex range, the Day-Date (see page 138), and a few men's and women's Datejusts (see page 192). The colours available were yellow, pink, burgundy, coral, cherry red, turquoise, blue, green and white, and the name came not from the American artist Frank Stella, but rather from the supplier of the lacquer used – a Swiss firm named Stella SA Fabrique de vernis (Stella Limited, manufacturers of varnish, colours and printing inks). The manufacturing technique used to produce this dial was, in principle, French polishing on a miniature scale. The metal dial blank was coated in a thin film of lacquer using a spray gun, and the lacquer was then dried in a low-temperature oven before being polished to a high gloss. This process was repeated up to a dozen times before a final coat of clear lacquer was applied and the dial given a final polish by hand. The result was a dial well over 1mm thick – more than three times the thickness of a regular dial. The depth of the enamel could easily be seen in the apertures for the day and date windows and, because of its depth, the dial almost appeared to be liquid; with the blue ones in particular it felt as though you could dive into it.

There were, however, several problems with the dials. The first was that the amount of hand labour needed in their manufacture made them inordinately expensive compared with conventional dials. Secondly, they were initially fitted to the most expensive Rolex model – the Day-Date – which tended to be purchased by more discreet clients, who showed little interest in flamboyant dials. Finally, the lacquer had a propensity to crack if the watch received a knock.

In launching the Stella dials, Rolex was trying to bring itself up to date and align with the current trends. If Rolex was a serious watch company, there was no more serious car firm than Porsche. Yet, in the mid-1970s, you could order your 911 in a choice of six different shades of green, or if that was not flamboyant enough, three different yellows or perhaps one of the four reds. These were colourful times, and Rolex was not going to be left out.

SUNDAY
ROLEX
OYSTER PERPETUAL
DAY-DATE
25
SUPERLATIVE CHRONOMETER
OFFICIALLY CERTIFIED
T SWISS T

1972

DAYTONA

The screw-down pushers on these watches were a mixed blessing in my opinion. When screwed down it meant that the watch was now genuinely waterproof, but they made spontaneous use of the pushers impossible.

- **Model number: 6265**
- **Date: 1972**
- **Dial: Brass, silvered, applied white gold indices**
- **Movement: Calibre 727**
- **Case material: Stainless steel**
- **Dimensions: 37mm**

Two years after the launch of the 6239 (see page 154), Rolex introduced two new versions of the Daytona, the numerically progressive 6240 and 6241. They had one feature that differed from the 6239: the bezel was no longer flat metal with engraved tachometer measurements. Rather, a black plastic insert with the tachometer indications printed in white on the underside was placed in a recess. Ironically, it had taken Omega exactly the same amount of time to switch from a metal bezel to one with a plastic insert on its Speedmaster chronograph. However, unlike Omega, Rolex did not make the switch – it kept both bezel configurations in production. The 6240 and 6241 differed from each other in that the 6241 was identical to the 6239 apart from the bezel, while the 6240 introduced screw-down chronograph pushers to accompany the screwed crown. The 6240 also carried the word Oyster on the dial and was advertised by Rolex as being safe down to 50m (165 ft).

The 6240 can be seen as a prototype for the 6263/6265 models, which were introduced at the start of the 1970s. Only the movement differed from the 6240, which transitioned from the 722 to the 727. This was the final update on the Rolex Valjoux 72-based movement, and it was hardly a trivial revision. Ten components were changed from the previous version, but they included major items such as the main plate, balance complete, second wheel, balance cock and mainspring. In fact, it might be safe to call it almost a new movement. The balance now swung at 21,600 bph rather than the 18,000 of its predecessors (the only movement fitted in a men's Rolex to beat at this frequency).

The 6263/6265 pair had one strange claim to fame – the movement is different in the steel and in the gold versions. The steel watches have movements regulated in three positions, while all the gold ones are COSC-tested chronometers, although it was only in the last few years of 6263 and 6265 production that the dials were marked to reflect this.

I mentioned that the manual-wind Daytonas used a movement from Valjoux, but what is not so well-known is that Rolex did not make the cases, dials or hands either. Cases came from Charles-René Spielmann, which also made many of the cases for Omega's Speedmaster. The companies Singer, Beyeler or Stern made the dials. Hands came from Universo and other Swiss suppliers. The screw-down crowns came from Boninchi (which was purchased by Rolex in 2001). However, the watches were assembled, timed and tested by Rolex.

→ The screw-down pushers on the 6240/6263/6265 solved one of the major problems with the previous Daytona – it wasn't really waterproof, despite having a screwed back and a screw-down crown. But they introduced another problem, as you had to prepare to use the pushers by unscrewing them, and often when you wanted to use the chronograph, you wanted to use it at that moment.

ROLEX
OYSTER
COSMOGRAPH
DAYTONA
T SWISS T
UNITS PER HOUR

1972

KING MIDAS

In 1970, there was only one Rolex in the catalogue which weighed more than the King Midas. And that was the model 5100 Beta 21 'Texano' Quartz.

- **Model number: 9630**
- **Date: 1972**
- **Dial: 18ct gold, black enamel text**
- **Movement: Calibre 650**
- **Case material: 18ct gold**
- **Dimensions: 27mm wide**

I have often wondered how the Rolex King Midas came about. Did Gérald Genta, the Swiss watch designer, approach Rolex, or was it the other way around? And, if it was the latter, what brief did Rolex give the young designer? 'We want to change our image completely, design us something radical, almost crazy!' I cannot imagine that conversation ever taking place, but something like it must have occurred because when the reference 9630 was launched in 1962 it was not just unlike any preceding watch from Rolex, it was unlike any other watch on the market.

By the early 1960s, Rolex was well established. Then, as now, you knew what you were getting when you bought a Rolex: an Oyster case, a circular dial, automatic winding and a little window for the date covered by a Cyclops magnifier. The King Midas offered none of these, every Rolex 'rule' went out of the window. It was not circular or even square or rectangular – it was the first pentagonal wristwatch. It was not waterproof or automatic and certainly had no room for a date window. Even the winding crown was on the 'wrong' side of the watch. It was not just different, it was radical. But there was a certain logic to the whole thing. If you placed the watch vertically on its edge, it looked like the pediments of a classical Greek temple. The winding crown was recessed into the tip of the pediment but engraved with a sunray motif, representing the sun shining down on the temple; by recessing into the pediment, it left the watch with an unbroken outline.

But, radical as the watch might have been, it was the bracelet which stood out even more. It appeared to be made from slabs of solid gold with a concave surface at one end and a convex one at the other. They nested inside each other perfectly to form an almost seamless band of solid gold around the wrist of the wearer. The links, like the watch, were asymmetric; they tapered towards the clasp and were a similar thickness to the watch. There was asymmetry too in the feel of the watch. The incredibly slim case and the movement – which measured just 4mm – seemed almost delicate, while the solid gold bracelet links of the same thickness appeared to be massive.

I used the phrase 'solid gold' a lot in the previous paragraph, and I meant to, as the watch weighed around 200g (7oz) and almost all of that weight came from the gold in the bracelet; the wafer-thin Piaget-based calibre 650 would have weighed a few grams at most. No wonder it was the most expensive watch in the 1972 catalogue. The Day-Date (see page 138) on a concealed clasp bracelet was $1,400 in the US, the King Midas was almost twice the price at $2,600. When Rolex claimed in its King Midas advertising that 'You may not be able to afford one', they certainly were not kidding.

→ The Midas was a watch of contradictions – its design was pure and rectilinear, almost austere, yet in yellow gold it was positively flamboyant. It was the flagship of the Rolex range, yet it didn't look like any Rolex before or since. This looked like a watch designed for a drug kingpin, but it was designed long before anyone had ever heard of drug kingpins.

1974

LADY-DATEJUST

No other Rolex can be personalized like the Lady-Datejust – the choice of case size, bezel design, dial material and design and bracelet are almost endless, and that's before we start to place precious stones in any conceivable location.

- **Model number: 6917**
- **Date: 1974**
- **Dial: Brass, gilt plate, applied faceted indices**
- **Movement: 2035**
- **Case material: Stainless steel, 18ct gold bezel**
- **Dimensions: 26mm**

In 1970, Rolex introduced a new version of their Lady-Datejust, the 6917 powered by the new self-winding calibre 2035, replacing the 1035 in the first version of the model. The two watches looked very similar but the new movement was much more modern, looking like a ¾ scale version of the 1535. It had a free-sprung balance with regulation via Micro-Stella screws and even a Breguet overcoil on the hairspring. Unlike its predecessor, every model, no matter what the case material, was a certified chronometer.

Riding on the heels of its predecessor the 6517, sales of the new watch took off like the proverbial rocket. This happened not because it was a horological breakthrough, but because of the world in which it was launched. By the late 1950s and early 1960s, the Western world was changing; the austerity of the immediate postwar years was gone, and European economies as well as the US were booming. And while lots of women had joined the workplace, they were still expected to perform the majority of domestic chores as well. It was assumed that it would be the woman of the house who would wash the dishes, bathe the baby and prepare the family's food. A watch that did not have to be unstrapped every time you went near liquid was a godsend. And there was one other advantage to the Lady-Datejust, particularly the two-tone version: it was sporty enough to wear when playing tennis and, with its gold accents, elegant enough to wear to a cocktail party.

The watch was available on a leather strap, or a variety of Rolex bracelets: the Oyster, the Jubilee or – for the noble metal versions – the President bracelet, either with or without a concealed clasp. The variety of dials available was even more extensive, not only the usual white, silver, blue and black, but the watch was also available with a variety of brightly coloured 'Stella' dials. And, all of these dials were available with diamond indices, if desired. The watch became a blank palette from which the purchaser could create the watch of her desires.

It is difficult to pinpoint the moment that the two-tone Lady-Datejust slipped from being a practical everyday object to becoming an icon, but that is what it became and where it remains to this day.

→ This century has seen men's watches increase in size from an average of 36mm to over 40mm, but what hasn't been mentioned is that the exact same thing has been happening to lady's watches. When the very first Lady-Datejust was launched, it measured 24mm, a few years later it moved to 26mm, where it remained for most of its existence. But now the current model measures 28mm.

1974

MILITARY SUBMARINER

It's refreshing to see a Military Submariner complete with all its original constituent parts – the dial, the hands and the bezel insert are no longer available from Rolex – so often civilian examples are substituted if the original parts get damaged.

- **Model number: 5513**
- **Date: 1974**
- **Dial: Brass, black matt paint, tritium indices**
- **Movement: 1520**
- **Case material: Stainless steel**
- **Dimensions: 40mm**

→ Why is the Military Submariner so highly sought after? It's not just because it's rare – there are rarer Rolex watches which are nowhere near as eagerly collected. I believe it is because it is a highly visible watch: it immediately stands out from all other Submariners by the NATO band, the unique bezel, dial and hands. It isn't just that it is different – it is a watch which shouts that it is different.

The divers of the British Royal Navy (RN) were the first military users of Rolex watches, but they did not wear Submariners. No, the first Rolex military dive watches were reference 6150 Explorers issued in 1953 (see page 98). The following year, they switched to 6538 Submariners, which were used until 1968, when the RN followed the lead of the British Army and switched to the more modern Omega Seamaster 300. The lack of a screw-down crown on the Omegas was a problem for them, and pretty much all RN examples were withdrawn and retrofitted with screw-down crowns and tubes. These can be easily recognized as they have an 'A' engraved before the issue number on the case back.

In 1972 the Ministry of Defence switched back to Rolex and ordered a batch of 5513 Submariners from Rolex UK. Known as 'MilSub' these closely followed the specifications of the Omegas. Like all military watches, they had fixed strap bars, not spring bars, but the design of the hands and the bezel insert were almost identical to the Omega designs. There are claims that these watches were specially ordered for the famed Special Boat Service, but this is not true; they were issued to both mine clearance and maintenance divers, as well as to divers in the British Army's Royal Engineers whose tasks often required underwater work. The last group to receive the MilSub were, oddly, British Army helicopter pilots.

Between 1972 and 1979, three batches of MilSubs were ordered from Rolex. They were dispatched to Herstmonceux Castle is Sussex, the site of the Royal Observatory at Greenwich after World War II, and which was now a Royal Navy establishment and the site for the Admiralty's watch and clock makers. There the watches were tested for their depth rating and timekeeping. When this was completed, Rolex London was asked to collect the watches together with a list of which one was destined for which dockyard. This information was supplied to me by Henry Hudson, an apprentice Rolex watchmaker in the 1970s who was dispatched to Herstmonceux to deliver the MilSubs for testing and subsequently responsible for sending them to the dockyards. As a watchmaker, he was a meticulous soul and, for his own records, kept a ledger of when every MilSub arrived at London, when it went to Herstmonceux, when it came back and to which dockyard it went. When he rose to the position of General Manager at Rolex London he was always generous with his knowledge.

ROLEX
OYSTER PERPETUAL
660ft = 200m
SUBMARINER
SWISS - T<25
10
20
30
40
50

CHAPTER EIGHT

1976–1985

ROLEX
OYSTER PERPETUAL
660ft=200m
SUBMARINER
SWISS - T < 25

1976–1985

ROLEX EMBRACES QUARTZ

But discovers it was only a passing affair... and walks away.

In 1973, the Swiss watch industry had reached its peak, exporting around 75 million watches. A decade later, the figure was less than half that, at 35 million. Yet Rolex did not just survive this period, it thrived and continued to introduce new models.

When it came to quartz, Rolex made what seems in retrospect to have been a very smart decision. While the rest of the Swiss watch industry rushed headlong into quartz watches, Rolex decided to wait and see how it all played out. To keep its options open, it decided to develop its own quartz movement, but – being Rolex – it ignored the route chosen by most other brands. They all value-engineered the movement so that it could be produced as cheaply as possible with the minimum amount of human intervention. Rolex decided to produce a quartz movement which would be almost identical in size to its contemporary mechanical movements. The logic behind this was that if the quartz movement proved overwhelmingly popular, it could be fitted to current models without needing to modify the cases. Rolex also decided to construct the movement from metal, like all other Rolex movements, and, crucially, to make it modular and easily serviceable. Both decisions ran against the current thinking that quartz movements should be nothing more than a circuit board, some chips, a stepper motor and a couple of wheels, and that if any component failed, the whole thing was so inexpensive that it could be discarded and a new movement slotted into place. Rolex went so far in the opposite direction to everyone else that they did not even use the ubiquitous stepper motor. This is the motor which pulses the seconds hand in conventional quartz movements and moves it in discrete one-second steps. Rolex chose to use a lever escapement to stop and start its seconds hand; I believe that this one component in the Rolex quartz movement probably cost considerably more than the entire quartz movement found in most of its competitors. Yes, Rolex was going to make a quartz movement – but it was going to do it the Rolex way.

It is important to point out that Rolex was not the only firm that saw the future of the quartz watch as following two distinct paths: the high end, where Rolex was most comfortable, and the mass market, where it was not. While Rolex was developing its quartz movement, two engineers at Ebauches SA were also working on a new movement, once again using a blank sheet of paper. André Beyner and Maurice Grimm reworked the design of the quartz movement to produce a watch called the Delirium, which – when it launched in 1979 – was remarkable for two things. At 1.98mm it was the thinnest watch in the world and at 20,000 Swiss francs it was the most expensive quartz watch in the world. For example, the 18-carat Oysterquartz Day-Date (see page 216) was less than half the price at 9,000 Swiss francs.

← Military Submariner, 1976 (see page 208).

Yes, Rolex was going to make a quartz movement – but it was going to do it the Rolex way.

But Rolex was not going to put all its eggs in the quartz basket. While one development team worked on the quartz movement, another was developing a new mechanical movement to replace the tried and trusted, but already long in the tooth, 15XX series (see page 182). This was the new 30XX series (see page 220), the first fast beat movement from Bienne, with a balance that oscillated at 28,800 bph rather than the 19,800 of the 15XX. The new movement had another Rolex first, a rapid date adjustment. All of these improvements were worthwhile, but the big change was how the new movement was designed and constructed. Since the 15XX series had been conceived in the 1950s, there had been a complete change in manufacturing technology. The new series of movements was the first to be designed and built using computer-aided design (CAD), electro-discharge machines (EDM) and computer numerically controlled (CNC) multi-axis milling machines. This new technology enabled components to be produced not only faster and with less human intervention and therefore at a lower cost, but also – crucially – to much finer tolerances.

It was also at this time that Rolex continued its progress upmarket, with the launch of the Crown Collection (see page 258). These were Day-Dates and Datejusts with stone set-bezels, exotic dials and even stone-set bracelets. The range was not available from all Rolex agents, only its more important outlets with high-spending clients. It was by far its most extravagant and ostentatious product line, and Rolex considered it important enough to have its own catalogue. Meanwhile, at the other end of the ostentation scale, Rolex produced the military Submariner for the British armed forces (see page 208). Proof, if it were needed, that Rolex was now producing watches for everyone.

One of its clients during this period was the author of this book. In 1980 I was living in London and had a business with a friend in California. Back then, all communication was done by telephone, and I decided that I needed a watch with two time zones. I was not a watch nut back then, so I asked around and everyone I trusted told me to get a Rolex GMT-Master (see page 128). One afternoon I went to the Watches of Switzerland store on Bond Street (Patek Philippe's London boutique is located there now) and I asked to see one. I slipped it on my wrist, admired it and reached for my wallet to extract my credit card, as I did so I paused for a moment and asked the salesman, 'If I pay by cash or cheque, is there any discount?' He shook his head and told me, 'Sorry sir, we don't discount Rolex – except if you want one of the Daytonas, we can give you 20 per cent off them.' I took the GMT-Master, my first Rolex.

→ Another Rolex tennis ambassador in the 1970s was the Australian champion John Newcombe. In this 1970s brochure, he is linked to the Rolex Explorer II – seen with the brochure here and on page 205.

JOHN NEWCOMBE's centre court style is unmistakable. His dazzling court coverage, precision ground stroke and flawless timing have won him three Wimbledon crowns and two U.S. Open titles. It is a style matched by his choice of timepiece: Rolex.
THE ROLEX EXPLORER II (l), a superlative stainless steel self-winding chronometer, is built to withstand a championship singles match, and also face the rigors of pressure-proof precision down to 330 feet. Its special red hour hand points time on a fixed 24-hour bezel.
THE ROLEX COSMOGRAPH (r) in stainless steel with matching bracelet, and 17-jewel manual winding movement, has screw-down push buttons to time sequences to 1/5 second. And it is pressure-proof down to 165 feet.
1655s/B9315
OFFICIALLY CERTIFIED SWISS CHRONOMETER

1976

MIDDLE EASTERN DIALS

Royal familes, government departments, armed forces, police forces, airlines and oil companies are just some of the Gulf-based organizations who have commissioned Rolex to produce watches featuring their crest or logo.

- **Model number: 1500**
- **Date: 1976**
- **Dial: Brass, silvered, applied gold indices, Iraqi armed forces logo**
- **Movement: Calibre 1575**
- **Case material: 18ct gold**
- **Dimensions: 34mm**

→ I believe that the Omani royal family were the first to have their crest on watch dials and the practice then spread all across the region. However, it wasn't just royal families who had their watches emblazoned with crests, I have seen Rolex watches with the logos of construction companies and airlines, both – incidentally – Saudi-based firms.

Things were different when I started collecting watches back in the early 1980s. For a start, you could walk into any Rolex dealership and buy pretty much any watch you wanted right off the shelf. And, if you were lucky – or persistent – you could even get a discount. Also, the used Rolex business existed not to provide hard-to-get models at a premium, but to supply a Rolex to people who wanted one but could not afford a brand-new model.

The problems facing the used Rolex dealer then were the same as they are today – where to obtain watches to sell. Back then, lots of watches came from the grey market, retailers who had been sitting on stock for a long time and who were happy to get rid of it at a tiny profit. Or, when a nation's currency collapsed, secondary market dealers would swoop in with hard currency and empty the stores – I remember this happening during the Asian economic crisis of the 1990s and the Icelandic economic collapse a decade later.

In central London there was one other source: the Middle East. Back then, visitors and expatriates headed to antiques markets with warrens of small shops buying and selling antiques and used watches. Many of these visitors brought with them watches that they had been given by members of various royal families in the region. These invariably had special dials featuring the crest of the donor and they were quietly exchanged for envelopes of £50 notes. The watches were sent to local jewellers, the dials removed and replaced with standard production dials. If you wanted you could walk into the London Rolex service centre and buy as many dials as you wished. The special crested dials would be unceremoniously thrown in the bin.

These dials started to appear towards the end of the 1970s, after the 1973–74 oil crisis had caused oil prices to rise by 100 per cent in the West. For the oil producers of the Middle East, production costs remained constant, but incomes doubled. This sudden influx of wealth transformed the region irrevocably. Allied to this newfound prosperity was a long-established tradition in the region of gift-giving as a reward, to build or reinforce a relationship.

The great irony about many of these dials ending up in London is that is where most of them originated. The famous London jeweller Asprey had a long-term relationship with many of the region's ruling families, particularly Oman. On well-preserved examples, you can still see the Asprey engraving on the outside of the case back.

I always found it interesting that these crested dial watches ranged from basic steel Air-Kings to diamond-encrusted platinum Day-Dates. And I have always wondered who decided the level of watch a recipient might receive.

ROLEX
OYSTER PERPETUAL
DATE
26
T SWISS MADE T

1976

EXPLORER II

Initially thought of as a poor relation to the GMT-Master 1675, the Explorer II now commands a loyal following of its own, as a very different Rolex 'tool' watch with an interesting history.

- **Model number: 1655**
- **Date: 1976**
- **Dial: Brass, matt black paint, tritium indices**
- **Movement: 1565**
- **Case material: Stainless steel**
- **Dimensions: 39mm**

→ I have always liked the 1655 Explorer II, probably because it never received the love showered on to its near relative, the GMT-Master 1675. I like the outliers, the different ones, and the 1655 is different. With a unique bezel, handset and dial it looks completely unlike any other watch in the catalogue.

The Rolex Explorer II was introduced in 1971 as the answer to a question nobody had ever asked. The watch is, essentially, the Rolex 1675 GMT-Master (see page 182) but with a fixed bezel. Its unique feature is its ability to tell the current time in both 12-hour and 24-hour formats. The story goes that it was designed to meet the demands of cave explorers, who are underground for so long that they lose track of whether it is daytime or nighttime. Sorry, but that just does not make any sense; how many cave explorers are there who spend multiple days underground? Is that a viable market?

My belief – completely unfounded, I must declare – is that Rolex had nothing new to introduce at the Basel Spring Fair (as Baselworld used to be called) in 1971 – and so this was a comparatively easy product to develop and launch.

The need to tell time simultaneously in 12- and 24-hour formats is not in high demand, so the reference 1655 was never a high-volume seller for Rolex. This meant that when the Rolex collecting craze took off and Italian dealers saw how well the 'Paul Newman' versions of the Daytona were selling, they picked on the 1655 as the next big thing. So some bright spark came up with the theory that if they could sell Daytonas by attaching the name of an iconic film star to the watch, why not do the same with another model? Someone, I know not who, renamed the 1655 the 'Steve McQueen'. That is how the watch is listed in the 1993 US vintage price guide and somehow the name took off, even though there is absolutely no record of Mr McQueen ever wearing an Explorer II. He was a Rolex wearer, but a Submariner 5512 (see page 160) was his watch of choice.

Despite all the above, the 1655 is an interesting watch. It has a unique aesthetic with hands, dial and bezel unlike any other Rolex watch. Its standout feature – the bright fluorescent red 24-hour hand – has a very unique characteristic: over time and exposure to light, it fades. First to an orange tone, then to yellow and then to a cream colour.

It may have been developed as a stopgap, but I really like the watch. A nicely used one on a 7836 bracelet, with a faded 24-hour hand and an original bezel with most of the enamel numerals gone, is one of the great everyday wearing watches.

ROLEX
OFFICIALLY CERTIFIED
T SWISS < 25 T

1976

OYSTER PERPETUAL DATE 1530

This was a collection of firsts – the first sapphire glass Rolex Oyster, the first steel-integrated bracelet Oyster, the first new Oyster case design for decades. The case soon became home to the Oysterquartz and 50 years later influenced the design of the 2025 Land-Dweller.

- **Model number: 1530**
- **Date: 1976**
- **Dial: Brass, silvered, applied white gilt batons**
- **Movement: 1575**
- **Case material: Stainless steel**
- **Dimensions: 36mm**

Rolex launched its versions of the Oysterquartz (see page 210) in Basel in 1977. People might have been shocked to see the firm that believed in automatic movements develop its own quartz movement; but they should not have been shocked by the new angular case – it had already been on sale for two years, but with a mechanical movement.

The references 1530 and 1630 – the only difference between them is that the first was only made in stainless steel, while the second was only available in steel and yellow gold – are two of the strangest watches ever to come from the Geneva giant. Identical in appearance to the Oysterquartz models 17000 (see page 210) and 17013 (see page 210), they were launched in 1975 and powered by the venerable calibre 1575 (see page 172), a movement directly developed from the calibre 1530 (see page 146), launched in 1957. They were the last watches to be launched with a 15XX movement, apart from one of the strangest watches ever produced by Rolex which I will discuss below.

Rolex collectors talk a lot about transitional models, watches which are the bridge between two generations. No watches are more transitional than the 1530 and 1630. They were not only the last watches to use the old movement, but they were also the first automatic Rolex watches to use sapphire glass.

Collectors have always discussed why Rolex launched the two models. Was it to get rid of the last of the old movements, or was it to test the aesthetics of the new case? I tend to favour the latter explanation, because if you are running a test, it is important to have a control group to measure success or failure against. And that is what Rolex did. The 1530 and 1630 watches were only sold in the US. This meant that, at the turn of the new decade, an American client who wanted a two-tone Datejust had three options – the 1630, for $1,975, the new 3035 powered 16013 for $2,100 or the Oysterquartz 17013 for $2,325. Incidentally, the Oysterquartz version was the only one which was not chronometer certified, even though it was the most accurate of the three.

I mentioned an even stranger model. This was the bizarre reference 1831, produced in single figures for the Shah of Iran. One of his representatives had approached Rolex as he was looking for a unique model which would be given to the highest-ranking visitors and friends of the Shah. Rolex produced the body of the 1530 in platinum with a diamond bezel, then added a platinum bracelet which mimicked the appearance of that used on the King Midas (see page 190). The movement was the final version of the 15XX, the Day-Date calibre 1556. And to top it all off, the watches had a Stella dial with round and baguette diamond indices. At 290g (approximately 10¼oz), it was almost certainly the heaviest watch ever made by Rolex, and is certainly one of the most rare.

→ The unique features of the 1530/1630 are the distinctive case shape and the unusual sloped minute track. Neither of these had been seen previously on a mechanical Rolex watch and they were never to be seen again. Until 2025, of course, when the new Land-Dweller was launched and it copied both of these unusual attributes (see page 324).

ROLEX
OYSTER PERPETUAL
DATE
8
SUPERLATIVE CHRONOMETER
OFFICIALLY CERTIFIED
T SWISS T

1976

MILITARY SUBMARINER

The most instantly recognisable version of the Submariner, with its unique case, bezel, dial and hands, to say nothing of the obligatory NATO strap.

- **Model number: 5517**
- **Date: 1976**
- **Dial: Brass, black matt paint, tritium indices**
- **Movement: 1520**
- **Case material: Stainless steel**
- **Dimensions: 40mm**

This watch is one of the last batch of Submariners purchased by the British Ministry of Defence (MoD) prior to them changing to much cheaper British-supplied watches.

Over the course of almost a decade, between 1972 and 1979, Rolex made three deliveries of Submariners to the MoD. The first were 5513s, and were modified from normal 5513 watches at Rolex Geneva. Four years later a second batch was built at Rolex's UK headquarters in Bexley, Kent, from normal 5513 watches held in stock there. This watch comes from this second batch. They are interesting in that although they have the model number 5513 stamped between the lugs at 6 o'clock, the rear of one of the lugs is also stamped, with the reference 5517. This batch is known as 5513/5517 or as 'Double stamped'. The final batches in 1978/9 were produced at the company's Swiss operation; these were stamped with the unique model number 5517.

These final watches are seen as the most desirable by collectors, because of their unique model number, but any Rolex military Submariner (the preferred nickname is 'MilSub') is desirable. Like Paul Newman Daytonas, they are easily recognized at a glance, and their oversized 'sword' hands, fully marked bezel and circled T mean that they are instantly recognizable. But those are just the surface identifiers of the watches. There are others hidden from view. If the watch is turned over, there will be engraving on the outside of the case back. The top line will identify if it was issued to the Royal Navy or to the British Army; Royal Navy watches will have an identification beginning with 0552, while Army issue watches will have codes starting with W10. Below this will be an engraved broad arrow, or 'pheon', showing that this item is the property of HM's government. And the last line will have an issue number and the last two digits of the year in which the watch was issued.

Inside the case back, once it is opened, you will find the serial number of the watch. The case backs were sent away in batches for the outer case back to be engraved, so having the serial number inside the case helped to ensure that cases and backs were not mixed up. Inside many case backs you can also find the date of manufacture – or, at least, the year and quarter. This can often be several years apart from the issue date on the outside of the case, as the watches were purchased in large batches but only issued in much smaller ones.

It is generally accepted that Rolex produced around 1,200 military Submariners; how many survive is unknown. I believe there is somewhere between half and two-thirds of the original number as:

a. the people who used these watches lived much tougher lives than almost anyone who will read this book, and
b. they did not have to pay for the watches.

The following is an excerpt from an email from a gentleman who sold me his MilSub over a decade ago:

When the Regiment left Fallingbostel [a British army base in Germany], I went to ATDU (Armoured Trials and Development Unit) as the Co-Ord WO. Major (later Brigadier) Peter Barry was one of the trials officers. Every time we were due to carry out an amphibious trial (from Land Rovers to AFV`s [armoured fighting vehicles]), we had to rely on safety cover being provided by R.N. Divers. Which held up the trials for a considerable time. Peter saw a way out of this by sending six guys from the unit on the RE diving course at Marchwood (Southampton). He volunteered himself and, needless to say, me as part of the six. We passed the course (that's gotta be a story in itself), and the diving kit came through. Top of the range in every respect, including Rolex Submariner Diving Watches, and we were warned – on pain of death – to look after them.

The team were doing a practice dive on an old Tank Landing Craft off Chesil Beach between Weymouth and Portland. After the dive, we returned to ATDU and checked the kit, and a little 15/19H Geordie lad (whose name eludes me) reported he had lost his Rolex. "Fecking hell I thought we`re gonna be toast". I saw the RQ (Regimental Quartermaster) and he told me to write an incident report he would submit it, and told me not to worry as it was lost on hazardous duty. "Feckin, Feckin Hell I thought that`s a relief."

It`s amazing over the next six months, we lost another two.

Added to this, around 35 years ago, when I had a stand at Portobello Road Market in London, there was a guy who would turn up five or six times a year with trays of MilSubs – somewhere around 10 or 12 watches in a tray – for sale. He would buy them from Ministry of Defence disposal auctions and then hawk them around the markets. Back then, a 5513 was worth around £300, these MilSubs were about £200, if I remember correctly. There was one London watch dealer who would often buy the entire tray, convert the watches to civilian specification and then sell them. Back then, if you had a parts account with Rolex, you could buy anything you wanted.

↑ In the US there is a phrase 'stolen valor' for someone who wears military decorations or awards that they are not entitled to. I have to be honest and say that I always feel a bit of a fraud wearing a Military Submariner, much more so than when wearing any other military watch. These were very special watches worn by guys performing very specialized and very dangerous tasks, tasks which I could never even contemplate.

1978

OYSTERQUARTZ

The strongest bracelet ever made by Rolex, attached to a watch with the most accurate movement Rolex have ever made. Why wasn't the Rolex Oysterquartz a huge success?

- **Model number: 17000**
- **Date: 1978**
- **Dial: Brass, gloss black paint, applied indices**
- **Movement: Calibre 5035**
- **Case material: Stainless steel**
- **Dimensions: 36mm**

→ When the Oysterquartz was launched it was the most accurate watch that Rolex had ever made, yet the dials of the Datejust versions did not bear the SCOC text certifying the accuracy. But I much prefer these original-style dials, as they give the watch a much more 'pure' appearance, which goes well with the austere design of the 17000, with its massive bracelet.

No matter how you look at it, the 5100 (see page 184) was a failure in the eyes of Rolex – sure, the production run sold out, but 1,000 watches is hardly a historic achievement.

By this time, Rolex was thinking of its next step in quartz movement design, and at the Basel Spring Watch Fair in 1977 it was ready to launch three new models. They were the reference 17000 in steel with a massive Oyster-style bracelet, the 17013 in steel with a gold bezel and a steel and gold Jubilee-style bracelet and the flagship of the range, the 19018 in 18-carat gold on a President-style bracelet. All three proudly bore the new name Oysterquartz. They were presented in an angular case, which had more than a passing resemblance to the 5100 but was considerably slimmer. The Oysterquartz was also the first mass-produced men's Rolex Oyster with a fully integrated bracelet, meaning that there was no way to attach a leather strap. However, it was not an entirely new design; two years earlier the case design had been introduced in the reference 1530 and 1560 models (see page 206), powered by the old 1535 non-quickset movement.

Some people say that these interim models were only produced for two years and then dumped as soon as the Oysterquartz movements became available, but I beg to differ. My library includes a 1980 US Master catalogue, which shows the 1530 and the 17000 on sale simultaneously, with the 1530 listed at $1,050 and the 17000 at $1,350.

There was an even greater price difference between the quartz-powered 17000 and the 3035-powered 16030 Datejust. On an Oyster bracelet, this quickset steel Datejust sold for just $900. By 1980 Japanese quartz watches were already making serious inroads into the watch market. The stainless steel Seiko Grand Quartz 9943-802 was a similarly styled Genta-inspired high-precision quartz watch with an integrated bracelet, which had a guaranteed accuracy of 10 seconds per year and it sold for only 25 per cent of the price of the reference 17000.

By the time the Swatch was launched in early 1983, buyers could not grasp the logic of paying more for a quartz Rolex than for a mechanical one, and sales of the 17000 and the 17013 fell off the proverbial cliff. Ironically, the 19018 Day-Date (and its 19019 white gold cousin) did not suffer the same fate and continued to sell well, even into the early years of the 21st century. The Oysterquartz models made their final appearance in the 2003 catalogue, where all of the models were still shown as available; there was no sign of them in the following year's listings.

ROLEX
DATEJUST
31
OYSTERQUARTZ
T SWISS T

1978

COMEX

After the Military Submariner 5517, the COMEX 5514 and 1665 watches are among the most desirable of all vintage Rolex diving watches. Much of this desirability can be laid at the feet of the huge COMEX logo slapped across the dials of these watches.

- **Model number: 1665**
- **Date: 1978**
- **Dial: Brass, black pad printed, tritium indices**
- **Movement: Calibre 1575**
- **Case material: Stainless steel**
- **Dimensions: 40mm**

Henri-Germain Delauze founded COMEX (Compagnie Maritime d'Expertises) in 1961, after working with Jacques Cousteau and being the head of the project building the revolutionary underwater Havana Tunnel in Cuba. He started the company in response to the increasing demand for professional divers who could perform underwater engineering tasks for oil and telecommunications firms. But COMEX was more than an employment agency for divers, it developed and produced the specialist kit they needed and conducted research into the tools, technology and systems they used.

Watches were vital for divers working at depth; they needed to time not only how long they had been at the bottom, but also how long they must spend at each level of the decompression process. This process was the major restraint on how long a diver could work before nitrogen narcosis occurred. Delauze had spent some time in the US, and would have been aware of the US Navy's experiments with saturation diving. In this technique, a diver enters a chamber where the pressure is gradually increased to the level that they will experience during the dive. Once reached, they transfer to a diving bell (kept at the same pressure) and are then lowered to their work level. After completing their shift, or the entire job, they return to the bell and back to the chamber, where they will spend a few days decompressing back to the surface pressure. Delauze was one of the first to build these chambers and install them on his diving ships.

COMEX were in the right place at the right time as two unexpected events happened: in 1966 oil was discovered in quantity under the North Sea, between Britain and Scandinavia, and the major oil producers in the Middle East massively restricted oil exports after the 1973 Yom Kippur War. Suddenly, the search was on for underwater oil resources in less volatile areas of the world.

I have talked about watches and saturation diving, and now I am going to explain why mixing the two is a bad idea. In a saturation chamber, you breathe a mixture of helium and oxygen so that no nitrogen enters your bloodstream, which could cause nitrogen narcosis at depths. The downside is that, unlike nitrogen, helium is formed from microscopic particles. This means that it can penetrate the tiniest apertures, such as the ones between a seal and the back of a watch case. This is not a problem in itself – helium causes no harm to the movement or the lubricants. But, when the diver is decompressing, the helium cannot escape the watch as quickly as the pressure in the chamber is reduced. This means that the pressure inside the watch is higher than the external pressure. We are all taught at school that nature abhors a vacuum – it also abhors a pressure differential and will do anything to equalize the two. The easiest way out for the pressurized helium to escape is to blow out the watch crystal, which is where the Rolex gas escape valve comes in.

→ Henri-Germain Delauze began as a diver himself, working with Jacques Cousteau, but he was much more than a diver, not just an entrepreneur who built one of the largest sub-sea contracting firms in the world. He was also a dreamer – he was involved in the plans to build the world's first commercial nuclear submarine to enable divers to live and work at extreme depths for prolonged periods of time.

ROLEX
OYSTER PERPETUAL
16
comex
2000ft=600m
SUPERLATIVE CHRONOMETER
OFFICIALLY CERTIFIED
SWISS - T < 25
10
20
30
40
50

1979

SEA-DWELLER 16660

Another example of a transitional watch, where Rolex is slowly evolving from one model to the next. This has the new case, movement and bracelet, but the old-style matt dial.

- **Model number: 16660**
- **Date: 1979**
- **Dial: Brass, black pad printed, tritium indices**
- **Movement: 3035**
- **Case material: Stainless steel**
- **Dimensions: 40mm**

Rolex never expected the 1665 Sea-Dweller (see page 178) to be a major seller. Compared to its contemporary, the 1680 Submariner Date (see page 180), the 1655 was bulkier, more expensive and, without a Cyclops lens, more difficult to use. But it was a flagship project – the watch fixed Rolex in the mind of any potential customer as the dive watch company, so its very existence probably helped to sell lots of Submariners (see page 194 and 208), and possibly even quite a few Datejusts (see page 218).

Produced from 1971 to 1978, the Sea-Dweller, ref. 1665, led a very short life by Rolex standards. Yet the company thought enough of it to develop a completely new model, the 16660, which was the first Rolex sportswatch to feature a sapphire crystal. Like the 1665, it had the patented Gas Escape Valve. The new watch was substantially more robust than the previous model and was rated to 4,000ft (1,220m) – exactly twice the depth rating of the 1665.

The 1665 was a slow seller – it was still on sale three years after the new model was launched. The 1981 catalogue shows that the 1665 was less expensive than the 16800 Submariner Date (see page 222), which was only rated to 1,000ft (304m), half the rating of the 1665, yet the Sea-Dweller was priced at 1,850 Dutch Guilders while the 16800 cost 2,070.

At 2,575 Dutch Guilders, the 16660 was the most expensive steel dive watch available from Rolex. Powered by the newly introduced 3035 movement (see page 226), the sapphire crystal and a high beat and rapid date-change free-sprung movement brought the Sea-Dweller into the modern age. The other major improvement was the bracelet, which was now machined from solid steel. On earlier watches, the centre links had used folded or pressed steel; now even the end links, which attached the bracelet to the watch, were machined from a solid steel blank.

Only one change was made to the 16660 during its production run: in 1984 the matte dial was replaced with a new design featuring a high gloss finish and white gold enclosures around the luminous indices. While the reason for this switch to the finish on the dials is unknown, the tritium indices were given a gold enclosure to keep the luminous material in place. When subjected to certain environmental conditions, a few of the matt dials experienced luminous creep, where the luminous mixture absorbed moisture from the air, expanded and overflowed its allotted area. The white gold enclosures were designed to prevent this. The downside was that these new shiny dials with white gold indices gave the watch the look of a luxury product, not the professional tool it so obviously was. This is why the early matt dial versions are so collectable now.

→ Rolex, if they are known for anything, are known for their practice of gradual evolution, rather than drastic changes. The watch opposite is a perfect example of what we call a transitional watch, where the new case is married to the dial design of the previous model. This can also be seen in the first versions of the GMT-Master 1675 (see page 182), which used the dial layout of the 6542, and in several other models.

ROLEX
OYSTER PERPETUAL DATE
30
SEA-DWELLER
4000ft=1220m
SUPERLATIVE CHRONOMETER
OFFICIALLY CERTIFIED
SWISS - T < 25
10
20
30
40
50

1979

OYSTERQUARTZ 19019

The Oysterquartz Day-Date was a premium watch, selling for 15 per cent more than the mechanically powered model 18038 Day-Date on a concealed clasp President bracelet.

- **Model number: 19019**
- **Date: 1979**
- **Dial: Brass, blued finish, applied white gold indices**
- **Movement: Calibre 5055**
- **Case material: 18ct white gold**
- **Dimensions: 36mm**

The 5035/55 movements in the Oysterquartz watches were truly radical. They were not just the first-ever quartz movement from Rolex, but also the first Rolex movement to be decorated with the Geneva stripes since the final Rebberg movements 40 years before (see page 16). They were also totally different from any other quartz movement of the day. Not only were they constructed completely from metal – just as single-chip, plastic-mounted movements became common – but they were also designed to be serviceable with replaceable parts and modules, just like their contemporary mechanical counterparts. But the biggest divergence from the norm was the absence of a stepper motor to control the seconds hand as Rolex decided to use a conventional escapement to drive the seconds hand. There was a regular pallet fork, but instead of locking the escape wheel, it locks and releases a pallet wheel which drives the seconds hand. The advantage over the stepper motor is that the seconds hand steps precisely on top of each individual seconds index, without any backlash as the escapement locks the hand in place and then releases it exactly one second later. The hour and minute hands are also driven from this pallet wheel. There was one disadvantage to this system: a conventional pallet fork and escape wheel operates eight times per second and the individual lock/release sequences are indiscernible from each other; the once-per-second sequence in the Oysterquartz can be easily heard.

It was also one of the first quartz movements with both thermal compensation and a rate-trimming adjustment, which enabled the on-wrist accuracy to be adjusted by the Rolex service department up to plus or minus two seconds a day.

The movement was introduced in 1977, at the same time as the new high-beat 3035 movement, with which it shared more than 20 components, including the complete date and Day-Date mechanisms and even the winding stem. In fact, the Rolex parts catalogue from this period shows that almost half the individual components of the 5035 movement are shared with its 3035 mechanical sibling.

When the Oysterquartz was launched, only the Day-Date version was sent to the Contrôle Officiel Suisse des Chronomètres (COSC) for chronometer testing. The Datejust versions –both the steel and two-tone versions – had simple dials with just three words on them: 'Rolex' and 'Datejust' above the centre post, and 'Oysterquartz' below it. After about two years all of the movements made a visit to the COSC and all the dials had this reassurance printed just below the centre post. This change happened when Rolex decided to swap the initial simple quartz crystal for a tuning fork-shaped one. I do not believe that the early watches were any less accurate than the COSC-labelled ones, I think the inclusion of COSC was carried out for aesthetic and marketing reasons.

Rolex was a late entrant to the quartz race. But when it joined in 1977 with the 5035/5055 movement, it did so in its own idiosyncratic way. This movement used a technology not found anywhere else – the vibration frequency of the crystal is directly related to the voltage fed to it. Rolex used a thermistor to measure temperature variations; this was then fed into a compensation circuit which varies the voltage by tiny amounts – just enough to force the crystal to vibrate at the correct rate, irrespective of the temperature.

→ This is my everyday watch – well, one of them – but it is the one most often found on my wrist. As someone who automatically glances at my wrist whenever I hear the Greenwich 'pips' on the radio, I love its unwavering accuracy. But the contrarian in me loves that it isn't the 'normal' Rolex. I like the heft of the white gold and the clean lines of the integrated bracelet with its hidden clasp.

TUESDAY
ROLEX
OYSTERQUARTZ
DAY-DATE
SUPERLATIVE CHRONOMETER
OFFICIALLY CERTIFIED
SWISS MADE

1980

DATEJUST PROTOTYPE

The hole in the dial of this watch hides a secret. Not only is the watch not what it seems to be, but behind the date window is a second secret.

- **Model number: 1600**
- **Date: 1980**
- **Dial: Brass, silvered**
- **Movement: Rolex 2135**
- **Case material: Stainless steel**
- **Dimensions: 36mm**

My interest in Rolex, its products and its history has led me down some interesting paths and introduced me to some fascinating people. One of them was a gentleman who lived in Switzerland and was as fascinated by the firm as I was. He had built up a massive collection of ephemera, documentation and prototypes. Over the years I bought a few things from him, but mostly we traded items between us. By far the most bizarre piece I received from him was a Rolex Datejust (see page 82) with a giant hole in the dial which had been made for one purpose only.

By the late 1970s, Rolex knew that there was a problem with its women's watches, and the issue was its clients. There was a tendency for women to wear a watch loose, like a bangle, not tight, like a bracelet. This meant that the watch did not move with the wrist and so it did not get wound properly. Rolex service departments were flooded with complaints that the watches would stop running, even when worn on the wrist. And so a team at Rolex's Bienne facility took the existing 2035 movement and worked on all the parts of the winding gear to reduce friction wherever they could, even adding an extra jewel. But then came the question of how to test these new movements in real life. You could put them on the winding machines and then remove them and see how long it took for the watch to run down, but the engineers were more interested in how quickly the

→ This is a weird watch, no two ways about that, but what I love about it is that it gives us a view into how projects are developed at Rolex. Because the firm just releases a brand-new model or movement, we rarely gain any insight into the interim stages which bring us to the final product. This watch may look amateurish, but it's actually an impressive answer to a difficult problem.

new movements would wind and how much effort was needed to do that.

Rolex watches do not have power reserves, so how could the engineers tell how long one would work for? They fitted the new movements inside full-size men's Datejust cases and used a modified movement plate to hold the new movement centrally. Then they altered the new movement, adding a small hand to the centre of the winding barrel and modifying the date mechanism. The additional hand acted as a winding indicator, and each drilled dot on the periphery of the hole represented another hour of autonomy for the watch. Each time the little hand hit 8, it flipped over the date. The Research and Development department noted the position of the wind indicator and the 'date' at the start of each experiment. At the end they noted the new positions and were able to tell the state of wind of the mainspring.

What this all means is that when you wind the watch manually, the 'date' flips over following every few revolutions of the crown. But if you set the time, no matter how many times you pass 12 the 'date' never changes.

This movement eventually became the 2135.

1982

SINGLE 'QUICK' DAY-DATE

For the first time in 20 years, the Day-Date receives a new movement, and with it comes both sapphire glass and a new level of usability.

- **Model number: 18038**
- **Date: 1982**
- **Dial: Brass, gold-plated, gold indices**
- **Movement: 3055**
- **Case material: 18ct gold**
- **Dimensions: 36mm**

The 15XX series of movements (see page 182) were at the heart of the watches that made Rolex's name – the 5513 Submariner (see page 174), the 1016 Explorer (see page 156), the 1603 Datejust (see page 142) and, of course, the 1803 Day-Date (see page 186). The movement soldiered on until the end of the 1980s, more than 30 years since its launch, but by the early 1970s Rolex knew that it was due for replacement. In 1977 it introduced the new 30XX series of movements, and bravely chose the firm's flagship watch as the launch platform. The new 18038 was a genuine breakthrough – the first Day-Date with sapphire glass, it also benefitted from one major addition to the movement, the Quickset date change. Now, there were four positions that the winding crown could be moved to. The first was firmly locked in position then in the first unscrewed position, it allowed the movement to be hand-wound. Pull it one more click and the date could be quickly adjusted. The final position allowed the hands to be set to the correct time; this was aided by the fact that in this position the seconds hand would stop, allowing the watch to be synchronized to a time signal.

This new feature solved the biggest practical problem with the old Day-Date model. If you did not wear it for a few days and the watch stopped, you had to move the hands through countless revolutions to reset the watch to the correct day and date. At the end of a month with less than 31 days, when you advanced the date forward one day you also advanced the day, which meant that the watch now read the wrong day. To rectify this you had to turn the hands back 24 hours (the date wheel did not go in reverse, but the day wheel did). This was such a complex procedure that many people wore their watches with the correct date but the incorrect day, making the whole point of the feature irrelevant. Now, because advancing the date with the new watch did not affect the day disc, most users could keep their watches completely correct.

The watch looked completely different from its predecessor, but one connection to the old model remained – the choice of bracelets. It was possible to order the watch with a President bracelet, but you still had the choice of the concealed clasp or the old-style adjustable bracelet. Believe it or not it was still possible to order the watch with a leather strap and a normal pin buckle.

→ One of the great features of Rolex watches is that the appearance rarely changes, you can wear a ten-year-old model, and as long as it is in good condition it is difficult to tell it from a new one, except under very close examination. However, when the Single 'Quick' Day-Date was introduced with its sapphire glass, all previous Day-Dates were now visibly different to the new model. So, a profitable sideline developed for some less-than-scrupulous watchmakers; new bezels for plastic glass Day-Dates which could mount the new sapphire glasses. Unfortunately, many of these bezels were not sufficiently watertight, with disastrous consequences.

THURSDAY
ROLEX
30
OFFICIALLY CERTIFIED
T SWISS MADE T

1984

COMEX

Along with everyone else, the COMEX Submariners and Sea-Dwellers received new movements, dials and cases. None of which had any deleterious effect on the desirability of the watches.

- **Model number: 16800**
- **Date: 1984**
- **Dial: Brass, gloss black paint, white gold index surrounds**
- **Movement: 3035**
- **Case material: Stainless steel**
- **Dimensions: 40mm**

As well as the likelihood that he was aware of the work the US Navy (USN) had done on saturation diving, it is probable that Henri-Germain Delauze also knew about Rolex's work with the USN on projects such as SeaLab and Tektite and therefore about the pressure equalization problem with watches (see page 212).

Nobody knows the origins of the relationship between Omega and COMEX. Still, they began working together towards the end of the 1960s to develop the ultimate professional divers' watch. Omega wanted a watch that was totally impervious to helium, and this was the Ploprof or Professional Diver.

It was used successfully by COMEX until 1971, when Rolex director general André Heiniger approached Delauze with an offer he could not refuse: Rolex would supply COMEX with watches for every diver – free of charge – in return for feedback from the firm. The Sea-Dweller was already in production, so some of these were supplied. But when Rolex received the copies of the dive logs and the diver reports, they realized that the divers needed neither date displays nor chronometer-class timekeeping, so the decision was made to provide basic 5513 Submariners. They looked like normal Submariners (see page 208), but had the word 'COMEX' engraved on the case back, a smaller issue number, and the addition of a Mk1 Sea-Dweller gas escape valve on the side of the case.

These fulfilled all the requirements that a diver might need and, as COMEX expanded and recruited more divers, the demand for watches increased. When Rolex received the new orders, it was decided that these unusual watches deserved their own model number, and they were given one – 5514. These watches not only had the gas escape valve, but 'COMEX' was printed boldly on the dial and engraved on the case back along with an issue number in large numerals. An external contractor carried out the engraving. I assume this was because the case number was engraved inside each case back so that the correct back would be reunited with the watch when it returned.

Rolex continued to provide watches to COMEX for a few years after the diving branch of the firm was sold to Stolt Seaway in 1993, and a batch of 15 presentation watches was delivered to COMEX in September 2006. Prior to the launch of the Sea-Dweller Deep Sea, COMEX built a pressure chamber for Rolex to test the integrity of the watches, which were rated to 3,900m (12,795ft). ISO 6425 regulations for dive watches insist that a watch must be able to withstand a pressure 25 per cent more than its declared rating so, courtesy of COMEX, the Deep Sea watches were actually tested to 4,875m (15,994ft).

→ As a firm who built their reputation on saturation diving, COMEX bought quite a lot of Submariners without gas escape valves and I always wondered why. But further investigation revealed that the majority of everyday work for COMEX divers was done at depths between 100 and 200m (328–656ft), where there was no need for either saturation divers or gas escape valves.

ROLEX
23
comex
SUBMARINER
1000ft=300m

1985

JEWELLED DAYTONA

I have always preferred understated, discreet watches, but even I have to admire the craftsmanship and quality of the stones fitted to this most opulent of Daytonas.

- **Model number: 6269**
- **Date: 1985**
- **Dial: 18ct gold, pavé diamonds, sapphire indices**
- **Movement: Valjoux 727, signed Rolex**
- **Case material: 18ct gold**
- **Dimensions: 37mm**

→ Over the years I have had the experience of visiting several jewellery workshops of world-famous brands. What is impressive about them is how little modern technology is employed and how much delicate hand work is used instead. The jewellery workshop on the top floor of Rolex Chêne-Bourg is no different – everything is still done by incredibly skilled hands.

In the car business, when a model is about to be replaced and the public knows that there is a new one on the way, there is one way to shift the remainder of the existing model – load it with every option on the list and sell it as a special edition. I do not know if that was the sales tactic that Rolex had in mind when it launched the 6269 and 6270 models of the Valjoux Daytona at the 1984 Basel exhibition, but it certainly feels like it. The 6269/70 were the final and numerically highest models of the four-digit model number chronographs, which began 20 years earlier with the 6234, and they certainly lacked for nothing.

The difference between the two versions is that the 6269 has a bezel set with 44 round brilliant-cut diamonds, while the 6270 has 28 much larger baguette-cut diamonds. The dials are often set with a field of over 200 identical small diamonds, broken only by the three registers and two raised plates, one for the maker's name and one for the model's name. The hour indices are nine tiny sapphires, only nine because there are none at the register positions.

The two models are interesting because they were Rolex's first production off-catalogue watches. It had offered diamond-laden men's watches as far back as 1957, with the platinum Day-Date, model 6613, which had 46 diamonds on the bezel and a mixture of baguette and round ones on the dial. They were listed in detail in the catalogues, but these new chronographs differed in that they were not listed in any catalogue. I assume that selected – important – retailers were made aware of the existence of the watches and they contacted potential clients about them. We know the identity of at least one retailer and its client – Asprey of London, whose client the former Sultan of Oman, Qaboos bin Said Al Said, purchased at least eight of the 20 known examples of the 6270, for about 70,000 CHF each.

The movements were the final Rolex version of the venerable Valjoux 72 (see page 114), the 727, which was chronometer-regulated but otherwise absolutely standard. That was not something you could say about the case or dial. Like most Valjoux Daytonas, the case was made in Chêne-Bourg, Switzerland, at the factory of C R Spillmann. The jewel setting for the dial and case was done in-house at Rolex, which maintains one of the most complete jeweller's workshops in Geneva. The ironic touch is that in 1988 Rolex bought the Spillmann business, the factory was demolished and a new one built on the site. Subsequently the jewel-setting workshop moved to the new Chêne-Bourg facility.

ROLEX
COSMOGRAPH

1985

EXPLORER II 16550

This is a watch where the small details matter – does the bezel retain its radial brushing, have its tritium indices faded to cream or brown, and does the tritium in the hands match that on the dial?

- **Model number: 16550**
- **Date: 1985**
- **Dial: Brass, white lacquer, white gold indices**
- **Movement: 3085**
- **Case material: Stainless steel**
- **Dimensions: 40mm**

The 16550 may have been the unluckiest watch Rolex ever made. Launched in 1985 as a replacement for the unloved 1655 Explorer II (see page 204), Rolex tried to widen its potential market by making the new model a true two-time-zone watch. It also broadened its appeal by offering the watch with a choice of black or white dials and a much more conventional appearance.

Unfortunately, these new dials were problematic. Like the new versions of the Sea-Dweller, Submariner and GMT-Master, the new Explorer II had dials with a high gloss finish and white gold surrounds for the tritium indices. Rolex used a gloss lacquer topcoat to obtain a shiny appearance, but the lacquer had flaws. On the black dial watches the lacquer tended to crack, leaving the surface looking like a random spider's web. The lacquer on the white dials was unstable when exposed to bright light, and in a short period of time would gradually discolour from a bright white to a subtle cream. Ironically, this results in a much more attractive appearance and so these defective watches are eagerly sought-after by collectors. The so-called Ivory Dial Explorer became the first watch from the sapphire glass era to become collectable. It is still eagerly sought and commands a significant premium over its black dial cousin.

The watch was launched at the same time as the new 16750 GMT-Master. Both had grown from 39mm to 40mm, featured sapphire glass and were driven by the new 3085 movement. This was the GMT version of the 3035 calibre, a high-beat movement with an independently movable 24-hour hand in place of the quick-set date feature. The 24-hour hand allowed the watch to be used to display two time zones, making it attractive to travellers and to anyone needing to make international phone calls.

The 16550 had a comparatively short production life – from 1985 until 1989 – so there was only time for one variation. In around 1987 Rolex switched to a new dial manufacturer and the problems with the dials were fixed. It is easier to identify these new dials on the white versions as in order to be more visible, the white gold circles now have a black finish. The material used for luminosity also changed from tritium to LumiNova, although many of the dials were still printed with 'SWISS MADE T<25'.

→ I have always liked this version of the Explorer II, probably not as much as I like the 1655, but the discoloured cream dial on the 16550 has an attraction of its own and is much nicer than the bright white of the later dials. One of the nicest features of this model is that often the tritium luminous finish fades to a very similar shade as the dial, giving it a near monochromatic appearance.

ROLEX
SUPERLATIVE CHRONOMETER
OFFICIALLY CERTIFIED
SWISS – T < 25

CHAPTER NINE

1986–1995

ROLEX
OYSTER PERPETUAL
SUPERLATIVE CHRONOMETER
OFFICIALLY CERTIFIED
COSMOGRAPH
DAYTONA
UNITS PER HOUR
T SWISS
MADE T

1986–1995

ROLEX DISCOVERS COLOUR

A period remembered more for its flamboyance than the technical excellence of the new Automatic Daytona.

Rolex is an important watch company. It is possible to argue that it is the most important watch company in Switzerland, but that is all it is, a watch company – it does not have a role in society other than to reflect it. The period under discussion here, the 1980s and '90s, is a perfect example of Rolex reflecting the society around it. In the English-speaking world this was the era of Reagan and Thatcher, a time of financial deregulation, corporate takeovers and more than a touch of insider dealing. Michael Douglas won an Oscar for playing the corrupt financier Gordon Gekko whose motto was 'Greed is good'.

This was the period when Rolex went full steam ahead into the luxury market, with three collection launches, all at the top end of the market. First was the Crown Collection; these were 18-carat gold or platinum Day-Dates and Datejusts in standard cases but with precious stones liberally sprinkled on them. Jewelled bezels were de rigaeur, but you could also find stones on the lugs, completely covering the dials, set as hour indices, or even on the bracelet. The typical Crown Collection watch might be a Day-Date with a white gold case, yellow gold bezel set with baguette diamonds, sapphires as hour indices and a bracelet made from white, yellow and rose gold – the so-called 'Tridor'.

The Crown Collection proved such a success that Rolex took it even further and added another, more flamboyant line, which was colloquially known as the Pearlmaster range. The Pearlmaster name at that time only applied to the smaller Datejusts, intended for female clients, but the name has stuck for all models. They are distinguished from the rest of the range by their slightly larger cases, unique five-link bracelets and a liberal sprinkling of precious stones. The bracelets used on these watches are among the nicest and most comfortable that Rolex has ever made, and I think it a great tragedy that the design was never used elsewhere.

If you want to see how much Rolex was pinning its flag to the luxury market, look at the only new model Rolex introduced during this period, the Rolex Yacht-Master (see page 246). Produced in 18-carat yellow gold only, this was a watch for someone who found the 18-carat gold Submariner 1680 (see page 180) with blue dial and bezel to be too discreet. The Submariner was born as a dive watch, and even though probably less than 1 per cent of Submariner owners ever put on a diving mask, the watch – even the 18-carat versions – met all the ISO 6425 qualifications of a true diving watch. The Yacht-Master did not, despite looking as solid and substantial as the Submariner. Rolex rated it as capable of surviving at a depth of only 100m (328ft), the same as a Datejust and one-third of the Submariner's rated depth of 300m (984ft).

For a couple of decades Rolex had sponsored sporting events and recruited sporting personalities as ambassadors.

← Automatic Daytona, 1988 (see page 236).

This was the period when Rolex went full steam ahead into the luxury market, with three collection launches, all at the top end of the market.

The sports and pastimes involved were aspirational ones associated with well-off middle-class participants, such as golf, tennis, motor racing and opera. But now Rolex gave its name to a sport which was confined to the super–rich: yacht racing. And not the kind of yachts that the owner might potter about in and occasionally use to enter a local regatta. These were Maxi Yachts, 18m (60ft) in length and crewed by professionals. Rolex sponsored the annual races held off the island of Sardinia's famed Costa Smeralda. Over the previous couple of decades, the Aga Khan had developed the area as a resort area for the ultra-wealthy. There were polo fields, yacht clubs, heliports, homes worth millions of lira and, to add to the exclusive feel of the place, in 1980 the Aga Khan established the Maxi Yacht World Championship. In 1984 Rolex gave its name to the event and it became the Maxi Yacht Rolex Cup. For over 40 years Rolex has remained an integral part of the event. It was to this group and those who aspired to join it that Rolex launched the Yacht-Master.

When the Yacht-Master was launched it was powered by the most important movement Rolex had produced in decades, the 3135. Despite the similarity in model numbers to the now discontinued 3035, this was not a modification of the previous movement but an entirely new calibre. The obvious difference was the abandonment of the conventional balance cock and the substitution of a balance bridge, but the changes went much deeper. The balance wheel was now larger, and the inner end of the hairspring was laser welded to the balance staff, rather than glued as it had been previously. The jewel count rose from 27 to 31, yet despite all these improvements the movement was actually 0.35mm slimmer than the 3035. The movements shared the exact same diameter, 28.5mm, so that no changes were needed to the case design when models were switched from the 3035 to the new calibre.

Speaking of movements, in 1987 Rolex filed the patent for a rather unusual new quartz movement. It was a full perpetual calendar which could be completely adjusted and set via the conventional winding crown, without the need for correctors or cocktail sticks. What was even more unusual about the movement was that it featured an independently adjustable hour hand. This meant that when the clocks went forwards or backwards, or the wearer crossed time zones, the hour hand could be moved without affecting the timekeeping of the minute and seconds hands. If Rolex had included all of these features in a watch, it would have been the most advanced one in the catalogue, but it was not to be. The firm made a few prototypes but went no further. It is believed that the decision not to proceed with the new movement was made because it would have meant that a firm renowned for its mechanical watches would have had a quartz watch as its flagship model, and André Heiniger simply would not allow it.

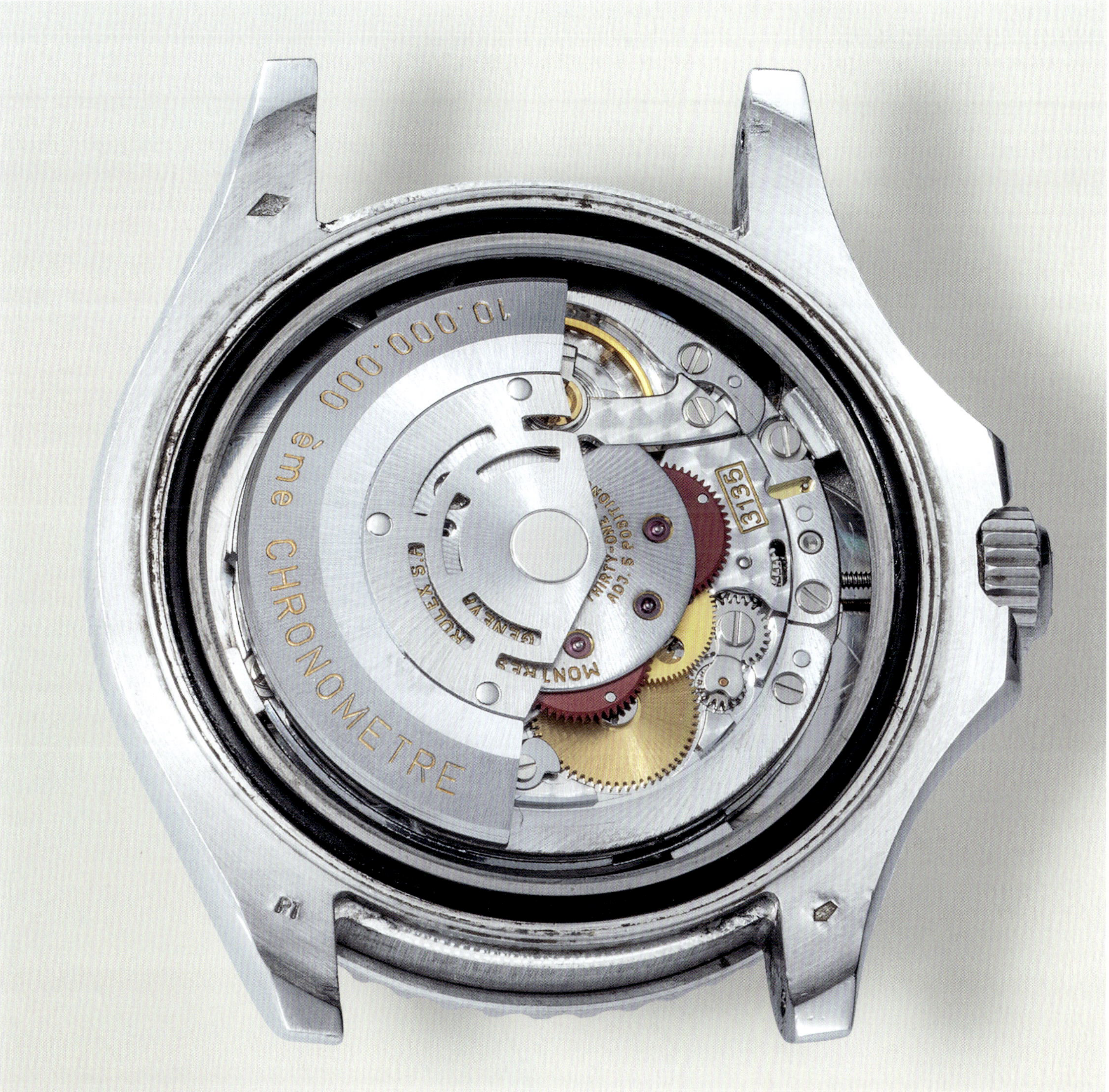

↑ This may look like a conventional 3135 movement, but in fact it is the only known 3135 with a custom engraved rotor. It was produced to celebrate the construction of the ten millionth chronometer by the firm (see page 244).

1988

STONE DIALS

Dials for the newest Rolex watches were made with centuries-old lapidary techniques and technology.

- **Model number: 18038**
- **Date: 1988**
- **Dial: Brass, thin slice of rubellite, gold and diamond indices**
- **Movement: 3055**
- **Case material: 18ct gold**
- **Dimensions: 36mm**

→ One of the great ironies of these dials is that, despite being made from incredibly strong and solid materials, they are very delicate. This is because the slice of the stone is so thin that it easily shatters when drilled for the attachment of the indices or even by unequal pressure on the dial feet – to say nothing of accidental knocks or other impacts. Despite all this, there is a constant demand for these watches.

At almost the same time as it was launching its Stella dials (see page 186), Rolex released another range of exotic dials. Rather than using new technology, it chose a technique going back centuries, and materials that were millions of years old. These dials are known by several names such as 'mineral', 'gemstone' or just 'stone'. For simplicity's sake I am going to call them 'stone'.

The first dials, introduced in the early 1970s, seem to have been made from lapis lazuli and destined for the Middle East, a market where a little flamboyance was not out of place. Lapis was one of the more restrained or discreet stones Rolex used. It is deep blue with gold flecks from the pyrite impurities within it. The stone principally comes from Afghanistan and had been coveted for centuries – it has been used as a jewel since the days of the Egyptian Pharaohs. But it became famous during the Renaissance when it was ground to a powder and mixed with oil to become ultramarine, the most expensive pigment of the time, which was reserved by artists for painting the robes of the Virgin Mary.

Stone dials remained very much a one-off, not listed in the catalogues but available to those in the know. This all changed in 2000 when Rolex relaunched the Daytona 'Beach' collection with four versions of the watch in 18-carat white gold with the reference 116519. They had brightly coloured dials in yellow, green, pink and turquoise, each with lizard-skin straps to match the dial colour. But what was extra special about these watches was that each coloured dial was made from a different semi-precious material. The yellow was listed in the catalogue as 'Champagne Nacre' and was made from yellow-toned mother-of-pearl. The green dial was made from a stone known as chrysoprase, a type of quartz with a green tone from the presence of nickel. The blue dial was natural turquoise while the pink was another shade of mother-of-pearl.

The introduction of these watches, and their instant popularity, nudged Rolex into launching a much wider range of stone dials; it was helped in this endeavour by having a new factory at Chêne-Bourg, Switzerland, where both dial manufacture and gem setting were now under one roof.

The dials are made from a brass plate as normal, and the mineral to be used is machined into a cylinder with the same diameter as the dials. Thin slices are then cut from the cylinder and attached to the brass plate using a strong adhesive, then the stone dial surface is milled down to less than half the thickness of the original slice. It is done in this way because it would be impossible to cut such a fine slice from the original mineral.

WEDNESDAY
ROLEX
OYSTER PERPETUAL
DAY-DATE
30
SUPERLATIVE CHRONOMETER
OFFICIALLY CERTIFIED
SWISS MADE

1988

AUTOMATIC DAYTONA

Nowadays known as the Zenith Daytona, this was the model which changed the Daytona from a frequently discounted shelf-sitter to the most desirable watch in the Rolex catalogue.

- **Model number: 16520**
- **Date: 1988**
- **Dial: Brass, black enamel, white gold indices**
- **Movement: Calibre 4030**
- **Case material: Stainless steel**
- **Dimensions: 40mm**

By the mid 1980s, Rolex knew from the sales figures that the writing was on the wall for its Valjoux-powered chronographs. The question was what to replace them with. Rolex knew two things: the new chronograph would have to be automatic, as manual-wind chronographs just did not make sense, and the market was not big enough to justify it making its own movement. Where movements were concerned, there were just three contenders: the Valjoux 7750, the Heuer/Breitling Chronomatic and the Zenith El Primero. Rolex had worked with Valjoux for decades, and so it was the obvious choice. However, the 7750 was one of the new styles of movement designed to be churned out by the factory. It was mostly made from stamped components and too many modifications would be required to enable it to be used by Rolex. The Heuer/Breitling Chronomatic was more like it, but Heuer was mainly a chronograph maker, and it was hardly likely to be interested in helping one of its biggest competitors. It came down to the Zenith, but – once again – there was a problem. Zenith had ceased production of the El Primero in 1975 after the firm's American owners decided that the future belonged to quartz watches. However, Zenith had several hundred movements and movement kits sitting around when a small watch company in the neighbouring town of La Chaux-de-Fonds asked if it had any El Primero movements for sale. Zenith assembled movements for it and the resulting watch, the Ebel 1911 chronograph, proved to be a huge success for both firms when it launched in 1982.

Enter a man named Oscar Waldan, a New York-based watchmaker who also saw the benefits of the El Primero. He purchased several hundred triple-calendar moonphase versions from Zenith and set them in 18ct gold cases, selling them principally to Tiffany in New York City. These watches bore the store's name rather than Waldan's. At the time, Tiffany was a major Rolex retailer. Waldan, who had trained, lived and worked in Switzerland, knew both René Dentan, head of Rolex in New York, and Diether-Heinrich Kübel-Wilsdorf, a nephew of Hans Wilsdorf (see page 11) who had worked in senior management at Rolex Geneva and sat on the board of the Hans Wilsdorf Foundation. Waldan showed the Zenith movement to both of his Rolex contacts and, before long, Rolex was in touch with Zenith. It took two years to modify the original Zenith movement to make it compatible with Rolex servicing procedures. Almost 200 alterations were made; the most significant was that the unique feature of the movement, its 36,000 bph beat rate, was discarded in favour of Rolex's usual 28,800 bph free-sprung balance. The entire auto-wind system was replaced with the regular Rolex one, and many of the smaller components were modified for ease of production. These changes needed to be made – previously the movement had been produced in batches of a few hundred at a time, Rolex needed thousands.

→ This was the watch which changed everything at Rolex – from the moment that it was launched, it was unavailable. There was always a waiting list for the watch – initially prospective buyers were quoted 'several months' as the possible wait time; this then stretched to 'several years' and now retailers won't even quote what the delay might be between requesting one and finally taking delivery.

ROLEX
OYSTER PERPETUAL
SUPERLATIVE CHRONOMETER
OFFICIALLY CERTIFIED
COSMOGRAPH
DAYTONA
UNITS PER HOUR
T SWISS
MADE T

1989

DOUBLE 'QUICK' DAY-DATE

A new movement changes everything for the Day-Date, now it is the ultimate user-friendly wristwatch, as well as being a quiet statement of power.

- **Model number: 18206**
- **Date: 1989**
- **Dial: Brass, silver sunray finish, diamond indices**
- **Movement: 3155**
- **Case material: Platinum**
- **Dimensions: 36mm**

When Rolex introduced the Single 'Quick' Day-Date in 1977 (see page 220), it was immediately distinguishable from its predecessor by its aesthetics. The old organic-looking plastic glass was gone, replaced by flat sapphire glass. When the new 18238 Day-Date arrived in 1988, it took an expert with a pair of callipers and a loupe to tell the difference between it and the expiring 18038.

The only visible difference, and then only visible to the experts, was that the new watch was just under 0.5mm thinner than the previous model. This was thanks to the new 3155 movement, which measures 0.66mm less than the 3055. The 3155 was a much more modern movement and used a balance bridge instead of a balance cock. This was a much more robust method of securing the balance in place and preventing end-shake of the balance staff, which can have a negative effect on timekeeping.

The major change was not the watch's aesthetics, but its usability. It was now possible to instantly change both the date and day from the same crown position: one direction for day, the other for date. This meant that even if the watch had stopped for days or weeks, it was but a matter of a moment to synchronize the time, day and date and then get the watch back on the wrist.

An interesting introduction was that, for the first time in more than 30 years, the Day-Date was available on an Oyster bracelet which – like the President bracelet – had a concealed clasp. Making a welcome return to the catalogue, the Day-Date was available in pink gold once more. Interestingly there was no price difference between the yellow and pink gold watches, while buyers paid a 12 per cent premium for white gold.

The biggest change was the increased availability of jewel-set models. Historically, a diamond-set bezel and/or diamond indices had been options, but now that the jewellery atelier at Rolex was in full operation, Day-Dates were listed in the catalogue with baguette bezels, diamond-set lugs and even bracelets. Dials became available with not only pavé diamonds, but red or blue sapphires as hour indices, or with tiny diamonds set all over the dial like a starlit sky, a technique called Pléiade. All of this created the stepping stones to the next flagship Rolex watches – the Pearlmasters (see page 304).

→ **When the watch was launched at Baselworld in 1988, my first glimpse of it was through the windows of the stand, but I got to see it close up when I found myself standing next to Stewart Wicht, CEO of Rolex USA and a good friend. He was wearing a white gold version on the Oyster bracelet, with a dark-coloured dial and I thought it the nicest Day-Date I had ever seen – it looked imposing, yet still discreet.**

SUNDAY
ROLEX
OYSTER PERPETUAL
DAY-DATE
28
SUPERLATIVE CHRONOMETER
OFFICIALLY CERTIFIED
T SWISS MADE T

1990

STONE DIALS

The colourful alternative to Stella dials, but much rarer and more desirable.

- **Model number: 18238**
- **Date: 1990**
- **Dial: Brass baseplate, coral surface**
- **Movement: 3155**
- **Case material: 18ct gold**
- **Dimensions: 36mm**

The probably unexpected success of the Daytona 'Beach' watches (see page 234) convinced Rolex to expand the availability of the stone dials. Within a couple of years, onyx and lapis dials were available, either with or without diamonds on the Day-Date and precious-metal Ladies' Datejusts. Sodalite became available, but only with diamonds, on both watches, and on the steel Datejusts with a white-gold fixed or rotating bezel.

The addition of diamonds to these dials shows how confident Rolex had become in the manufacture of stone dials; mounting eight square diamonds and two baguettes on each dial involved drilling four tiny holes through the stone and brass of the dial for each gem. Making every hole could cause a crack, yet Rolex was confident enough to drill up to 40 holes through each dial. The diamond itself is held in a precious metal frame, the base of which has a number of pins. These pins fit into the drilled holes and are then secured in place on the back of the dial. Every operation on the dial carries the risk of it cracking and becoming worthless.

By the second decade of this century, Rolex expanded its stone dial options. It no longer offered just the three mentioned here, but now bloodstone or jasper, coral, malachite, tiger eye, jade, meteorite, chrysoprase, grossular garnet rubellite, eisenkiesel, fossil or Jurassic/ammonite, howlite (known as marble) and ferrite became options. Some of them you will recognize, but most may need some explanation. Jasper is a dark green stone that sometimes has red inclusions of ferrite; when these are present, it is known as bloodstone. Eisenkiesel is a dark brown quartz with random veins of ferrite spreading through it; only introduced to the Rolex range in 2021, it looks its best with Everose cases. Fossil or Jurassic dials are made from chunks of fossilized tiny bivalves, while a variant features fossilized ammonites in the dial surface. Howlite looks like white marble but is actually a silicate crystal with darker veins. Most of the stone dials have veins or inclusions which are unique to that particular dial, so no two dials will ever be alike.

So far, I have only mentioned Day-Dates and Datejusts, but for a short period at the end of the twentieth century, Rolex offered both lapis and onyx dials on the 18ct yellow gold Submariner 16618 (see page 284). As this model did not come with any diamonds on the dial, at a quick glance it could pass for a common gold Submariner – not that any gold Submariner is common.

→ **Of all the optional materials for Rolex dials, it is ironic that two of the most common and one of the rarest are not actually 'stones' of any kind. Neither mother-of-pearl nor meteorite could accurately be described as minerals, and Coral most certainly isn't. I have to be honest and say that I have never really liked Rolex watches with stone dials. But I would make an exception for a white gold Submariner with a lapis dial.**

TUESDAY
ROLEX
OYSTER PERPETUAL
DAY-DATE
15
SUPERLATIVE CHRONOMETER
OFFICIALLY CERTIFIED
SWISS

1991

STELLA DIALS

Stella dials didn't vanish, they just took on a new and rather more sober appearance as Ombre dials, sometimes also known as Vignette dials.

- **Model number: 18346**
- **Date: 1991**
- **Dial: Brass, multi-coat enamel, diamond indices**
- **Movement: 3155**
- **Case material: Platinum**
- **Dimensions: 36mm**

→ As a contrarian, I always found the Vignette dials more attractive than the monochrome Stella dials. Perhaps it is because they are not as flamboyant as the Stellas, usually being in a darker tone. Rolex produced watches with these dials for over a decade, but ceased before the end of the century. However, in the last few years practically every brand, including Rolex, has reintroduced them to their catalogue.

The dials were produced by Cadran Stern Frères in Geneva. However, it is intriguing that it did not manufacture this style of dial for any other watch brand. Was this because no one else was willing to purchase these very expensive dials, or because Rolex paid Stern a premium to gain exclusive access to them? Like many aspects of vintage Rolex, there are more questions than answers.

While the Stella dials disappeared from the catalogues over 30 years ago, the technique used to produce them did not. Shortly after they appeared, a variation known as 'vignette', 'ombre' or 'dégradé' also turned up in the Rolex catalogue. Instead of using just one colour, a darker shade was added to the edge of the dial and feathered as it came inwards, resulting in a shadow effect. These dials were produced until as late as the 1990s, and while they were made using the same techniques as the Stella dials, they were more complex to create as the method involved using a slowly rotating turntable. Possibly due to their more sombre tones they are not – as yet – as highly valued.

By the end of the last century, these watches were little more than a footnote in Rolex's history. But then, in the first half of the 2000s, Italian women began wearing them, not with their gold President bracelets, but with brightly coloured leather straps to match the dial. Never underestimate the importance of stylish Italian women on the watch market. The oversized Panerai watches (see page 72) are almost a cliché nowadays, but they first gained widespread acceptance on the wrists of Italian women, not men.

The reappearance of the Stella dial watches sparked an interest in them among collectors, and as they began to appear at auction, prices inevitably rose. When production ceased at the end of the 1970s, a yellow gold Day-Date sold for 7,500CHF (worth £2,112 then); now, these watches have sold for over 100,000CHF at auction.

The renewed popularity of these watches seems to have caught the eye of someone at Rolex and, in 2013, it launched a series of five Day-Dates (see page 290) with eye-catching dials – green and cognac in yellow-gold cases, cherry-red and blue in white-gold cases, and chocolate in Everose (the Rolex name for its own alloy of red gold) – each watch fitted with a leather strap to match the dial. What I find really interesting was that the contemporary Day-Date II measured 41mm but like the original Stella watches, these new coloured-dial Day-Dates were only available in 36mm and seemed to be aimed at a female clientele. As I have said – never underestimate the importance of stylish women (Italian or not).

ROLEX
OYSTER PERPETUAL
DAY-DATE
SUPERLATIVE CHRONOMETER
OFFICIALLY CERTIFIED
SWISS MADE

1992

NON-CATALOGUE WATCHES

During his tenure as CEO of Rolex, Patrick Heiniger was extremely generous to friends and colleagues, gifting unique platinum pieces to a number of them.

- **Model number: 16626**
- **Date: 1992**
- **Dial: Platinum, pad printed, diamond and sapphire indices**
- **Movement: 3135**
- **Case material: Platinum**
- **Dimensions: 40mm**

I have talked almost exclusively about about Patrick Heiniger in relation to non-catalogue watches (see page 176) because I believe that understanding Patrick is the key to understanding the off-catalogue watches launched during his tenure. Look at any photograph of the man, and you will see a very elegantly dressed gentleman, but I guarantee one feature will catch your eye: the knot in his tie. I genuinely do not know how you can get a knot so large. This, I believe, is the key to Patrick – elegant but with a touch of flamboyance.

And that was definitely how I would describe many of the bespoke watches that were produced during his reign, and usually on his command. Almost all of them were made in platinum, a very discreet material, but its weight constantly reminds the user that this is something special.

Seven weeks after Patrick passed away in 2013, and in the surroundings of the recently completed Messe Basel (trade fair building), Rolex launched the platinum Daytona (see page 276) to celebrate the 50th anniversary of the model. This was the first time it was possible to buy the Daytona in the most noble of metals – but not the first time that it had been made. Patrick got there first. In 1999 he commissioned five Daytonas to be made in platinum, each with a different dial and each bearing the model number 16516. Rolex was only months away from launching its new in-house movement, so these were some of the last Daytonas to carry the Zenith-based movement.

Of the five watches, he kept one for himself and gave the other four to friends and business contacts – one of these watches surfaced in 2018 at an auction at Sotheby's in Hong Kong, where it sold for a hammer price of HK6.84 million. The watch was a wedding gift to a young couple; the bride was a member of the Gobbi family, Milan's largest and oldest Rolex retailers.

However, these were as nothing compared with the watch he had made to commemorate the production of the firm's 10 millionth chronometer. This was an all-platinum version of the Yacht-Master (see opposite), the only new model introduced during his stewardship. A platinum version was unique, but that was just the start – the dial was silvered with a sunburst finish, and it had sapphire baguette and triangle quarter-hour markers with round diamonds for the balance of the indices. Above the 6 index was the text 'Dix Millioniéme Chronometre' (ten millionth chronometer), to celebrate the unequalled achievement. On the movement, the rotor had a similar engraving – this is the only Rolex I have ever seen where the rotor has a unique engraving. I do not know how the watch left the family, but it appeared at an auction in Monaco in 2023 where it sold for over €2.3 million (Monaco Legend Auctions).

→ What else is there to say about this watch, the ultimate in off-catalogue watches? It is a watch that I would love to own, not for its value, but for its uniqueness, although if I – by some strange event – did own it, I would replace the dial with a plain blue one and make the watch even more idiosyncratic.

ROLEX
DIX MILLIONIEME
CHRONOMETRE
SWISS - T<25

1993

YACHT-MASTER

If you considered the 18-carat Submariner with blue dial and bezel to be too discreet, Rolex now had a watch specifically designed for you.

- **Model number: 16628**
- **Date: 1993**
- **Dial: Brass, white paint, gold indices**
- **Movement: 3135**
- **Case material: 18ct gold**
- **Dimensions: 40mm**

→ My taste has almost always been towards the discreet end of the spectrum, and the first-generation Yacht-Master sat proudly at the other end. But I am the exception, the watch has been in production for over thirty years now and not only has the 18 carat version never been out of production, but this is the only Rolex sports watch produced in three sizes – 37, 40 and 42mm.

The Yacht-Master is one of the stranger watches from Rolex. Essentially, it was a more luxurious version of the Submariner (see page 180), but – as the Submariner was by that time already available in 18-carat gold with the option of either stone- or diamond-set dials – was a more luxurious version required? Rolex firmly believed that it was, and launched the reference 16628 in 1992 in 18-carat gold with a white dial. It differed from the Submariner in both aesthetics and function; there was no insert to the bezel, the numerals and indices were cast into the solid-gold bezel and stood proud of the matt-finished base. The surfaces of the numerals and indices were highly polished, making them stand out even more at a glance. Also, unlike all Rolex dive watches, the bezel could be rotated in both directions. Although the case appeared identical to the gold Submariner, and used the identical 8mm Triplock crown, the Yacht-Master was depth rated at 100m (328ft), while the Submariner carried a 300m (984ft) rating.

I have no proof of this, but I believe that the Yacht-Master was an attempt to reposition Rolex in the market, to make it even more upscale than it already was. Yachting had always been the preserve of the moneyed classes, and Rolex already had connections with the activity. These went as far back as Sir Francis Chichester's solo circumnavigation of the world in 1967, when his Rolex Oyster Perpetual served as his marine chronometer for navigational purposes. Rolex is very active in sponsoring yacht racing, and you can tell the kind of client it is trying to attract when you realize that one of the oldest yachting events it sponsors, the Maxi Yacht Rolex Cup, is for single-hulled yachts over 18m (60ft) – in other words, multi-million-pound boats.

Despite all this, the Yacht-Master, was not an initial success and so – just two years after the launch – Rolex did something that it had never dared to do with the Submariner – it brought in smaller versions, a 35mm and a 29mm, both with white dials, now discontinued. This still did not set the sales charts on fire, so Rolex introduced two-tone versions of the two smaller versions, leaving the full-size version as 18-carat yellow gold only. In 1997 Rolex introduced a version which finally broke the dam and brought the Yacht-Master to the fore – a full-size stainless steel version with an all-platinum bezel and, for the first time for Rolex, a satin-finished platinum dial. This version, the 16622, became a hot item immediately after its launch.

ROLEX
YACHT-MASTER
SUPERLATIVE CHRONOMETER
CERTIFIED
SWISS

1994

AUTOMATIC DAYTONA

Officially there were only two dials on the steel Daytona, but soon collectors began to notice slight differences and these variations became collectable in themselves.

- **Model number: 16500**
- **Date: 1994**
- **Dial: Brass, black enamel, white gold indices**
- **Movement: 4030**
- **Case material: Stainless steel**
- **Dimensions: 42.5mm**

When the new model 16520 Daytona was launched in 1988, it sold out immediately. In retrospect, it is easy to see why – the Daytona (see page 236) was now really a Rolex – not just automatic, but also an Oyster and a Chronometer. And, with the shoulders enclosing the winding crown, it now shared the DNA of the GMT-Master and Submariner. It was a radical transformation, the only thing carried over from the Daytona 6265 (see page 188) was the metal bezel that held the tachometer scale.

The contrasting colour subdials for the registers on the dial were replaced. Now they were the same colour as the dial, with the perimeter of each register encircled by a slim band of a contrasting colour – black for the white dials, white for the black ones – and the numerals for the registers were contained within these bands. The most obvious difference in the dials was that there was now a lot of text on them. The red printed Daytona around the 12-hour register at the base remained, but everything up top had changed. On the steel watches, there had been three words on the dial – 'Rolex Oyster Cosmograph'. Now the dials flaunted eight as descriptions for both the automatic movement and chronometer status were used.

The case not only had shoulders, it had also grown in almost every dimension. Compared with its 6265 predecessor, it was 42.5mm in diameter, up from 37mm, and it was 47mm from lug to lug rather than 44mm. The most interesting measurement is that the thickness had shrunk from 13.5mm to 12.5mm, despite the fact that the movement now had a rotor, which could be expected to add considerably to the height. This can be explained by the fact that, even with the rotor and automatic works, the new movement was 0.4mm slimmer than the old manual Valjoux movement – 6.55mm rather than 6.95mm.

↑ The outer circle in the three registers on black-dial Daytonas was originally white, but some fault in the lacquer used caused them to gradually darken from white to cream, and eventually, to a dark brown. Watches so affected are known as 'Patrizzi' dials, after the founder of the Antiquorum auction house, Osvaldo Patrizzi, who first raised awareness of these changes.

For the first time, the Daytona was now available in what had become the signature Rolex material – steel and gold. But an even bigger innovation was to come in 1992, when the 18-carat yellow gold version became available on an alligator-skin strap; this was the first time any of the sapphire glass sports watches had been available on a strap. Then, in 1997, the yellow gold watch was joined by its white gold cousin. As if to emphasize that these strap versions were more formal than their bracelet versions, they had completely different dials with applied Arabic numerals rather than the batons normally seen on these models.

CHAPTER TEN

1996–2005

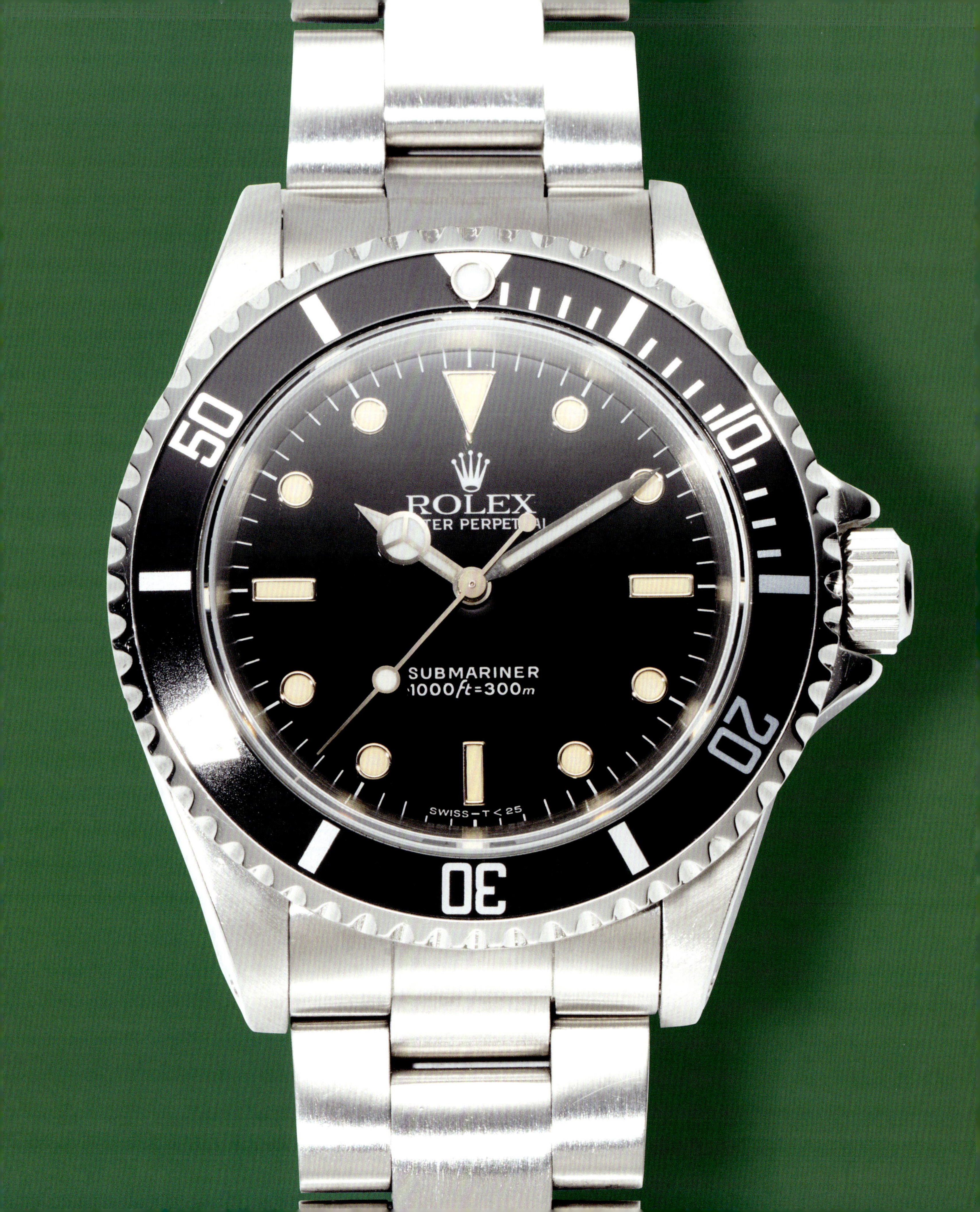

ROLEX
SUBMARINER
1000ft=300m
SWISS-T<25

1996–2005

ROLEX REMEMBERS

This was when Rolex introduced their first anniverary model, the 'Kermit', and reintroduced two discontinued models: the Prince and the Turn-O-Graph.

It can be argued that the biggest change at Rolex during this period was the introduction of the in-house movement for the Daytona (see page 266). I can understand the logic behind this argument but, while the 4130 movement (see page 266) marked the end of Rolex relying on external movement suppliers, I believe that the structural changes in the company were much more important.

I make no bones about it, the 4130 was a big deal. It was the first mechanical chronograph designed in Switzerland since the Valjoux 7750 was introduced in 1973. It was revolutionary because it completely reimagined the layout and workings of a chronograph. It was this that allowed a parts reduction of around 40 per cent, thereby increasing the available space, which allowed for much larger balance wheels and mainsprings, each with its own benefits. Unusually for Rolex, the movement was revolutionary, not evolutionary, but it has benefitted from the firm's programme of constant evolution with the recent addition of the Chronergy escapement. Even after 25 years, the 4130 (or 4131 as it is now called) is still the most advanced chronograph movement in the world.

This period marked the start of Rolex introducing anniversary models. In 2003 it was the Green Submariner (see page 262), model 16610LV. The name used by Rolex at the launch was the Maxi dial, referring to the oversized indices which were a feature of the watch, but collectors and dealers soon came to refer to it as the 'Kermit', after the Muppet character whose theme song was 'It's Not Easy Bein' Green'. Green, after all, is Rolex's corporate colour, and so the green theme continued in 2005 when the 50th anniversary GMT-Master II (see page 280), model 116718LN was introduced. This time the green was on the watch dial, not the bezel – although the bezel did have a surprise of its own. It was made from Cerachrom, the in-house developed ceramic compound, and this was the first watch to use it. This was an incredibly flamboyant design, only made in 18-carat yellow gold on an Oyster bracelet. It proclaimed itself with its bright green glossy dial, oversized luminous indices and a polished bezel with recessed hours coated with 24-carat gold.

This was also the period when Patrick Heiniger assumed full control of the firm from his father, André. Patrick had joined the company in 1986 as commercial director, became managing director six years later and in 1997 became Chairman. In the early days of his running the company he convinced the shareholders – the Wilsdorf Foundation – to embark on a reorganization of the firm which would change it for ever. Rolex had been headquartered at Les Acacias (a district of Geneva) for more than 20 years, but watches were still being made the way they were when the firm was located in the centre of Geneva, with components and sub-assemblies obtained from several suppliers in and around the city. Over the years, Rolex had purchased many of these

← Submariner 14060M, 2002 (see page 260).

Rolex is a privately owned company that does not have to worry about how the stock market will react to this quarter's result. Most firms think that five-year plans constitute long-range forward planning. Rolex can think in 25-year terms, or longer.

suppliers, but they still remained in their original workshops. The idea Patrick sold to the Foundation was that Rolex could improve its quality if everything was centralized, and if the quality improved, it would be possible to charge more for the product.

This was a multi-billion-Swiss franc project, and it was made possible only because Rolex is a privately owned company that does not have to worry about how the stock market will react to this quarter's result. Most firms think that five-year plans constitute long-range forward planning. Rolex can think in 25-year terms, or longer. This was made clear to me when I visited the giant operation at Plan-les-Ouates (the French translates as 'field of oats', although the locals now call the area 'Plan les Watches', due to the number of horological factories there). I was shown around the facility shortly after it opened in 2005 by Dominique Tadion, who was the head of PR for the firm and, incidentally, my first friend at Rolex Geneva. What amazed me was the width of the corridors between the workshops. I asked her why they were so wide and whether it was a wasteful use of space. Her response said more about how Rolex thinks than anything else anyone has since said to me. She told me that the architect's brief was to look at the largest piece of equipment due to be installed in the factory and imagine that one day that equipment will need to be removed so that a replacement machine twice the size of the original can be substituted. The building was designed to allow this changeover to happen without removing walls, ceilings or partitions. She told me, 'This building wasn't designed for the next five years, it was designed for the next 50 years.'

This was the path that Rolex embarked on during Heiniger's leadership, but it was only possible because of the unique ownership structure of the firm. I often hear people say that Rolex has only been able to grow because unlike every other watch firm it is owned by a charity so it does not have to pay taxes. Not only does Rolex SA have to pay taxes, just like every other watch firm, it is actually the single largest taxpayer in Geneva – not just the city, but in the entire canton. Rolex pays taxes and its employees also pay taxes – the firm is a major contributor to the coffers of the canton and the nation. Once the taxes are paid, the employees paid and the suppliers and overheads paid, whatever is left is profit and it is this profit which is paid to the shareholder – the Foundation.

The consolidation of the manufacturing sites into the three giant factories, and the purchase of Rolex Bienne from the Aegler-Borer family, are Heiniger's immortal legacy. The firm changed more under his leadership than it had under his two predecessors, each of whom had around 40 years at the helm. The Rolex we see today actually owes more to Patrick Heiniger than it does to his father, André or to Hans Wilsdorf.

→ Not for the retiring type, this Submariner 16613 from 2004 with its resplendent blue dial and bezel makes a change from the conservative all-steel black-dial version.

ROLEX
SUBMARINER
1000ft=300m
SUPERLATIVE CHRONOMETER
OFFICIALLY CERTIFIED
SWISS – T < 25

2000

OYSTERQUARTZ PROTOTYPE

We may never know where this path could have led Rolex if they had decided to fully embrace advanced quartz technology as featured in this prototype.

- **Model number: 17000**
- **Date: 2000**
- **Dial: Brass, white paint, applied white gold Roman numerals**
- **Movement: 5335**
- **Case material: Stainless steel**
- **Dimensions: 36mm**

As I mentioned earlier (see page 210), the Oysterquartz made its last appearance in the 2003 catalogue, although some lingered in retailers' windows and safes for many years. A UK Rolex agent offered me a brand-new Oysterquartz Day-Date in around 2010 at a very substantial discount – foolishly I declined.

Rolex had most likely ceased production of the Oysterquartz movements by around 1995, but as far as the company was concerned this was not the end of the line for the movement; it was a pause before the new model could be introduced. The plan was for the 5035 and 5055 movements (see page 216) to be replaced by two brand-new ones: the 5335 and the 5355. The 5035 movement bore no resemblance to the previous Beta-21 movement, and these new movements were nothing like their predecessors. They incorporated all the developments in ultra-high accuracy timekeeping which had occurred in the twenty-plus years since the 5035 was developed. It used two quartz crystals, a conventional 32khz tuning fork-shaped one for basic timekeeping and a ZT cut, 2.4mhz one which monitored the accuracy of the 32khz one and adjusted it if required. Rather than a conventional button-sized alkaline battery, the new movements were powered by a huge lithium one which filled the case back. The new movement's low power requirements, coupled with this high-capacity battery, meant the watch could run for a decade before the battery needed to be replaced. For the user, all of these features were hidden. What they saw was a watch with an independently adjustable hour hand, meaning that when you crossed timezones or daylight savings time came or went, the hour hand could be moved as needed while the minutes and seconds hands kept perfect time. The watch was also a full perpetual calendar, with the date wheel jumping instantly to the first of the month, no matter whether the previous month had 28, 29, 30 or 31 days. What was even more impressive was that the initial programming of the watch was all done via the screw-down crown.

This could have been the ultimate set-it-and-forget-it watch. It had everything: its accuracy was guaranteed by the ZT cut 2.4mhz monitoring crystal, it had a battery life of more than ten years, an independent hour hand adjustment and full perpetual calendar. Nevertheless, after making several prototypes Rolex decided not to put it into production. Some sources say that just over 20 were produced, while others claim that as many as 400 were made. The existence of these watches was confirmed when the patent for them was published in 2011, and when one or two of them appeared at auction. Over the years I have seen five or six of the Day-Date versions and two of the Datejusts. I think it is a shame that Rolex chose not to put them into production, but I can understand why – it would have meant that the best watch from the firm was quartz-powered at a time when Rolex was reinforcing its position as the saviour of the mechanical watch and was universally acknowledged as the firm which emerged best-placed out of the 'quartz crisis' (see page 168).

→ Rolex never acknowledge the occasional prototype watch which escapes from its clutches, except for this one. In 2004 a similar watch to this appeared in an Antiquorum auction, but was withdrawn before the sale. It was withdrawn because Rolex claimed the watch was stolen. The case went to court and was thrown out as a police report was never filed, but in claiming the watch was stolen they proved that it was real.

ROLEX
OYSTERQUARTZ
DATEJUST
SUPERLATIVE CHRONOMETER
OFFICIALLY CERTIFIED
SWISS
MADE

2001

CROWN COLLECTION

When the Crown Collection was launched, the most popular shows on TV were 'Dallas' and 'Dynasty', and Rolex could see that ostentation was king. They responded with their most flamboyant watches to date.

- **Model number: 18239B**
- **Date: 2001**
- **Dial: Brass, stamped design, diamond indices**
- **Movement: 3055**
- **Case material: 18ct gold**
- **Dimensions: 36mm**

→ The watch shown opposite is often refrred to as a Tridor; but it isn't – the watch itself is white gold with a yellow gold bezel. It is the bracelet only which is Tridor (made from three (Tri) shades of gold (d'or) – white, pink and yellow). These watches had a unique model number, 18239B – the B standing for 'BiColour', referring to the yellow gold bezel on a white gold watch.

Towards the end of the 1970s, not long after Rolex introduced the quick-set 3055 movements for the Day-Date (see page 220), it launched its most flamboyant watches yet. Listed as the Crown Collection, they were instantly recognizable by their jewelled bezels and dials; sometimes the jewel settings spread to the lugs and even to the bracelets.

At this time, it was still possible to drop into your local Rolex retailer and ask to see a selection of bezels and dials, make a choice and have them fit the new parts. Not only was it possible, but Rolex actively encouraged its salespeople to offer clients the option to upgrade their watches by supplying the dealers with an assortment of bezels and dials. The Crown Collection put an end to this practice; watches were delivered to the retailers as finished products with no alterations possible. But they were not delivered to every Rolex retailer; only the best-performing outlets in high-net-worth locations.

The old plastic glass Day-Dates had a four-digit model number, and the final digit designated the bezel fitted to the watch: the 1802 had a smooth bezel, the 1803 the classic milled bezel, the 1804 the diamond-set one, the 1805 was the pyramid bezel and so on. The advent of the five-digit model numbers gave Rolex a chance to be much more descriptive. The final digit designated the case material:

0 steel
3 steel and yellow gold
4 steel with a white gold bezel
5 pink gold
6 platinum
8 yellow gold
9 white gold

This meant that a watch reference 18038 was a single quick Day-Date with a milled bezel in yellow gold. However, Rolex decided that the two numbers in the middle of the reference were a missed opportunity and, with the launch of the Crown Collection, began to use it to describe the bezel fitted to a watch. For example, take a watch with the reference 18188: the first two digits tell us that it is a Day-Date and the last that it is in yellow gold, but the intervening two digits tell us that this has a multicoloured jewelled bezel. Reference 18168, on the other hand, is an 18-carat yellow gold Day-Date with a baguette-set bezel.

The Crown Collection was not just Day-Dates, it also included the two smaller sizes of the Datejust. These were clearly intended for women, as they were even more extravagantly set with precious stones than the Day-Dates. Looking through contemporary catalogues, the most expensive watch in the Crown Collection was a 31mm Datejust with a pavé diamond dial, sapphire hour markers, square-cut sapphire bezel, diamond case lugs and a concealed clasp bracelet set with round diamonds and baguettes. It was 30 per cent more expensive than the costliest Day-Date.

MONDAY
ROLEX
5
DAY-DATE
T SWISS MADE T

2002

SUBMARINER 14060M

The long reign of the Submariner 5513 finally comes to an end, but its replacement evolves into a new version of the Submariner 5512.

- **Model number: 14060M**
- **Date: 2002**
- **Dial: Brass, gloss black paint, white gold indices**
- **Movement: 3130**
- **Case material: Stainless steel**
- **Dimensions: 40mm**

When I wrote about the Submariner 5513 (see page 174), I described it as the archetypal Submariner. Part of the reason for this was its longevity; it was produced between 1962 and 1989 – the better part of three decades. Seven years before its demise, the 5513 lost the iconic matt dial, which was replaced by a high gloss one with white gold circles around the luminous plots. Rolex traditionalists may have objected to the new look, but their woes were magnified when the 5513 was replaced by the completely new 14060 in 1990. They may not have liked the glossy dial, but it was the only component carried over from the 5513. The case was brand new, as was the Sapphire glass, and the watch was powered by the new calibre 3000 movement. The calibre 3000 was a strange movement. It was essentially a less sophisticated version of the 3035 (see page 226): it was denied the Breguet hairspring fitted to the balance of all other 30XX movements and was not sent for chronometer certification. But, like the rest of the 30XX movements, it was robust, reliable and the perfect movement for a watch unlikely to be coddled. The 14060 was in production from 1990 until 2001, when the model number received the letter 'M' after its numbers. This either stood for 'modified' or 'movement' because the watch was modified by the replacement of the simplified calibre 3000 by the much more modern calibre 3130.

The 3130 was distinguished from the 3000 by several features. While it still beats at 28,000bph, it now uses a balance bridge rather than the old-fashioned balance cock, and it also has a Breguet overcoil hairspring, both classic Rolex signatures. Also introduced in the 3130 was a new style of reversers for the automatic movement. These are much more efficient than the original ones and were derived from the ones introduced in 1999 on the 2235 lady's movement. But the biggest difference was that the 3130 movement was chronometer certified. It was probably more efficient for Rolex to make all its movements to one standard than manufacture a specific movement for a watch that was not even a big seller. This theory was supported by the fact that the list price for the 14060 and the 14060M remained the same.

Although the 14060M movement was chronometer-certified, the dial made no mention of this; the bottom half simply stated the model name and its depth rating, '1,000ft=300m'. But this changed in 2007, and the dial now bore 'Superlative Chronometer Officially Certified' below the original text. This change came alongside the fitment of the engraved rehaut, which had 'ROLEX' engraved around its perimeter and the serial number at the bottom.

In 2012, the 14060M was replaced by the 114060, which used a bigger case and a ceramic bezel insert, signalling an end to the classic Submariner. I think that the 14060M – particularly with the 'Superlative Chronometer Officially Certified' marking – was this century's equivalent to the 5512, and – like the 5512 – will be regarded as a classic in the years to come.

→ One of the most common questions I am asked, and one I hate, is 'Which Rolex do you think will be the next to rise in value?' I hate it because it looks at watches as investments, which I disapprove of, and because it assumes I can see into the future – which I can't. But if I had to make a guess, I would go for this model; either the early one shown with the creamy tritium lume, or one of the last ones with the SCOC text on the dial.

ROLEX
OYSTER PERPETUAL
SUBMARINER
1000ft=300m
SWISS – T < 25
10
20
30
50

2003

SUBMARINER 16610LV 'KERMIT'

Whether it is after a soft drink, a coffee house chain, a movie star or an amphibian, you can tell the popular Rolex models as they are the ones with a nickname.

- **Model number: 16610LV**
- **Date: 2003**
- **Dial: Brass, black gloss paint, white gold indices**
- **Movement: 3135**
- **Case material: Stainless steel**
- **Dimensions: 40mm**

Rolex introduced the 16610 Submariner in 1988. It had the ever-reliable 3135 movement, a high gloss dial with white gold surrounds for the luminous indices and a uni-directional bezel. It was the natural successor to the 16800 and the 168000, and continued the same workmanlike, discreet, almost austere appearance which had been a signature of the Submariner since its first appearance in 1953 (see page 102). So in 2003, the arrival of the 16610LV to celebrate the 50th anniversary of the Submariner did not just come as a surprise, it came as a shock.

Obviously, the green-coloured bezel insert was the first thing that hit the eye, but once you diverted your gaze from it, something else was strange: the dial looked like every Submariner dial, yet different. On the Rolex stand at the Baselworld fair it was referred to as the 'Maxidial' Submariner, and this was the difference: both the dial indices and the luminous hands were significantly larger than on any previous Submariner.

Rolex knew that the watch was going to be controversial, so it played safe and kept the previous model with the old-style dial and black bezel insert, the 16610, in production. However, it now bore a new model number, 16610LN, the LN standing for Lunette Noir (Black Bezel), while the newly introduced version bore the suffix LV for Lunette Vert (Green Bezel). It may have been controversial, but it certainly was popular, as – within days – it acquired a nickname. It became the 'Kermit', evidently named after the puppet amphibian whose theme song was 'Being Green'. The first line of every verse began, 'It's not easy being green'.

Rolex has never been one to celebrate anniversaries. When I asked how it planned to celebrate the firm's centenary in 2005 (or 2008, depending on when you think it began) I was told, 'We prefer to look at the future, not the past.' That is what made the Kermit so unusual. Plus, while it was an anniversary edition, it was not a limited edition and it stayed in the catalogue alongside its black-bezel colleague until both were replaced by the 116610 in 2010. The end of the 16610 signalled the end of the aluminium bezel insert on the Submariner Date.

Looking back, it is strange to think how long it took Rolex to launch a green watch – after all, it is its corporate colour – and now there are so many of them, GMT-Masters, Daytonas and Day-Dates – and we have come to accept them as part of the firm's DNA, yet I will never forget the shock of seeing my first Kermit at Baselworld.

→ The model was collectable from the moment it was launched. Part of this was because it was launched as an anniversary edition and people didn't know if it would be discontinued at the end of the anniversary year. When it continued in production, collectors began to notice subtle differences in the printing of the bezel inserts and of the dials. This soon turned into an entire field of research which is still continuing.

ROLEX
PERPETUAL
13
SUBMARINER
1000ft=300m
SUPERLATIVE CHRONOMETER
OFFICIALLY CERTIFIED
SWISS MADE
10
20
30
40
50

2004

NEW TURN-O-GRAPH

Rolex attempted to move away from the sedate, almost austere look of the Datejust with this variation. In the end, it didn't go well.

- **Model number: 116264**
- **Date: 2004**
- **Dial: Brass, black gloss paint, pink gold indices**
- **Movement: 3135**
- **Case material: Stainless steel, pink gold**
- **Dimensions: 36mm**

→ I feel that this watch was a lost opportunity for Rolex. I think that if they had used the earlier design of bezel from the 1625, and linked it to the new case, bracelet and dial designs, it would have been more successful than it was. This new bezel was neither one thing nor the other and ended up looking as though someone had taken the classic milled bezel and randomly scattered some numbers on it. It looked mixed up, not coherent.

Rolex are great on timekeeping, having produced more independently certified chronometers than the rest of the Swiss watch industry combined. But they are not so good at reading calendars. In 2004 it launched a new version of the Turn-O-Graph (see page 100), telling us that it was to celebrate the 50th anniversary of the watch. The only problem is that in 2003 it had launched the Kermit (see page 262) to celebrate the half-century of the Submariner (see page 102). The generally accepted timeline is that the Turn-O-Graph was launched before the Submariner, or – perhaps – simultaneously with it. I do not think that anyone believes that the Submariner came before the Turn-O-Graph, but I will not argue with Rolex.

The new reference 116264 Turn-O-Graph was so much more than a regular Datejust with a rotating bezel; it was the first step on the way to a brand new Datejust. It was the classic 36mm size but with a completely different bezel design to the old one; the new bezel was the midpoint between the classic Rolex fluted bezel and the sports watch version. It had fluting around 70 per cent of its surface, with the numbers 10 to 50 recessed into five evenly spaced plateaux. There was an inverted triangle where the 60 would have been and all the numbers were enamelled in black. That was the sedate part of the watch, the dial was much more fun. Like all the early Datejusts, the date numbers were in red, and so was the model name and the sweep seconds hand.

While the appearance was new and different, the big change was the way the watch was worn. It was the first Datejust to receive the new bracelet configuration introduced on the new Daytona (see page 266). The new bracelet featured not only the long-desired solid end links but also solid centre links and a new clasp design, which finally did away with the holes on the side of the clasp, which had been seen on Rolex Oyster bracelets for almost 70 years. The new clasp had a half link, which can be used or hidden without tools, for when your wrist expands – it proved particularly useful in hot weather. The finish of the bracelet is also quite different, with polished centre links and edges to the links.

The Datejust Turn-O-Graph had a new case design which utilized a flat surface to the end of the lugs. With this, all of the sharp edges on the watch had now been removed, making the watch much more comfortable in use.

The great irony is that after all the research, interesting design and effort that went into the new Turn-O-Graph, it left the catalogue just seven years after its introduction and has not – so far – returned.

ROLEX
OYSTER PERPETUAL
DATEJUST
19
TURN-O-GRAPH
SUPERLATIVE CHRONOMETER
OFFICIALLY CERTIFIED
SWISS MADE
10
20
30
40
50

2004

DAYTONA 116500

Rolex designs its first ever automatic chronograph movement and gives birth to the most advanced chronograph movement yet seen.

- **Model number: 116509**
- **Date: 2004**
- **Dial: Brass, blue sunburst finish, white gold indices**
- **Movement: 4130**
- **Case material: 18ct white gold**
- **Dimensions: 40mm**

The Zenith-based 16520 (see page 236) was a massive success for Rolex, but it could have been an even bigger one if it had more movements. Within a few years, Rolex knew that it had to produce its own chronograph movement, and so development began. The results of that development were not released on 23 March 2000, at 2pm, the moment on the Basel fair preview day when the new 116500 Daytona was released. They were first shown about five years earlier, on 31 October 1995, when patent number 03077/95 was filed in Geneva. Rolex holds around 1,000 patents on almost all aspects of horology, but this was the first complete movement it had patented in over 50 years. The patent was notable because it displayed many of the innovations Rolex would launch in the 116500, including a new layout for the chronograph mechanism, a considerably reduced parts count and a massive increase in the running time of the watch.

The great thing about the new movement was that it combined the best of the old with some remarkable innovations. The large central rotor and the column wheel actuation are classic solutions that have never been bettered. The new stacked design of the chronograph mechanism and the lever operation of the stop/start/reset mechanism are truly innovative. The advantage of the stacked design is that it takes up much less space in the movement, allowing much more room for the mainspring barrel and also for the balance wheel; the larger the balance, the more consistent the performance of the watch will be.

At first glance, the new Daytona dial looks very similar to the Zenith-powered version, but a closer inspection reveals several differences. First, the continuous seconds dial has moved from the 9 position to the 6 position. This is the most logical place for it, and it means that the two timing registers are now at the 3 and 9 positions. Well, not exactly, as both have been raised slightly. Previously, the centre holes of these two registers and the main centre hole were in a straight line; now, both the subsidiary registers have been raised to an angle of 7° above the horizontal. The advantages of this new layout are obvious: the sub-dial that is most likely to be used is the continuous seconds one, and the next most used one would be the 30-minute register. The least used register is the 12-hour one, and this is the one that is at the least visible 9 position.

Apart from the dial, there were changes to the aesthetics of the watch head itself. It retained the asymmetric case, with wider lugs on the left side, but the way the lugs were finished had changed. Like all previous Rolex models, the tops of the lugs on the Zenith Daytona had a brushed finish, while the new Daytona was highly polished. The major change was to the complete bracelet. The new Oysterlock clasp had a new and simple adjustment system, which no longer relied on moving a spring bar between the holes on the outside of the clasp and a new method of resizing which could be done without tools.

The new movement was not just a more modified version of the Zenith design, it was a truly radical reinvention of the chronograph. The main innovation was in the way it operated. Historically, a mechanical chronograph with hour and minute registers had two separate mechanisms, one to drive the seconds and minute registers and another to drive the hour register. These were separate from each other and usually arranged on different sides of the movement. Obviously, the more space they used, the less was available for the watch movement itself. In the new, much-simplified system, everything was integrated into a single chronograph module with one power input – from the seconds wheel. As it was much smaller than all previous versions, there was now space for a larger mainspring barrel and balance. This resulted in the watch now

→ For every model of the 11650X Daytona, including the 116509 white gold version shown here, there exists a massive imbalance between supply and demand, which affects the waiting list and the subsequent resale value. Because of the waiting list, it is possible to resell a Daytona at an immediate profit, which results in most of the people on the waiting list being investors or 'flippers', rather than someone wanting to own a chronograph.

having a 72-hour power reserve, up from the 42 hours of the old movement. This meant that an owner could take his watch off his wrist on Friday evening and not wear it again until Monday morning and it would still be running and keeping time.

The movement had two major design changes. The rotor was now mounted on ceramic ball bearings rather than a simple bushing. The ball bearings were sealed inside a lubricated casing, so – unlike a bushing – they would rarely need servicing or replacement. They also supported the rotor over a larger surface, so it was much less likely to come into contact with the movement plates or the case back. Finally, the new movement had a bridge for the balance rather than a balance cock. The main advantage of this was that it gave a more stable location for the top end of the balance shaft, which in turn meant that there was less end shake on the balance staff.

The other major innovation was that the new movement may have been the first chronograph designed with after-sales service as one of its main design criteria. Service employees were consulted during every stage of the design, and this resulted in a much simpler movement to work on. For example, the Zenith Daytona had 40 different screws, while the 4130 had just 12.

2005

LEOPARD DAYTONA

This is one of those occasions when my personal taste shouldn't be allowed to direct my readers' own judgement. So, on this occasion, I will refrain from comment.

- **Model number: 116598SACO**
- **Date: 2005**
- **Dial: Brass, multicoloured lacquer, diamond indices**
- **Movement: 4130**
- **Case material: 18ct yellow gold**
- **Dimensions: 40mm**

→ The ultimate love it or hate it watch. When we first glimpsed the watch in 2004, it was unanimously hated and on the forums universally reviled. Yet, it stayed in the catalogue for 15 years and still sells at a considerable premium over retail. We were wrong, we were purists who saw everything in monochrome, when it's really a multicoloured world with enough outrageous people in it to make the watch a success.

When Rolex launched the in-house Daytona in 2000, visitors to the stand at Baselworld were open-mouthed in shock – alongside the regular models were a group of four watches with coloured dials and matching coloured reptile-skin straps. I wonder how they reacted four years later, when Rolex introduced the model 116598SACO, otherwise known as the Leopard Daytona.

The Beach models (see page 234) had the regular 18-carat white gold case and only the brightly coloured dials and straps differentiated them from the more restrained models. Not so the Leopard – it was about as in-your-face as it was possible to get, while still vaguely resembling a watch. Only made in 18-carat yellow gold – the most ostentatious material used by Rolex – it sacrificed function for form. Gone were the classic tachometer engravings on the bezel and in their place were 36 cognac baguette-cut sapphires. But, compared with the rest of the watch, they were restrained. The dial was no longer the monochrome colour seen on the Beach models. No, it segued from yellow to orange, and a series of black lacquered blotches, a passable representation of a leopard's skin, were printed on it. This pattern overflowed from the dial and continued along the entire length of the strap, although the path from the dial to the strap was interrupted by the hoods which concealed the strap attachments. These were home to 48 brilliant-cut diamonds, which were not the only diamonds on the watch. As well as the leopard skin print, the dial had room for eight square-cut diamond hour markers, each set in a gold chaton. It was outrageous, and it was meant to be.

The rumour was that the watch was designed for the Rolex CEO Patrick Heiniger's girlfriend, Nina Stevens, which might be true, but it does not explain why the model was produced in series and was listed in the catalogue for 15 years. I believe that it was made as a proof of concept. Rolex had previously produced equally outrageous gem-set pieces, but they were off-catalogue, special order items. The Leopard was proof that Rolex could produce watches like this in series. Take the 2008 Rolex catalogue, where the Leopard Daytona looks almost restrained next to four other white gold Daytona models with diamond pavé dials and bezels set with round or baguette diamonds interspersed with rubies or blue sapphires. The Leopard is listed at just over £30,000, while these are almost double at over £55,000. This shows that Rolex was now able to produce gem-set masterpieces on a production line.

ROLEX
OYSTER PERPETUAL
COSMOGRAPH
SWISS
MADE

2005

CELLINI PRINCE

Rolex tries to reintroduce a watch half a century after it withered on the vine for lack of interest, and doesn't do a very good job of it.

- **Model number: 5443/9**
- **Date: 2005**
- **Dial: White gold, machined sunburst effect, white gold indices**
- **Movement: Calibre 7040**
- **Case material: 18ct white gold**
- **Dimensions: 47mm long**

When the Cellini Prince was launched in 2005, I wrote that of all the discontinued models which Rolex might reintroduce that year, I could have given you a list of a dozen before I got to the one that turned up on their stand at the Basel fair. The Prince (see page 50) had been in production from the mid-1920s to the mid-1940s, and was Rolex's flagship watch until the Oyster Perpetual arrived (see page 56). Introduced in 1928, the Prince was a hugely important watch for Rolex – it was its first watch with unique styling, and the first designed with accuracy in mind. By placing the large balance wheel and the oversized spring barrel at opposite ends of the movement, they could both be significantly larger than in a conventional circular movement. And the movement was inside a slim, elegant case, devoid of decoration.

The new Prince was the opposite of all this – it was chunky with decorated cases, movements and dials. The only thing resembling the original Rolex Prince was the duo-dial with the top one showing the hours and minutes while the bottom one handled the seconds.

The original Prince had always been restrained, almost austere, in its styling. The new models featured gadroons, horizontal milling or sunburst effect machining. The dials were, if anything, even more ornate: sunburst finishes (yes, there was more than one), hobnail effects or full diamond pavé. What was even more bizarre than the dial finishes was that each one was then repeated on the movement's back plate.

Up until this moment, Rolex had never been concerned about the finishing of its movements, they were about accuracy and robustness. They were not badly finished – far from it – they were just workmanlike. Everything needed to reduce friction or to improve longevity was done, but form came a distant second to function. The new watch had a sapphire back, a genuine first for a Rolex production watch, and this gave a window onto a novel movement. Ten years after its demise, the calibre 7040 is pretty much forgotten, but it showcased a couple of features which have now become standard across all Rolex movements: a balance bridge rather than the centuries-old balance cock, and the new Rolex-patented Paraflex shock protection system for the balance. If you looked beyond the heavy-handed decoration, it was one of the most interesting movements from Rolex for years.
In retrospect, the Cellini Prince was doomed from the start. Rolex had spent almost 80 years telling the world that what made Rolex watches special was that they were waterproof. It had spent 70 years eulogizing the massive advantages of self-winding watches, and 50 years extolling the benefits of a date window in the dial. The Cellini Prince had none of these. Because of this, it could never be the heart of a one-watch collection, a role fulfilled by millions of Datejusts, Explorers and Day-Dates. The Cellini Prince positioned itself as a second or third watch, something you wore at the weekend or to go to a dinner party, not for washing the dog or changing the baby. This meant that the watch faced an array of competition that other Rolex models never did. Everyone from Cartier to Jaeger-LeCoultre made nice rectangular or square dress watches. When faced with the choice between one of them and the Cellini Prince, it was rarely the Prince that triumphed.

The watch was solid and substantial, but most buyers are looking for elegance and restraint in a dress watch, not heft. Compared to most of the competition, the Prince came off as heavy-handed; it measured almost 47mm long lug to lug, which was too big for many wearers, and although the height off the wrist was just 10mm, it felt bulkier.

When it came down to detailed comparisons, there was little in the Prince's favour. Everything about the watch was busy, everything seemed to be decorated. Even the most restrained

→ I never 'got' the Cellini Prince. It was launched in 2005, exactly a century after Wilsdorf & Davis opened their doors, so I asked a friend in the Public Relations department at Rolex how they planned to celebrate the centenary. I was told that there were no plans as Rolex looks to the future, not to the past. Yet what was the new Prince, other than disinterring their past?

model, the white-gold 5441 had deep machined grooves on the case above and below the dial. The dial itself had a guilloché effect, but not the classic rose engine finish. Instead, the dial looked like a close-up of a vinyl record, with deep concentric grooves. The dial's numerals and indices were too thick and, once again, heavy-handed. Turning the watch over to reveal the movement via the sapphire back was not really recommended – the well-executed, high-quality movement with blued steel Breguet hairspring and the new Paraflex on both the balance and the escape jewels was disfigured by the same deeply etched concentric grooves as the dial.

The day the watch was launched in Basel, I was introduced to many other brand-new Rolex models. As is my norm, |I took photographs of the watches on my wrist and later posted them online. When I looked back at the shots I took that day, I noticed that I took none of the Prince – I did not like it then, and I have not changed my mind.

CHAPTER ELEVEN

2006–2015

ROLEX
OYSTER PERPETUAL
MILGAUSS
SUPERLATIVE CHRONOMETER
OFFICIALLY CERTIFIED
SWISS
MADE

2006–2015

SIZE MATTERS

A 36mm watch was no longer the norm for Rolex. Watches introduced during this period ranged from 40 to 44mm.

This ten-year period saw more changes at Rolex than the previous half-century. When it began, the century-old firm was on its third CEO in its history; when it ended, it was on its sixth. On 17 December 2008, Rolex announced the retirement of Patrick Heiniger for 'personal reasons'; the date was significant as only six days previously the financier Bernie Madoff had been arrested and accused of orchestrating the world's largest Ponzi scheme. The world saw two plus two and came to the sum of 493, assuming that there was a link between the two events. Rolex was forced to issue a statement that it had no funds invested with Madoff, but the rumours persisted. They should have disappeared once Patrick's replacement was announced – it was the firm's Chief Financial Officer, Bruno Meier. His role as CFO meant that he was the person who signed off all major investments; if Rolex had put money into Madoff's operation, it would have been Meier who approved it.

← New Milgauss, 2008 (see page 282).

The Madoff arrest was just one in a series of financial catastrophes that seemed to be happening at a dizzying rate; Lehman Brothers investment bank collapsed, UK banks had to be rescued by the Bank of England, then the economies of Greece and Iceland seemed likely to implode. It was a bad time to be a major brand focused on luxury, but the storm seemed to have almost no effect on Rolex. In 2008, as the height of the crisis loomed, Rolex introduced the new oversized 41mm Day-Date II, the white gold Submariner (soon nicknamed the 'Smurf') (see page 284) and the giant Sea-Dweller Deepsea (see page 286), which measured 44mm in diameter.

Following the success of Panerai, the entire watch world embarked on a programme of bigger is better. While Rolex was not one of the first to jump on the bandwagon, it was certainly the firm which embraced it most wholeheartedly. The Yacht-Master II (see page 288), with its innovative countdown complication, had been introduced in 2007 – it measured 42.6mm; in 2009 it introduced a new 41mm Datejust II. It seemed that Rolex was determined to add the suffix 'II' to all its watches, but only after giving them a dose of steroids. The trend peaked in 2011 when it introduced a new version of the Explorer II, with a diameter of 42mm. But that year is primarily remembered for another dramatic change at the top of Rolex – in May, Bruno Meier was replaced by Gian Riccardo Marini, who had spent all his working life with Rolex in Italy, ending up as the CEO of Rolex Italia.

Some eyebrows were raised at the appointment of a non-Swiss to the post, but I – as usual – differed, I saw it as Rolex returning to type. The firm had always been led by a marketer; Hans Wilsdorf was not a watchmaker or inventor, in legal documents he always gave his profession as merchant. His successor, André Heiniger, was head of sales in South America, before returning to

The entire watch world embarked on a programme of bigger is better. While Rolex was not one of the first to jump on the bandwagon, it was certainly the firm which embraced it most wholeheartedly.

Geneva to become worldwide sales director. And Andre's son Patrick, who – like his father – trained as a lawyer, was the firm's commercial director before being crowned CEO. Meier, on the other hand, had spent his life as a banker before joining Rolex as CFO. When Patrick resigned for health reasons in the middle of a worldwide economic crisis, it made sense for the firm to hand the reins of the company to a safe pair of hands. But, by 2011, economies worldwide were beginning to recover, interest rates were at a record low and confidence was starting to return. It was time to get back to normal and put a sales-oriented professional back in charge. But there was one problem. Marini was 64 years old when he was elevated to the Rolex throne, so it was apparent that he did not have long-term potential. I believe that the board saw the appointment of Marini as a temporary one until a search could be completed to find a long-term replacement. I am confident that Marini was fully aware of this plan and was an active participant. However, he never acted as if he was a mere placeholder; in fact he was responsible for signing the biggest sponsorship contract ever undertaken by Rolex: replacing Hublot as the official timekeeper and timepiece for Formula 1.

The links between Rolex and motorsport reach back decades, all the way to Sir Malcolm Campbell and his world land speed record Blue Bird cars, and Rolex was once again involved in land speed record attempts with its sponsorship of the British Bloodhound Supersonic record attempt. It signed on as timekeeper for the team and also provided instrumentation for the car's dashboard. This was not the only world record attempt that it was intimately involved with. It created a special watch that was attached to James Cameron's submersible which reached almost 11,000m (36,089ft) deep in the Mariana Trench, the deepest spot on Earth.

The world's economies were improving, and Rolex wanted the world to know that if you wanted a watch, it was the firm to know. Its market confidence was ably demonstrated at the 2013 Baselworld trade show when it introduced the Daytona in platinum to celebrate the 50th anniversary of the first Daytona. I think that this was the only 50th anniversary watch the firm ever released that did not have green somewhere on it. The launch price was $75,000 in the US.

If the platinum Daytona was unexpected, what happened in April 2014 was expected, but still a shock. It was announed that Marini was stepping down and his replacement was Jean-Frédéric Dufour, until that moment CEO of Zenith watches. Dufour was the first person ever to be appointed to the role from outside the company, but in many ways he was a continuation of the tried and trusted Rolex leadership profile – he was a marketer, not a watchmaker or banker. Apart from a few months as a banker, he had spent his entire business life selling watches, and he was Swiss – Geneva-born and bred. He was the right man for the job; having spent five years at Zenith sealed the deal. Plus Rolex had bought movements from Zenith for 15 years, so there was a good relationship to begin with. Also the fact that Zenith was a wholly owned subsidiary of LVMH was important, because while Zenith was a small brand compared to Rolex, it meant that Dufour was used to working inside a very large company. In the luxury industry there is no one larger than LVMH, and in the watch business there is no one larger than his new employer – Rolex. He was the perfect fit.

→ **This is a late model of the stainless-steel Yacht-Master II, featuring the blue Cerachrom bezel.** **See page 288 for the gold version.**

ROLEX
OYSTER PERPETUAL
SWISS MADE
YACHT-MASTER II

2007

GMT-MASTER II SARU

There is certainly no accounting for taste, not with me at least. I am not a fan of the Leopard Daytona, yet I absolutely love this watch.

- **Model number: 116759SARU**
- **Date: 2007**
- **Dial: Brass, black gloss paint, white gold indices**
- **Movement: 3185**
- **Case material: 18ct white gold**
- **Dimensions: 40mm**

→ To most people this is as disgustingly ostentatious as the Leopard Daytona (see page 268), but I beg to differ – I quite like this model, although only in white gold. Unlike the Leopard Daytona, it retains the original dial which is – unusually for a jewel-set piece – devoid of diamonds or other stones, and the bezel. At a glance it looks just like the classic blue/red bezel insert.

It is easy to look at the 2007 GMT-Master II 116759SARU as the epitome of bad taste. I beg to differ. On one hand, it is merely a continuation of a GMT practice going back to the early days of the model. And on the other, it is the only jewelled Rolex sports watch which retains its functionality.

The GMT-Master, reference 6542 (see page 128) was launched in 1956. Just a year later the watch was launched in solid 18-carat gold, so precious metal GMT-Masters are not a recent introduction. As for functionality, well, the bezel is enhanced with 18 rubies, 18 sapphires and 11 diamonds, all trapeze-cut in order to fit perfectly in the white gold bezel which also houses a triangle-cut diamond. This essentially turns the bezel from a 24-hour to a 12-hour one, but it does not take a genius to use the bezel as a 24-hour one, simply by identifying the centre of one of the blocks of three stones in between the diamonds and using it as an hour in the 24-hour cycle.

Like all previous GMT-Master SARU watches (SARU being the Rolex factory code for a bezel using sapphires and rubies) the jewel setting is not confined to the bezel. There are small clear diamonds set on top of all four lugs and even on the tops of the two crown guards. I prefer the white gold version of the watch as these diamonds do not look anywhere near as ostentatious as they do on the yellow or rose gold versions.

The majority of SARU-enhanced GMT-Masters have been in one of these flamboyant materials since the 1980s, the first being the 16758. It was, by far, the most ostentatious GMT-Master ever produced in series. Not only was the dial fully paved with white diamonds, it had round and bar-cut blue sapphires as hour indices and the first edition of the SARU bezel. But instead of the usual Oyster or Jubilee bracelet, the watch was fitted with a version of the concealed clasp three-link President bracelet – the first time this had been fitted by the factory on a sports watch – and each centre link was set with 12 white round diamonds.

This is why I regard the 2007 GMT-Master II 116759SARU as the most discreet of the SARU brethren. If you look closely at the dial, you will see that although the model name is in green, unlike other contemporary GMT-Master II watches, the SARU does without the green 24-hour hand.

The watch was never a limited edition in the sense that Rolex committed to only producing a certain number, but it was limited by the craftsmanship involved in producing it, and also by the problem of finding 18 perfectly colour-matched rubies and sapphires for each watch.

ROLEX
GMT-MASTER II
SUPERLATIVE CHRONOMETER
SWISS MADE

2008

GREEN GMT-MASTER II

Rolex goes all-in with the green anniversary theme this time, with the most audacious GMT-Master II released so far.

- **Model number: 116718LN**
- **Date: 2008**
- **Dial: Brass, green lacquer, white gold indices**
- **Movement: 3186**
- **Case material: 18ct yellow gold**
- **Dimensions: 40mm**

→ I am not a fan of yellow gold watches, but I like this one. The focus may have been on the new Cerachrom bezel and green dial, but I looked first at the dial itself and loved what I saw. It used the oversized 'Maxi-dial' luminous indices and the fat hands, both first seen on the Kermit Submariner. With 24 distinct click stops on the bezel, it showed that, despite being flamboyant, it was still a fully functioning 'tool' watch.

If you have read the previous pages, you will know that I was not the biggest fan of the re-introduced Cellini Prince (see page 270) when it was introduced in 2005. But it was not all gloom at the Baselworld fair. Rolex did launch a watch I really loved, the 50th-anniversary GMT-Master II, reference 116718. Two years previously it had shown the 50th-anniversary Submariner which had given it a green bezel insert to celebrate the event – green being the company's corporate colour. This time Rolex would not be so restrained, if you can consider the watch known as the Kermit restrained (see page 262). The 50th-anniversary GMT-Master II did not have a green bezel insert, no, it had a green dial the colour of a billiard table. And there was no need for the bezel to feel left out. In place of the screen-printed aluminium insert, which had graced the bezels of Rolex sports watches for half a century, the new bezel insert was made from high-tech ceramic produced from a zirconia-based compound containing a touch of cerium oxide. The proportions in the mixture and the firing procedures were patented by Rolex and, like most recent introductions, it received its own trademarked name – Cerachrom.

That was not the only new thing about the watch. The case was now much more substantial, bearing more than a passing resemblance to that of the Submariner, and the screw-down crown was now the Triplock variety, although – like the Yacht-Master – the watch was depth rated to only 100m (328ft). Inside was the new 3186 movement, the GMT version of the venerable 3135 (see page 232), but now equipped with the Parachrom hairspring which first debuted in the in-house Daytona movement back in 2000.

The Cerachrom bezel insert was the subject of most of the discussion I had with Rolex that day. It was obvious that they were very proud of the material, how it was made and how it was utilized, and although no comment was made it was evident that they planned to use the material on the rest of the sports range. But it was not just the bezel insert that fascinated me; the bi-directional bezel now had 24 distinct clicks, rather than being freely rotational, as it had been on all previous GMT-Masters.

So far, I have only talked about the green-dial version, although another one was launched simultaneously. It had a black dial, but even this one bore traces of green: both the 'GMT-Master II' text and the 24-hour hand were bright green. The black dial version with a matching colour bezel was somewhat more discreet than the green dial one – if any solid, 40mm, 18-carat gold watch on an Oyster bracelet with polished centre links could ever be described as such.

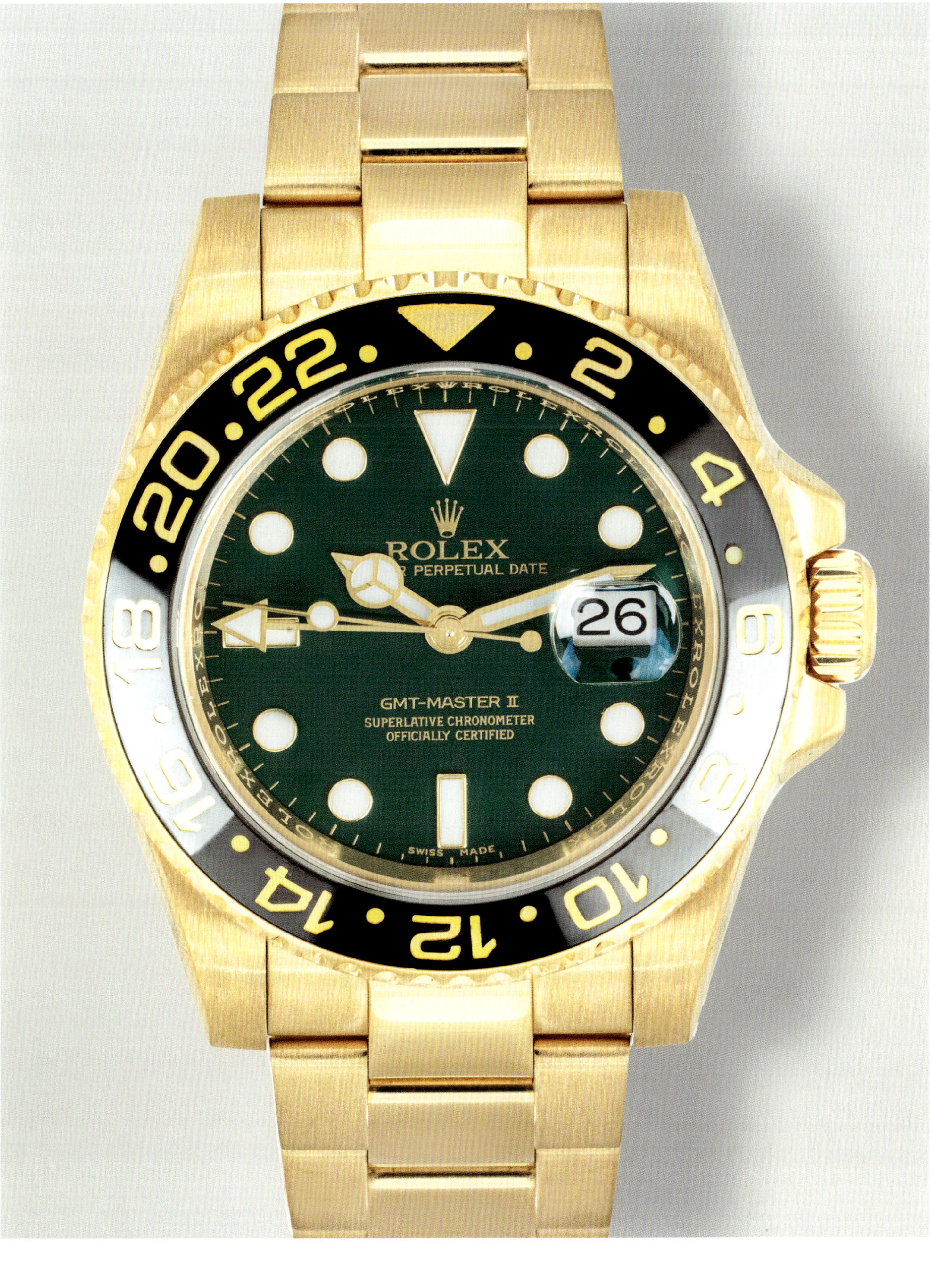
ROLEX
PERPETUAL DATE
26
GMT-MASTER II
SUPERLATIVE CHRONOMETER
OFFICIALLY CERTIFIED
SWISS MADE

2008

NEW MILGAUSS

Rolex resuscitates another long-lost model from the archives, eager to find out if anyone remembers the Milgauss and was waiting for its return.

- **Model number: 11640**
- **Date: 2008**
- **Dial: Brass, white anodized, applied gold indices with luminous infill**
- **Movement: 3131**
- **Case material: Stainless steel**
- **Dimensions: 40mm**

Nobody expected the re-introduction of the Milgauss (see page 158). But there it was in the windows of the 2007 Baselworld Rolex stand. Looking like the bastard offspring of the two previous models, with a pastiche of the 1019 dial (see page 160) and the lightning bolt-hand from the earlier 6541. The watch was brought up to date by the use of colour. Like the 1019, there were two dial colours, although this time they were black and white rather than black and silver. The only colour on the 1019 had been the single word 'Milgauss' printed in red. Red was banished from the new model 11640, to be replaced by orange, but it was not only the model name that was in this new colour, the indices were black anodized white gold and filled with orange luminous material, the perimeter of the dial had the numbers for each of the five-second intervals printed in orange, and the sweep seconds hand not only replicated the 'lightning bolt' design of the original 6541 watch but was also coloured bright orange.

The green anniversary theme continued. After the green bezel on the Kermit (see page 262) and the green dial on the GMT-Master II (see page 278), I had wondered what the next component to go green might be. I never expected it to be the sapphire glass. I was told that morning that Rolex had not even bothered to patent the process as making the green glass was so difficult. Two thoughts crossed my mind: I believed that the sapphire crystals are one of the few components Rolex did not manufacture itself in 2007 and why would anyone else want to make a green sapphire crystal?

The rumour was that the new Milgauss had been scheduled to launch simultaneously with the Geneva-based Large Hadron Collider at CERN (the European Organization for Nuclear Research) but that the decade-long construction of the particle accelerator had been delayed. Rolex decoupled the two events and went ahead with the launch.

The watch measured 40mm, like the new GMT-Master II, and I was told that this would be the new size for all Rolex men's watches from now on. It had the new Daytona-style bracelet with the Glidelock clasp and the half-sized extension link, and this too would be fitted to all the new models.

The watch was powered by the calibre 3131, which had the Parachrom-Blu hairspring. There were no ferrous metals in the proprietary alloys used to make it, so the watch is completely unaffected by electromagnetic forces. Also, several escapement parts and one wheel were made from a new and undisclosed alloy, which was as resistant to magnetism as the hairspring. Added to all of this, the movement is surrounded by the classic Faraday cage with a soft iron movement cap and a disc of the same material sitting between the dial and the movement's top plate.

But all of this effort was to little avail. Despite introducing a blue dial version in 2014, the new Milgauss was never a big seller and was discontinued in 2022.

→ I never understood why Rolex reintroduced the Milgauss – it wasn't as if there was a new cadre of people working in areas of high magnetism. Or demonstrations demanding the return of the model. Rolex had obviously put considerable research and energy into the new movement, but that was invisible and what was on display was just uninspiring. Despite a couple of updates it only lasted 15 years in the catalogue.

ROLEX
OYSTER PERPETUAL
MILGAUSS
SUPERLATIVE CHRONOMETER
OFFICIALLY CERTIFIED
SWISS
MADE

2009

SUBMARINER 116619 'SMURF'

The first-ever white gold Submariner surfaces and astounds everyone with a wonderfully fun bezel and dial combination.

- **Model number: 116619**
- **Date: 2009**
- **Dial: Brass, blue paint, white gold applied indices**
- **Movement: 3235**
- **Case material: 18ct white gold**
- **Dimensions: 40mm**

→ I keep thinking about buying a Smurf; my everyday Rolex watch is white gold with a blue dial, so it's obviously my taste. I love the incongruity of the watch, it's a 'tool' watch – but it's solid gold. It's made of white gold, so it's more discreet than a yellow gold one – but it has a bright blue bezel and dial. I think it's the most playful watch that Rolex has made in years.

Submariners with blue dials and bezels had been available since 1972, but only in yellow gold. Thus, the launch of model 116619 in white gold was completely unexpected. Even more unexpected was the shade of blue used on the new watch. It was lighter, brighter and almost playful, so it was not surprising when the watch was nicknamed the 'Smurf' after the Belgian comic characters.

It was not just the colour of the dial and bezel combination which was new; there was a new case, bracelet, bezel insert and even a new kind of luminous material for the dial and hands. This was the launch of the 'Super Case', still 40mm in diameter, but with heftier lugs which no longer had the polished 45-degree bevel on the outer edge. The bracelet was the new style which shared a clasp with the new Sea-Dweller Deepsea (see page 286) and featured the Glidelock which enabled the bracelet to be lengthened by up to 20mm (3⁄4in) without the use of tools. It also featured vertically brushed outer links but highly polished centre links, confirming – if there ever was any doubt – that this was a luxury watch, not a tool one.

The new bezel insert brought the firm's Cerachrom ceramic insert to the Submariner line for the first time, with the blue of the insert almost an exact match to the highly glossy dial.

The new luminous material which replaced Super-LumiNova was called Chromalight and was a Rolex invention, part of the long-term plan to bring as much of the manufacture of its components and suppliers in-house. It was launched on the Sea-Dweller Deepsea (see page 286) and the Smurf, which was rather apposite as the new material glowed blue at night, rather than the sickly green of the Super-LumiNova. It used a mixture of micro-fine oxides of various metals, most of which I had never heard of and could not find on the periodic table if my life depended on it. But it was much more efficient than Super-LumiNova, needed a shorter exposure to light to activate and the glow lasted longer. The ease of visibility was enhanced by the new Maxi dial indices which were much larger than the ones previously used.

The watch was also made in yellow gold as the reference 116618 and, like previous versions of the 18-carat Submariner, was available with a black or blue dial and bezel combination. I have always been a fan of white gold watches with blue dials, so if I had to pick one Rolex watch from everything it has produced in the 21st century so far, it would be a Smurf. You can imagine my dismay when it was replaced by a new model which disposed of the blue dial in 2020.

ROLEX
SUBMARINER
1000ft = 300m
SUPERLATIVE CHRONOMETER
OFFICIALLY CERTIFIED
SWISS MADE
13

2010

SEA-DWELLER DEEPSEA

After the Submariner, and after the Sea-Dweller, Rolex creates the ultimate diving watch – the Deepsea, safe to a depth of almost 13,000ft.

- **Model number: 116660**
- **Date: 2010**
- **Dial: Brass, matt black paint, white gold indices**
- **Movement: 3185**
- **Case material: Stainless steel, titanium**
- **Dimensions: 44mm**

Rolex prided itself on being known as the dive watch company; the Submariner (see page 260) was everyone's idea of a dive watch, and the Sea-Dweller benefitted massively from its association with COMEX (see page 212). But pretenders were starting to appear. In 2004, UTS, a small firm in Munich, Germany, launched a watch with a 3,000m rating (almost 10,000ft) when the Sea-Dweller's maximum depth rating was only 1,220m (4,000ft). Rolex decided to put the question to rest, once and forever, with a new watch – the Sea-Dweller Deepsea (SDDS), safe down to 3,900m (12,800ft).

Launched at the 2008 Baselworld fair, it caused a sensation. While its 44mm diameter size was the same as the previous year's Yacht-Master II (see page 288), that watch had an almost acceptable height of 14mm, but the Deepsea was 25 per cent taller at 17.5mm and measured a mammoth 51.5mm, lug to lug.

The construction of the watch was completely different to all current Rolex models, and bore a great similarity to the very first Oyster cases. In both models, the movement and dial are held in separate movement rings, brass in the 1920s watches and special nitrogen-treated steel in the SDDS. This assembly is placed inside the case on both models, and the bezels and backs are then screwed into place. But there the similarities end. On the new watch, half a dozen more components, all machined to micron tolerances, are needed to ensure the case is secure.

The sapphire glass on the watch is 5mm thick, the ring clamping the glass in place is titanium, and so is the case back, but they are different grades of titanium because each does a specific job. It is worth noting that the titanium back is used not because it is more pressure-resistant than steel, but because it will flex slightly under extreme pressure and then revert to its original form; steel will not.

The Cerachrom bezel insert on the SDDS has minute marks all the way around, like the old Military Submariners (see page 194) and unlike the Submariner or Sea-Dweller which only have them for the first 15 minutes. However, the bezel insert is not interchangeable with the one on the other dive watches.

The unique bracelet is a work of art. It integrates both the diving suit extension and the normal sizing adjustments in a new system which reminds me of the folding hard top on a Mercedes-Benz SL, in that it is double-hinged and totally undetectable when not in use.

Rolex watches have often attracted criticism for the amount of text on their dials, but the SDDS took things to the extreme; not only did it have 'Sea-Dweller' with 'DEEPSEA' in capital letters, the inner bezel – or rehaut – was also emblazoned with the words 'ORIGINAL GAS ESCAPE VALVE' at the top and 'RING LOCK SYSTEM' at the bottom.

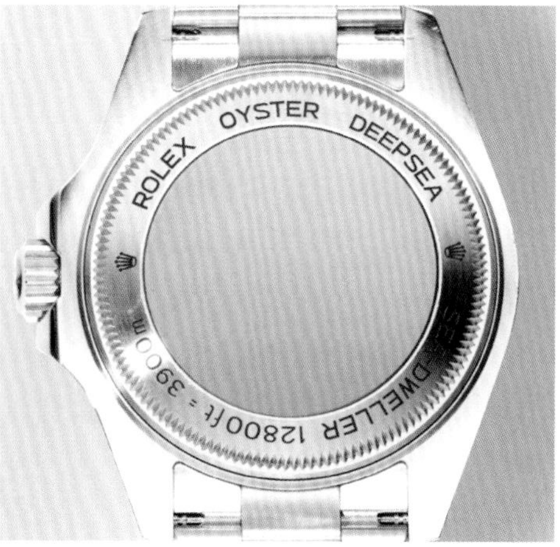

→ The Submariner had become the standard for all dive watches, and the Sea-Dweller was the choice of professional divers. So why did Rolex decide to make a watch capable of handling depths of almost 13,000ft? The climber Mallory was asked why he wanted to climb Mount Everest, his response was 'Because it's there'. It was a challenge and he accepted it. Rolex did the same, but rather more successfully.

ORIGINAL GAS ESCAPE VALVE
ROLEX
DEEPSEA
SEA-DWELLER
12800ft = 3900m
SUPERLATIVE CHRONOMETER
OFFICIALLY CERTIFIED
SWISS MADE
RING LOCK SYSTEM
10
20
30
50

2011

YACHT-MASTER II

The largest and most complicated watch from Rolex is, unfortunately, targeted at the nichest of markets.

- **Model number: 116688**
- **Date: 2011**
- **Dial: Brass, gloss white paint, applied gold indices**
- **Movement: 4161**
- **Case material: 18ct gold**
- **Dimensions: 44mm**

→ I have a love for the weird and the crazy and the Yacht-Master II is both. It is – by far – the most complicated watch Rolex had made until this point, and the most specialized. It was also the most 'in your face' watch the firm had ever produced – this was the opposite of discreet, after all it was 44mm of solid gold with a bright blue bezel. There is no way in the world I would ever own one, but I loved it.

The Yacht-Master II was probably the most niche watch ever manufactured by Rolex, but it was also one of the most interesting. It had the longest gestation time of any of its models; introduced at the 2007 Baselworld fair, it was not available for another three years. It was the first wristwatch with a programmable mechanical countdown timer, the first to use the rotating bezel as a switch and the first in-house complication from Rolex. But much more than that, it was the most unapologetic, in-your-face watch ever made by the firm, at 44mm diameter, it was the largest Rolex ever made before the Deepsea Challenge.

This was a watch made to do one job – time the start of a yachting regatta – and that was the first problem. The number of people interested in timing the start of regattas is pretty small to begin with. Essentially, only yacht captains race yachts, and they can be broken into two groups: family sailors with up to 20-foot boats or the big guys competing in major competitions. If you are in the former group, most boats cost around £20,000, so are you really going to spend £30,000-plus on a watch? If you are in the second group, competing for the Maxi Yacht Rolex Cup, your boat will have cost $30 million or more. Of course, you can afford the watch, but you are not captaining the boat – that is in the hands of a professional skipper and crew, all of whom will most likely be wearing something like a Suunto Yachtsman digital watch. As an owner, you will be on the terrace of a nearby five-star hotel watching the start from a distance and wearing your Yacht-Master II. That is who the watch was made for, yacht owners, not yacht skippers.

It is, however, an amazing watch. Its ability to alter the timing function backwards or forwards while it is running had never even been attempted previously, let alone manufactured. The movement is based on the calibre 4130 (see page 253), with the hour and minute counters discarded and the variable 10-minute timer in their place. The 4130 is a very lean movement with only 201 components, so you might think that the 4161 in the Yacht-Master II would have even fewer. Not so – there are 360 parts in this brand-new movement. The watch has the same 72-hour run time as the Daytona (see page 266) and also shares with it a depth rating of 100m (328ft). I find this really interesting, as the Daytona has screw-down pushers and the Yacht-Master II does without them, as users need to activate the pushers the instant they see the flag or hear the gun – they do not have time to unscrew them. It is well known that the majority of chronographs are used to time parking meters, eggs or pasta, and the Yacht-Master II is pretty useless for the first, with only a ten-minute timer; would be excellent for the second option; and just about cuts it for the role of pasta timer.

In 2024, the watch quietly disappeared from the catalogues. It had lasted less than a decade and a half, and – although I doubt if I would have ever owned one – I miss it.

ROLEX
OYSTER PERPETUAL
SWISS
MADE
YACHT-MASTER II

2013

COLOURED DIAL DAY-DATE

In this era of oversized watches, a new 36mm Day-Date was introduced specifically for women.

- **Model number: 118138**
- **Date: 2013**
- **Dial: Brass, electroplated, gold indices**
- **Movement: Calibre 3155**
- **Case material: 18ct gold**
- **Dimensions: 36mm**

→ Rolex followed fashion by introducing a range of Day-Dates with matching coloured dials and crocodile straps. This was also the first time that Rolex acknowledged the fact that women were regularly wearing men's watches.

One of the more interesting trends over the last few years has been the widespread opinion that there is no such thing as a woman's watch. As I understand this it means that we all should be free to wear whatever size watch we want. If this means that my wife can wear a 40mm watch if she wishes, then great – as long as it does not mean that I have to wear a 26mm gold watch with a mother-of-pearl dial. Women have been wearing men's watches for ages – even Chanel has a line of women's watches called the Boy·Friend– so you cannot be mad at Rolex for launching its own line of indeterminately gendered watches. They were 36mm Day-Dates with coloured dials and matching leather straps.

The watches came with five dial and strap colours and three colours of gold case. White gold watches were fitted with cherry red or deep blue dials and straps; the yellow gold with cognac or green; and the Everose a chocolate dial and strap combination. If you liked the idea of a Day-Date on a strap, but did not have the sense of style to wear one of the coloured combinations, Rolex also released an Everose gold version with a dark rhodium dial and a black alligator strap.

Since the 2010s, it had been fashionable to wear a vintage gold Day-Date on a leather strap, and it is worth remembering that, from its launch in 1956 up until the late 1990s, it was possible to buy a Day-Date on a leather strap. These straps had conventional pin buckles, while the new watches had folding deployant clasps with the Oysterclasp system, which made the length of the strap easy to adjust. Although the watches were notionally waterproof to 100m (328ft), I am unsure how well the alligator skin straps would have handled lengthy immersion. Despite this, the coloured straps gave the watches an informal, sporty look, particularly the white gold versions. There was, however, one problem: the people who had started wearing old Day-Dates on leather straps had done so because they were individualists who wanted to stand out from the crowd. Once Rolex launched its official version, the look was no longer unusual, and so these people – who we would now call influencers – moved on to newer styles and the new watches slowly lost their desirability. What people sometimes forget is that the very essence of fashion is its ephemeral nature; things change, and the caravan moves on. The coloured Day-Dates lasted a little over a decade, and now they are gone.

WEDNESDAY
ROLEX
OYSTER PERPETUAL
DAY-DATE
3
SUPERLATIVE CHRONOMETER
OFFICIALLY CERTIFIED
SWISS MADE

2015

NEW CELLINI

In the biggest ever cull of models, Rolex discontinues an entire range of watches and replaces them all with just three new watches.

- **Model number: 50525**
- **Date: 2015**
- **Dial: Brass, silver, machined finish**
- **Movement: 3180**
- **Case material: 18ct white gold**
- **Dimensions: 39mm**

Rolex officially launched the Cellini range in 1968 in an attempt to bring order to its range of watches. Oyster watches were pretty straightforward, but then there were men's dress watches with such names as Verithin, Veriflat and (believe it or not) Spider. Women's watches were being rationalized into Oyster, Chameleon (for watches with interchangeable straps) and Orchid (for watches with fixed straps), but there were still lots of jewelled pieces which did not fit into any category. So Rolex created a new product line and named it after the 16th-century Florentine sculptor Benvenuto Cellini. The Cellini line was distinguished by what it was not: it was not an Oyster, nor was it an automatic. The problem was that just as the Cellini line was being launched, J Walter Thompson's worldwide advertising campaigns and Mark McCormack's sports-linked promotions were both convincing the world that the best watch in the world was a Rolex Oyster.

Despite having dozens of models and even with the King Midas in the line-up, the Cellini line just did not sell and, over the years, Rolex gave it less and less attention. Then, in 2014, everything changed for the Cellini. The entire line disappeared and was replaced by one single model. Okay, there were two additional variations, but to all intents and purposes there was one model. It was 39mm in diameter and powered by a revised version of the 3130 movement used in 95 per cent of men's Oysters. But it was not just the movement that the watches shared with the Oyster line, the Cellinis had screw-down crowns, screwed backs and were rated to 5atm. Rolex was very clear that this was its rating, and 5atm does not sound very much, but it equals 50m or 165ft, and that was the depth rating for all the plastic-glass GMT-Masters, Explorer IIs and Datejusts. So it had a pretty good capability for a dress watch. Rolex did not call them Oysters because, from the late 1990s, a watch needed to be rated to 100m (328ft) or deeper to qualify for the title. The movements were certified by the Contrôle Officiel Suisse des Chronomètres to the same standards as an Oyster, but Rolex was going for a more discreet look, and so the mandatory 'Superlative Chronometer Officially Certified' was nowhere to be seen. In fact, the watches bore just three single words on their dials: 'Rolex', 'Geneve' and 'Cellini', while down at the very bottom of the dial in a tiny font were the words 'Swiss Made'.

I have written about all the things the new Cellini watches were not; now, I will talk about what they were. When the range was launched, there were three watches: the Cellini, the Cellini Date and the Cellini GMT. All three shared the same 39mm-diameter case with a slightly domed case back, which echoed the contours of the domed sapphire glass. They had a wonderful coin-edge bezel, which reminded me of the bezel on both the first Datejust 4467 (see page 82) and on the early cushion Oysters. Even though it was a screw-down model, the winding crown was shaped like the old World War I-era 'onion' crowns. Each of the three models was available in 18-carat Everose or white gold, meaning that there were six distinct models; each one was also available with a white or a black dial.

Although the watches obviously shared a common lineage, each one had its own dial design, which emphasized the differences between them all. The Cellini had a flat dial with incredibly elongated Roman quarter-hour markers painted in black enamel; the remaining markers were simple black painted lines but they were visually interesting because the seconds track bisected the hour markers. It was a wonderfully discreet – almost austere – watch, particularly when made in white gold with a white dial. The Date version was most unusual for a Rolex, yes, the date indicator was at the 3 position, exactly where you would expect to find the date aperture and Cyclops. Instead, there was a small subsidiary dial with the numbers

→ I never understood the last of the Cellini watches. There was a lot to like about them – I particularly loved how the sunray effect on the dial seemed to carry over to the fine coin edge milling on the bezel. I admired how the designers had found new ways to display the date or the GMT function, but my admiration was dulled by the realization that these new displays were not as functional as the originals.

1 to 31 printed around the periphery; the dial itself carried a sunburst guilloche effect, although I suspect that it was machine stamped rather than lovingly turned on a rose engine.

Out of the three watches, the GMT version was my favourite. Like the date version, it performed its role in a very un-Rolex-like manner. A subsidiary dial at the 6 position had the hour numbers around its edges, and the hour and minute hands could be set independently which allowed the watch to be set to the correct time in one of those strange locations which are 30 or 45 minutes ahead of the rest of the world. The subsidiary dial even had a window at 9 with a day/night indicator. It was a unique way to indicate a second time zone and worked perfectly for a dress watch without appearing too busy and sporty.

CHAPTER TWELVE

2016–2025

ROLEX
SKY-DWELLER
OYSTER PERPETUAL
SUPERLATIVE CHRONOMETER
OFFICIALLY CERTIFIED
SWISS
MADE

2016–2025

INTO THE FUTURE

Rolex launches its most technically advanced watches alongside some that are the most fun.

This decade has undoubtedly been the strangest for Rolex. It began smoothly enough, with Jean-Frédéric Dufour settling comfortably into his role as CEO and the brand introducing a series of understated yet elegant timepieces at the Baselworld fair. The 60th anniversary of the Day-Date (see page 124) was marked with a striking green dial, the Cellini range (see page 270) received fresh dial options, and the Air-King (see page 302) made a controversial return with an unconventional design. Overall, it was business as usual, as global economies continued their recovery from the recession of the late 2000s. Demand for luxury watches surged in developed economies, fuelled by full employment and historically low interest rates.

However, 2016 marked a turning point, not because of a new watch release, but due to a groundbreaking report from investment bank Morgan Stanley, produced in collaboration with Swiss firm LuxeConsult. This document, published in 2017, revealed that Rolex accounted for nearly a quarter of the entire Swiss watch market. While many had assumed Rolex was a major player, the sheer scale of its market share was astonishing. Rolex, true to form, remained silent on the matter, but industry insiders I spoke to confirmed that the figures were largely accurate.

Over the next few years, Rolex continued to outpace its competitors, gradually increasing its market share by a percentage point or so annually. Then, in early 2020, the world came to an abrupt halt. The COVID-19 pandemic forced Switzerland into a nationwide lockdown. Rolex lost over 20 per cent of its annual production and Swiss watch exports plummeted by 62 per cent in the second quarter of the year. Rolex, which typically maintains a delicate balance between supply and demand, now faced a massive imbalance. Even as production stalled, demand remained robust, driven by a unique set of circumstances.

Lockdowns left many people with disposable income but few opportunities to spend it. International travel, dining out and luxury shopping were off the table, prompting a shift in consumer behaviour. The nightly news, filled with rising death tolls, reinforced a live-for-today mentality and people began to prioritize immediate gratification over delayed purchases. At the same time, the rise of cryptocurrencies and NFTs created a new class of wealthy individuals who sought to convert their digital gains into tangible assets. Rolex watches, particularly models like the Rainbow Daytona and jewel-encrusted Day-Dates (see page 258), became highly sought-after. These timepieces were not only instantly recognizable, but also known for their value and scarcity. With supply further constrained by the pandemic, secondary market prices skyrocketed.

This surge in demand led to a new phenomenon: speculators began to join waiting lists for Rolex watches,

← Sky-Dweller, 2018 (see page 300).

This decade has been a rollercoaster for Rolex, marked by unprecedented challenges and transformative decisions. From navigating a global pandemic to redefining its relationship with the secondary market, it has demonstrated resilience and adaptability.

not as enthusiasts but as investors. Watches that once had waiting lists spanning weeks or months now had lists stretching for years. Amid the chaos, Dufour made a bold move that would reshape the industry. In 2020, as the Swiss government banned large gatherings, Baselworld's organizers opted to postpone the event rather than cancel it, retaining exhibitor fees in the process. This decision drew sharp criticism, particularly from smaller brands which relied on Baselworld to secure orders. The head of the exhibitors' committee, who also happened to be a director at Rolex, warned that the postponement would cause irreparable harm. When Baselworld refused to reconsider, Rolex quietly convened with three other major exhibitors – Chanel, Chopard and Patek Philippe – and collectively decided to withdraw from Baselworld. Instead, they announced plans to host their own event in Geneva, in partnership with Watches and Wonders. Notably, press releases from the other brands emphasized that this move was Rolex's idea.

The absence of Baselworld meant that new watch releases were delayed until September 2020. When they finally arrived, the launches were relatively subdued. The standout pieces were the Oyster Perpetual models with vibrant, colourful dials (see page 310). The following year, with lockdowns still in place, brands resorted to virtual showcases. Rolex introduced a two-tone Explorer, Datejust models with palm-inspired dials and a Daytona with a meteorite dial, but overall innovation was limited.

By 2022, the industry had begun to recover, and Rolex made a triumphant return with a physical show in Geneva. Notable releases included a left-handed GMT-Master (see page 314), a 42mm Yacht-Master in white gold with a 'Falcon's Eye' dial, an updated Air-King with a redesigned case (see page 302), and a completely revamped Sea-Dweller Deepsea. Just before Christmas, Rolex dropped a bombshell: the launch of its Certified Pre-Owned (CPO) programme, operated through select authorized retailers. This marked Rolex's official entry into the secondary market, a significant shift for the brand.

In 2023, Rolex continued to innovate, introducing its first titanium watch – a 42mm Yacht-Master (see page 318) – and a two-tone GMT-Master with a black and grey ceramic bezel. However, the standout release was a special edition white gold Daytona commemorating the 100th anniversary of the 24 Hours of Le Mans (see page 320). This model featured a dial reminiscent of the iconic 'Paul Newman' Daytona (see page 154), with a 24-hour register replacing the traditional 12-hour one and a tachometer bezel highlighted by a red '100'. Later that year, Rolex expanded its CPO programme to major retail chains, including the 1916 Group and Watches of Switzerland, further solidifying its presence in the pre-owned market.

By 2024, Rolex was in its third year of stagnant growth. While revenue continued to rise, production remained capped at approximately 1.2 million units annually, with manufacturing facilities operating at full capacity. In response, Rolex doubled down on premiumization, unveiling a series of high-end models at Watches and Wonders. Highlights included a steel GMT-Master with a grey/black bezel, a platinum 1908, a Sky-Dweller on a Jubilee bracelet in

18-carat gold, new ombré dials for the Day-Date, and, most unexpectedly, a Deepsea crafted in 18-carat gold. Notably, only one steel watch was introduced, with the rest being precious metal models.

This decade has been a rollercoaster for Rolex, marked by unprecedented challenges and transformative decisions. From navigating a global pandemic to redefining its relationship with the secondary market, it has demonstrated resilience and adaptability. While the brand's dominance remains unchallenged, the road ahead will undoubtedly bring new tests and opportunities. One thing is certain: Rolex will continue to shape the future of the Swiss watch industry, just as it has for 120 years.

→ **This is the new Calibre 7135, featuring the revolutionary Dynapulse escapement, as used in the new 2025 Land-Dweller (see page 324).**

2018

SKY-DWELLER

If you thought the Yacht-Master II was complicated, wait until you see the Sky-Dweller: annual calendar, two timezones and no fiddly corrector buttons.

- **Model number: 326934**
- **Date: 2018**
- **Dial: Brass, blue gloss finish, white gold indices**
- **Movement: 9001**
- **Case material: Stainless steel, white gold bezel**
- **Dimensions: 42mm**

In May 2004 Rolex filed a patent with the Swiss Patent Office describing a design for an annual calendar which performed its functions without cams or levers. It was not published until November of the following year, and once it was available chatter started on the watch forums about when Rolex might actually launch a watch with this feature. At that time I was editor-in-chief of Timezone.com and moderated both of its Rolex forums. The general consensus was that it would be great if Rolex did make an annual calendar, but that this was most likely another patent filed by Rolex that would not go any further.

Imagine the surprise when Rolex introduced the Sky-Dweller at the 2012 Basel Fair, not just an annual calendar, but also a two-time zone watch. Looking like a Datejust II on steroids, it measured 42mm in diameter, 14.5mm high and 51mm from lug to lug, but surprisingly it did not feel all that big once I had it on my wrist.

What really impressed me was that Rolex had developed an annual calendar without any of the pushers or correctors usually seen on these designs – everything was done via the crown. The date and time were changed as normal, except that you could now change the date in both directions for the first time in a Rolex production watch. But the real breakthrough was using the bezel as a switch to put the watch into programming mode. Depending on how you manipulated the bezel, you could set the month or the time on the second time zone. Although the bezel was not fixed and was free to rotate, the watch still bore the name 'Oyster', signifying that it was safe down to 100m (328 feet).

With the off-centre 24-hour disc on the face of the watch, as well as all the normal Rolex dial text features, the dial looked busy, particularly as it had only full Arabic or Roman numerals and not the usual baton indices.

It was powered by the calibre 9001, which was the first brand-new calibre from Rolex since the 4130 (see page 253) at the turn of the century (if we consider the 4160 to be a modification of the 4130). But, Rolex had a head start in designing it. Most of the unique features of the 9001 – setting the date backwards or forwards, one-hour jumps for the hour hand, and using the hours as month indicators – were all features of the calibre 5355 quartz perpetual calendar (see page 256), which Rolex had designed and put into pre-production in the 1990s but which never made it into the catalogue.

It was by far the most complicated watch that Rolex had ever produced, and – like most Rolex new introductions – was only available in noble metals. This made it an expensive watch and so not for everyone. But when the new two-tone versions, particularly the steel with white gold bezel, were launched in 2017 at a much more affordable level, the sales of this model took off and it became one of the most sought-after Rolex watches of the 21st century.

> → **'Rolex don't make complicated watches' is what everyone said until the Yacht-Master II, and then the Sky-Dweller arrived and we never heard it again. What made it so special wasn't the annual calendar, or the new method of displaying a second timezone; what was radical was that it had all these functions without the need for corrector pushers. Everything was controlled by the crown, and – like the Yacht-Master II – by the bezel.**

ROLEX
SKY-DWELLER
OYSTER PERPETUAL
SUPERLATIVE CHRONOMETER
OFFICIALLY CERTIFIED
SWISS
MADE

2018

AIR-KING

Almost certainly the strangest watch to have been (re)introduced in this century, the Air-King bore almost no visible connection to its predecessors.

- **Model number: 116900**
- **Date: 2018**
- **Dial: Brass, black paint, applied white gold indices**
- **Movement: 3131**
- **Case material: Stainless steel**
- **Dimensions: 40mm**

→ For a long time the Air-King was the least expensive watch in the Rolex catalogue; it was automatic, and an Oyster, but it didn't have a date or chronometer certification and it was smaller than the Datejust. But it was clean, it was unencumbered and it did its job, quietly in the background. Unlike the new one which seemed to me to be so busy.

During the 2016 Baselworld fair, Rolex introduced one of the stranger watches of the last few years – or should that be re-introduced? This was the model 116900 Air-King. While the Air-King had been in the catalogue for around 60 years, this was an Air-King like no other. All previous models had been 34mm or smaller; the new model was 40mm in diameter, in fact, it shared the main case body with the reference 116400 Milgauss. But it was not the new case that startled visitors to the stand – it was the dial. Not only was it unlike any previous Air-King dial, it was unlike any previous Rolex dial.

In my opinion, the watch should not have been called the Air-King; it should have been called the SSC or the Bloodhound, as the new dial was designed as a homage to the chronograph that Rolex designed and built in 2014 for the Bloodhound SSC supersonic land-speed record car. The problem facing Rolex was that by the time it was ready to launch the watch, the SSC project was facing financial difficulties, and I am sure that Rolex did not want to name its watch after a failure. And so Rolex resurrected the name Air-King – which it had abandoned in 2014.

I mentioned earlier that in the late 1930s, Rolex became the preferred watch of pilots, and during World War II, Royal Air Force pilots made it their timepiece of choice (see page 64). After the war, Hans Wilsdorf chose to honour these flyers with a new line of manual-wind Oysters; they were new because (like the new Datejust) they were much larger than the previous manual-wind watches in order to fit in with the new look of a bigger 36mm watch. Now, however, we would consider them quite small – they were 32mm to 33mm in diameter.

This new range of watches bore the names Air-Tiger, Air-Lion, Air-Giant and Air-King. They all used the legendary 10½''' Hunter manual wind movement with 15 jewels and without any shock protection on the balance staff. These watches remained in production from about 1948 to the mid-1950s but slowly lost popularity and were dropped from the catalogues. Only the Air-King remained and, in 1959, it gained an automatic movement as model 5500, the first of the modern Air-Kings.

It was not just the layout of the Air-King dial that was strange, it was also the complete lack of luminosity anywhere on the dial, other than the 12-index; the quarter hour indices were applied polished white gold and the remaining numbers were simply painted onto the dial.

However, in 2022 the watch was completely revised. A new case with crown-protecting shoulders and flat case sides was introduced, giving it a much more substantial look, and the plain polished quarter-hour numbers were now filled with Chromalight. In addition to this, the watch also gained the new 3230 movement, meaning that this was a completely new watch.

ROLEX
OYSTER PERPETUAL
Air-King
SUPERLATIVE CHRONOMETER
OFFICIALLY CERTIFIED
SWISS MADE

2019

CELLINI MOONPHASE

The last version of the new Cellinis to be introduced was the moonphase model. It was certainly the most conventional of the three, and the most attractive, but it wasn't enough to save the name.

- Model number: 50535
- Date: 2019
- Dial: Brass, white enamel, pink gold indices
- Movement: 3195
- Case material: 18ct pink gold
- Dimensions: 39mm

→ I thought that the white gold version of this watch was by far the nicest and most elegant of all the Cellini versions, but I still didn't get the point. The moonphase on its own just looked strange – I am used to moonphases being part of a calendar watch with indicators for both the month and the day at the top or centre of the dial. The moonphase sitting on its own at the bottom looked somehow abandoned to me.

Two years after the launch of the new range, Rolex broadened its appeal by adding two new dial colours for the Cellini: blue for the white gold watches and brown for the Everose versions. The blue-dialled white-gold watches were particularly attractive, but the new dials did not seem to have much effect on sales. There were a couple of problems, the main one being that when potential clients were looking for a dress watch, a Rolex dealer was not the usual starting point. And the competition at a similar price point was intense; you could go through the horological alphabet – Audemars Piquet, Breguet, Cartier, you get the picture – and everyone had an acceptable contender. The situation was not helped by Rolex's otherwise smart move towards mono-brand boutiques. If a potential client visited a multi-brand boutique, the jeweller might propose the usual suspects and, down the line, suggest the Cellini. But the same potential client would most likely avoid the Rolex boutique, assuming that there was nothing for them inside.

Rolex tried to broaden the range by adding a Moonphase version in 2017. It was an interesting experiment, and many observers thought that it harked back to the triple calendar moonphase watches that Rolex had produced in the 1950s (see pages 92 and 94). Although it had the same pointer date layout as the vintage models, it lacked both the day and month windows and also had the strangest moonphase indicator ever seen. While most moonphase indicators give you a rough visual approximation of how the moon appears as you look upwards, the Rolex version only offered an approximate idea of how many days it was since it was either a full moon or a new moon. There was nothing wrong with the design. It was a beautiful watch, the blue lacquered disc with the moon was gorgeous, and the full moon indicator was a slice of meteorite, but all of those who thought that the design harked back to the now fabulously desirable and expensive Moonphase Rolex watches of the 1950s seem to have forgotten an important fact. Those watches are valuable because they are rare, and watches only become rare by virtue of not selling many when they were new. That certainly described the vintage moonphase watches, and – unfortunately – it also described the new Cellini range. The Classic, Date and GMT were all discontinued in 2022, leaving the Moonphase as the solitary representative of the line. The following year it, too, had vanished from the catalogue.

ROLEX
GENEVE
SWISS MADE

2019

PEARLMASTER

This range took over from the Crown Collection as the epitome of over-indulgence. Rolex had a new jewellery workshop and were determined to put it to good use.

- **Model number: 86349SAFUBL**
- **Date: 2019**
- **Dial: White gold, pavé diamond set, applied white gold Roman indices**
- **Movement: 3235**
- **Case material: 18ct white gold**
- **Dimensions: 39mm**

→ I am not a fan of jewelled watches, but I always liked these with the oversized cases and I absolutely loved the bracelets. I never see myself wearing one, but that doesn't stop me admiring the skill and craftsmanship so obviously on display in the jewel setting. If you ever get a chance, take a loupe to one of them and you will see a level of craftsmanship normally associated with people like Graaf or VanCleef & Arpels.

André Heiniger (see page 87), the head of Rolex after Hans Wilsdorf (see page 12), was once asked by a friend how things were going in the watch business. He responded that 'Rolex is not in the watch business, we are in the luxury business.' Heiniger understood that a woman thinking about buying a two-tone Datejust is not deciding whether to spend the money on an Omega or a Rolex; rather, she is deciding whether to spend it on a Louis Vuitton handbag or a Rolex. Her husband, a potential purchaser of a new Day-Date, might also be choosing between updating his Porsche or his Rolex.

There is no better indication of Rolex's positioning itself as a luxury item than the launch of the Pearlmaster range and the Special Editions which accompanied it in 1992. The Pearlmaster was an enlarged version of the 26mm Lady Datejust; it measured 29mm, and had a completely different look. It was only available with a wide flat bezel set with diamonds or other precious stones, plus it broke a long-standing Rolex tradition. For over 40 years, the Rolex owner was offered only two bracelet options – Oyster or Jubilee – or, for noble metal watches, there also was the President bracelet. The new Pearlmaster did not just introduce a new bracelet design, it brought in two. The regular bracelet was, in many ways, a combination of the President and the Jubilee bracelets. Like the Jubilee it was five links wide, but like the President it had wide centre links, and all the edges were softly rounded for comfort. What was unique, however, was that the two-tone versions of the 29mm Pearlmaster – which were made from yellow and white gold, not steel and gold – had a unique bracelet, where the centre links were curved, not straight. It seems strange to have made a unique bracelet just for one model.

The Pearlmaster was not unaccompanied for long. Before the end of the decade it was joined by two companions: a 34mm and a 39mm version. Essentially, these were the 31mm and 36mm versions of the Datejust and Day-Date after a dose of steroids; they shared the same design of bezel and bracelets as the Pearlmaster, but bore the rather more mundane name of Special Edition. The market was having none of this discretion and immediately renamed them the Masterpiece line.

For a short period, Rolex made the white gold 34mm Pearlmaster, reference 81209, without diamonds or other jewels on the case, dial or bracelet. It was the only Masterpiece watch which enabled the design to stand on its own, and it stood up well. I would love to have owned a 39mm equivalent, but they never made one.

ROLEX
DATEJUST
10

2019

GMT-MASTER II METEORITE DIAL

Finally the GMT-Master II gets a 'Pepsi' Cerachrom bezel, but only on the white gold version. However, the bezel is almost overshadowed by the new meteorite dial.

- **Model number: 126719BLRO**
- **Date: 2019**
- **Dial: Brass, meteorite slice, white gold indices**
- **Movement: 3285**
- **Case material: 18ct white gold**
- **Dimensions: 40mm**

→ When I first saw these GMT-Masters at what was – unknown to us all, at the time – the very last Baselworld, I was knocked out. I love white gold watches and the blue dial. But I couldn't take my eyes off the meteorite dial. I loved how it shimmered, how it seemed to change its pattern depending on how the light struck. Everyone else raved about the bezel and the new Chronergy escapement, but I just looked at the dial.

Ever since Rolex launched the reference 116178 with the first Cerachrom bezel in 2005, Rolex fans had been wondering when the bezel would reappear in the iconic red and blue combination. It took 14 years for their wishes came true, and Rolex introduced the 126719BLRO (Bleu and Rouge) in March 2019. Like most recent introductions it was made in precious metal first, this time white gold. The reason why new models are made in gold first is that these will always be much smaller production runs than the steel versions, so the operatives in the factory have time to build up their expertise.

The new two-colour bezel was not the only thing about the watch that was new and different. It came with the option of two different dial styles, a deep blue one that almost matched the night-time half of the bezel and – most unexpectedly – a Meteorite version.

There were two very unusual things about the Meteorite dial. It was the first time Rolex had catalogued an exotic dial on a GMT-Master (previously individual, bespoke pieces had been made for special clients). But more surprising was that it was priced at only around 1,500CHF more than the blue dial; clients were accustomed to paying five figures for a semi-precious-stone dial. Not only was the Meteorite dial comparatively inexpensive, but what made it even more special was that each one was unique. The pattern is the result of the molten core of the meteorite cooling as it hurtles through the blackness of space. However this is only revealed when the meteorite is sliced open and the cut surface is treated with acid. The section is then cut into very thin slices, it is trimmed to fit the dial, holes are drilled to accept the white gold cages for the Chromalite luminosity, and a small square is cut for the date window. Then the wafer-thin slice of meteorite is mounted on a brass plate which already has the dial feet fitted. Finally the watch is assembled.

While everyone was looking at the new case and dial, the new movement was seemingly overlooked. The new watch was powered by the new 3285 calibre which featured all the recent improvements: the Chonergy escapement and the amagnetic Parachrom hairspring with Breguet overcoil. Like all the new models, these features enabled it to easily beat the existing Contrôle Officiel Suisse des Chronomètres timing standards and be guaranteed to be accurate to +2/-2 seconds per day.

ROLEX
GMT-MASTER II
SUPERLATIVE CHRONOMETER
OFFICIALLY CERTIFIED
SWISS MADE

2020

CERAMIC DAYTONA

Finally, the Daytona catches up with all other 'tool' watches and is equipped with a Cerachrom bezel.

- **Model number: 116500LN**
- **Date: 2020**
- **Dial: Brass, white paint, applied white gold indices**
- **Movement: 4130**
- **Case material: Stainless steel**
- **Dimensions: 40mm**

→ It has become common among collectors to give nicknames to popular Rolex versions – Kermit, Pepsi and Smurf among them – and it amazes me that nobody has ever bestowed one on the steel Daytona. I would like to propose one, the 'Unicorn', because the chances of being able to purchase one of these watches is similar to the chances of encountering the mythical beast, or so most folks assume.

The launch of the Daytona with a ceramic bezel had been anticipated since 2008 as, apart from the Explorer II, it was the only sportswatch without one. Still, it did not arrive until 2011 and, like most recent Rolex introductions, the new bezel was only available on the 18-carat gold model. What was different about the Daytona's new bezel was that ceramic was used without a metal bezel frame for the first time. On earlier models – the GMT-Master II, the Submariner and the Yacht-Master II – the ceramic structure was an insert in a metal bezel. Here, it was not only fitted without a support structure, the ceramic bezel itself was a structural part of the watch case. It held the sapphire glass in place as a key component of the ability of the watch to dive to 100m (328ft), if required. Concerns were raised that the unprotected edges of the bezel could chip or crack if it suffered an impact, but well over a decade since its introduction these concerns seem to have been unjustified.

The launch version was in 18-carat Everose pink gold and was available with a brown or cream dial, while the bezel itself was black ceramic. In 2016, to celebrate the 50th anniversary of the Daytona, Rolex surprised everyone by launching a platinum version with the ice blue dial which had been a signature of platinum Day-Dates for some time. It was also available with a brown ceramic bezel that complemented the brown rings on the edges of the subdials.

Historically there were two bezel layouts for the automatic Daytona – steel watches had the bezel tachymeter engravings in a vertical pattern, while precious metal versions had the numbers in a radial layout with the units between 100 and 60 linked by an underline. The ceramic bezel copied the precious metal design, and in 2016, when the 116500 steel Daytona was launched with a ceramic bezel, it too had the layout previously seen on the precious metal models. Many observers thought that the steel watches now bore a passing resemblance to the old 6240/6241/6263 manual wind Daytonas (see page 188) with their black plastic bezel inserts. I did not see the resemblance until 2024, when Rolex surprised nearly everyone by fitting metal rims to the edges of the ceramic Daytona bezels. To me the biggest surprise was that there were bracelet models in gold – yellow, white or Everose – that retained their gold bezels, as did the two-tone versions. The gold watches on Oysterflex straps had ceramic bezels. The reason why is another Rolex mystery.

ROLEX
OYSTER PERPETUAL
SUPERLATIVE CHRONOMETER
OFFICIALLY CERTIFIED
COSMOGRAPH
DAYTONA
SWISS MADE
UNITS PER HOUR

2020

COLOURED DIALS

The most attractive dials were no longer kept for the most expensive Rolex watches – this time they were on the brand's most affordable model.

- **Model number: 126000**
- **Date: 2020**
- **Dial: Brass, blue paint, white gold indices**
- **Movement: 3230**
- **Case material: Stainless steel**
- **Dimensions: 36mm**

When COVID-19 shook the world in early 2020, one of the less important casualties was the Baselworld trade fair, which had been scheduled for the end of April that year. It was postponed until the following January, although it never actually took place.

This left the watch world in a bit of a quandary. Although the watch factories were closed, the brands needed to show all the new models designed over the past year to the public. Most brands resorted to the internet, which worked pretty well as the basic information made its way to potential customers. But watches are tactile objects, the fit and feel are important and so by the summer, as restrictions were loosened, the brands invited the Press to their local offices to handle the new watches. And so it was that on 1 September 2020 I finally got to handle the new watches. I was not very keen on the new white-gold Submariner, which kept the blue Cerachrom bezel but replaced the blue dial with a conventional black one; it was more low key, but had lost its flamboyance. I thought that the new version of the Sky-Dweller on the (never call it rubber) Oysterflex strap was a combination that just did not work for me, a quite complex and expensive watch on a very utilitarian strap.

If the top-of-the-line pieces left me nonplussed, what really knocked me out were the least expensive Rolex Oyster models, simply labelled the Oyster Perpetual (see below and right). These were a success. They were great, simple, almost austere watches with the option of seven different coloured dials: turquoise, coral-red, British Racing Green, pink, yellow, silver and black. While most folks rhapsodized over the bright colours, my favourite was the black one as it allowed the design of the dial with its double-baton indices at the quarters to take pride of place, rather than be overwhelmed by the colour.

What was great about these dials was that they were painted using a high-gloss lacquer, giving them a shine reminiscent of the Stella dials of days gone by (see page 242), but without all the effort. They may have been the least expensive Rolex Oysters but they had the latest movement fitted, the 3230 with the new Chronergy escapement (see page 306).

It was obvious that Rolex wanted these watches to reach the widest possible audience as, for the first time, the same model was now available in five sizes: 28mm, 31mm, 34mm, 36mm and the new 41mm diameter.

The turquoise colour gained the nickname Tiffany (for its resemblance to the iconic blue of Tiffany & Co.) and soon became the hardest Rolex to buy, but all of them became very desirable – and they deserved to be. At a time when the world seemed to be coming apart, these watches brought a smile to the face of anyone who wore one, or even just glimpsed one on the wrist of a passerby.

→ These are my favourite watches introduced by Rolex this century. They are great fun – the colours can brighten up anyone's day. But, at the core, they are the purest essence of what Rolex is about; solid, reliable, tough and accurate. There is nothing extraneous on these watches, no date, no Cyclops lens, no milled or rotating bezel, just three hands, the latest movement and a vault-like steel case.

ROLEX
OYSTER PERPETUAL
SUPERLATIVE CHRONOMETER
OFFICIALLY CERTIFIED
SWISS MADE

2022

LEFT-HANDED GMT-MASTER II

It seems inconceivable that most watch brands have ignored 10 per cent of the world's population – the left-handed. But now Rolex have made their first true LH watch.

- **Model number: 126720VTNR**
- **Date: 2022**
- **Dial: Brass, gloss black paint, white gold indices**
- **Movement: 3285**
- **Case material: Stainless steel**
- **Dimensions: 40mm**

The year 2022 was not one for spectacular surprises from Rolex. A couple of precious-metal Yacht-Master models, the Day-Date 40mm in platinum and the 'butchification' of the Air-King (see page 302) all passed pretty much without notice. But what did raise the odd eyebrow was an exciting version of the GMT-Master II, designed to be worn on the right wrist by left-handed owners.

As approximately 10 per cent of the world's population is left-handed, it's interesting that less than 1 per cent of watches are designed to be worn by sinistrals. To give the company its due, Rolex has probably made more of them than most. One of the 1915 Mk1 calendar watches was left-handed, as were quite a few Datejusts in the 1950s, 20 of the 1680 Submariners in 18ct gold were also left-handed, as were a pair of 16660 Sea-Dwellers made for COMEX in the late 1970s. The dive watches had their winding crown at 9, not for left-handed divers but rather to be worn on the left hand, with the winding crown – which is the most easily damaged part of the watch – safely out of the way of danger. That they were designed to be worn on the left hand was obvious, as the date window remained at the usual 3 o'clock location.

Not so the new GMT-Master II. This was a full-on watch for the southpaws. The date window was next to the winding crown at 9 o'clock. If the watch was worn on the left wrist it would be almost impossible to read the date.

Making the watch was not in the least bit difficult. The watch case and movement were turned through 180-degrees and a new dial and date disc were printed and installed – that was all it took.

The other obvious change was that the Cerachrom bezel insert was now green and black, the first time that green ceramic had been used on the GMT-Master. US collectors, obviously keen to continue the soft drink nickname trend, which had started with different bezel versions of the GMT being known as 'Pepsi' and 'Coke', called the new watch 'Sprite', although I am at a loss to understand why, as the Sprite can in the UK is a monochrome green.

For the first time in ages, this new watch was launched with a choice of either Oyster or Jubilee bracelets (historically GMT-Master launches had been with only one style of bracelet and the alternative following on a year or two later). More than anything, this showed that Rolex was committed to the watch and wanted it to succeed. How much this can be attributed to the fact that Jean-Frédéric Dufour, the Rolex CEO, is left-handed, is open to discussion.

→ Where and when did the trend of wearing a wristwatch on your non-dominant wrist begin? I think it goes back to pocket watches. They came in two styles, open-face with the winder at 12 and Hunter with the winder at 3. When British cavalry officers began to wear these watches in holders on their wrists, they found having the winding crown facing out at 3 was the best configuration for winding and setting the watch.

ROLEX
OY… PERPETUAL DATE
20
GMT-MASTER II
SUPERLATIVE CHRONOMETER
OFFICIALLY CERTIFIED
SWISS MADE

2023

CELEBRATION DIAL

If you thought that the bright colours on the Oyster Perpetual range were fun, but you couldn't make up your mind which one to choose, then the Celebration dial had them all.

- **Model number: M126000-0009**
- **Date: 2023**
- **Dial: Brass, blue lacquer and multicolour bubbles, white gold indices**
- **Movement: 3230**
- **Case material: Stainless steel**
- **Dimensions: 36mm**

→ The fun inherent in the coloured-dial Oyster Perpetuals launched in 2020 was even more present in this variant, which used the most desirable of the lacquered dial colours, Tiffany blue as the base, and then spilled little bubbles of different colour lacquer all over the face. But all fun has to come to an end, and at the 2025 Watches and Wonders show, the Celebration dial was replaced by a range of muted pastel shades.

Earlier I mentioned how the coloured lacquered dials on the 2020 Oyster Perpetual watches became very popular (see page 310). However, within three years the most flamboyant of the colours had vanished from the catalogues. The coral-red and the yellow were gone, and the British Racing Green, the pink and the turquoise were restricted to particular sizes. Believe it or not, an even more flamboyant dial took their place and featured all five colours used on the previous lacquered dials in the form of bubbles on a turquoise field.

When it appeared on the Rolex stand at Watches and Wonders 2023 trade show in Geneva, it bore the name Celebration Dial. I am not sure what it was celebrating, or whether the bubbles represented the champagne bubbles often associated with celebrations. What was explained to me was that there were five sizes of bubble to represent the five sizes of Oyster Perpetual watches: 28mm, 31mm, 34mm, 36mm and 41mm. Despite this, the Celebration Dial was not available in two of the sizes – 28mm and 34mm.

Like the previous lacquered dials, this was a bright, cheerful face, with large, Chromalight-filled rectangular batons marking the hours and double batons at the quarter hours. If you looked really closely at the very bottom of the dial, between the words 'Swiss' and 'Made', there was a small Rolex coronet. This indicated that the watch contained the latest style of movement from Rolex, featuring its own in-house designed Chronergy escapement. This 3230 calibre was fitted to the two larger models, while the 31mm was powered by the 2232, which did not have the Chronergy escapement, but did feature a silicon hairspring as a concession to the 21st century.

The case was the latest version of the classic Oyster case, stripped of any decoration. It had a highly polished bezel, which stood out against the matt brushed lugs and bracelet. Speaking of the bracelet, it too featured all the latest modifications to the classic design – the flip-over Oysterlock clasp as well as the Easylink quick adjustment feature.

I began by mentioning that when the watch was launched I was unsure of exactly what it was celebrating. It was not long before I knew the reason for the celebration – its sales figures. The Celebration Dial proved to be even more successful than the coloured-dial watches had been. Along with almost every other Rolex model, it proved to be virtually impossible to buy from Rolex retailers, and secondary market dealers asked between two-and-a-half and three times the retail price for this flamboyant timepiece. But it was not – by a long shot – the most flamboyant watch that Rolex launched in 2023.

ROLEX
OYSTER PERPETUAL
SUPERLATIVE CHRONOMETER
OFFICIALLY CERTIFIED
SWISS MADE

2023

TITANIUM YACHT-MASTER

After hiding in plain sight for two years, the first titanium watch from Rolex finally breaks cover, and it's gorgeous.

- **Model number: 226627**
- **Date: 2023**
- **Dial: Brass, matt black paint, white gold indices**
- **Movement: 3235**
- **Case material: Titanium**
- **Dimensions: 42mm**

In 2021 a number of websites suddenly noticed that Sir Ben Ainslie, the world's most successful sailor, winner of two Maxi Yacht Rolex Cup races, countless Olympic medals and a Rolex testimonee, was wearing a most unusual Rolex watch. It appeared to be the Yacht-Master 42, but it was not the white gold version; his watch had an all-over matt finish and lacked a date window. The speculation was that the watch was made from titanium – Rolex had used titanium for the case back of the Sea-Dweller Deepsea (see page 286) and, of course, its sister brand TUDOR had been producing a titanium dive watch, the Pelagos, for years.

In 2023, the production version of Sir Ben's watch was launched at the Watches and Wonders trade fair in Geneva. Although it was not exactly the same watch: it had gained a date window – to bring it in line with all the rest of the Yacht-Master range – and lost the NATO-style strap that Sir Ben had worn.

Essentially, it was similar to the 42mm white gold version, but more than a passing glance showed that this was a very different, much more professional, watch. The case had a completely matt brushed finish all over, apart from four highly polished 45-degree bevels on the top edges of the lugs. These had been a feature of the Rolex sports watches up until the introduction of the maxi-cased watches and I, for one, was happy to see their return. It now felt like a proper tool watch; not only the case but also the dial had a matt finish, as did the Cerachrom bezel insert. Only the numerals, standing proud of the bezel, had a polished finish to enable them to be more easily read.

The watch had the first titanium Oyster bracelet ever made by Rolex with both the Oysterlock clasp and the Easylink expansion facility. The bracelet also featured ceramic liners in the links. These had been introduced several years previously in the Day-Date bracelet, and their role was to prevent undue wear on the gold bracelet links from the constant rubbing of the steel pins which held it together. I assume that they perform a similar job on the titanium bracelet.

With its matt-finish case, dial and bracelet and lightweight titanium construction, I would choose the new Yacht-Master over the Submariner any day, even though the Sub is rated to 1,000m (3,280ft) versus the 100m (328ft) for the Yacht-Master. The truth is I am not diving to either of those depths.

→ I love how low-key this watch is. The 2023 releases showed the Celebration dial and the genuinely bizarre Puzzle dial, so the all-matt finished Yacht-Master in titanium was almost lost in the glitz and the glamour. I say 'almost', because to me, this was the highlight of the event. It was a genuine 'tool' watch with nothing extraneous about it. It felt like a retrun to the Submariner 5513 or 1665 Sea-Dweller – a watch exuding quiet strength.

ROLEX
YACHT-MASTER
PERLATIVE CHRONOMETER
OFFICIALLY CERTIFIED
SWISS MADE
13
50
10
30
10

2023

DAYTONA 'LE MANS'

The best-looking Daytona of the modern era surfaced one Sunday afternoon and rapidly became the most desirable current Daytona ever produced.

- **Model number: 126529LN**
- **Date: 2023**
- **Dial: Brass, gloss black paint, white registers, white gold indices**
- **Movement: 4132**
- **Case material: 18ct white gold**
- **Dimensions: 40mm**

I do not remember ever getting a press release from Rolex on a Sunday afternoon. But 11 June 2023 was not just any Sunday; it marked the finish of the one hundredth 24 Hours of Le Mans. Le Mans and Rolex have a long history together, the Swiss firm has been the official timekeeper since the beginning of this century – but the relationship goes back a lot further. The watch we now call the Daytona was initially going to be called the 'Rolex Le Mans', and Rolex went as far as placing advertisements in magazines announcing the new watch in 1963. In 2023, it finally did receive that name, and that was what the press release told me.

To celebrate the centenary of the race, Rolex produced a very special edition of the Cosmograph Daytona, with a special dial, bezel and movement. The dial was the obvious differentiator; an initial glance took in the new subdials with indices almost – but not exactly – like the ones on the classic Paul Newman Daytona. A second glance noted that the left-hand register reads up to 24 hours, not the usual 12, a subtle homage to Le Mans. On the tachometer bezel, the number 100 is in red, again a further nod to the race.

Apart from the bezel, another part of the case is different. At the 2023 Watches and Wonders trade fair in Geneva, Rolex introduced a sapphire case back on the platinum-cased Daytona, but on no other metals. Yet this special-edition watch, in white gold only, also had an exhibition back to allow a view of the special 4132 movement. The 4132 differs from the 4131 fitted to every other Daytona by virtue of having a 24-hour register rather than the conventional 12-hour version. On most chronographs, going from a 12- to 24-hour register involves swapping the drive wheel – one with more teeth which revolves more slowly. Changing a single wheel would not merit a new movement number. But a new model number would be needed for the Le Mans, because there are seven extra parts in the movement. These parts are required because the design of Rolex 413X is so integrated that simply doubling the number of teeth on the wheel driving the 12-hour register is not possible, as the existing teeth are as small as it is possible to produce, so a satellite system is used instead to halve the rotation speed of the wheel.

The watch appeared on the market at the beginning of July, became the hardest watch to buy and the most desirable in the entire Rolex catalogue, then vanished from the catalogue in March of the following year. In its place Rolex introduced a yellow-gold version, and it was even more exclusive – it did not even make it into the catalogue, but was only available on request to select VIPs.

→ Forget the white gold case and bracelet, forget the special 24-hour register and get rid of the red paint on the bezel. You can even get rid of the Paul Newman-like indices on the sub dials, but please keep this classic reverse Panda dial with the solid colour subsidiary registers. For me, this is exactly how a Rolex chronograph should look.

ROLEX
OYSTER PERPETUAL
SUPERLATIVE CHRONOMETER
OFFICIALLY CERTIFIED
COSMOGRAPH
DAYTONA
SWISS
MADE
UNITS PER HOUR

2024

PUZZLE DIAL

This was the least Rolex-like watch that Rolex have ever sold. It also had one of the most creative and flamboyant dials ever made by the firm.

- **Model number: 128235**
- **Date: 2024**
- **Dial: Gold, champlevé enamel**
- **Movement: 3255**
- **Case material: 18ct rose gold**
- **Dimensions: 36mm**

→ Where do I start, this thing was so unexpected, so far out, that it would have made more sense to launch it in 2025, when Watches and Wonders opened on April Fools' Day. Yet, there it was undermining the belief that Rolex is the horological home of strict Genevan Calvinism. I would never wear one, but I raise my hat to the folks who designed and crafted it, and the executives who approved its release.

If the Celebration Dials (see page 316) on the 2023 Oyster Perpetuals evoked amazement from some of the visitors to the Rolex stand at the Watches and Wonders fair in Geneva, the 36mm Day-Dates with Jigsaw Dials brought open-mouthed astonishment.

Rolex has a century-old reputation as one of the most discreet and reserved of all Swiss watch brands. If it had a motto, it would be 'Success through evolution, not revolution'. Yet here was a revolutionary version of the firm's flagship, the Day-Date.

The dial on yellow- and white-gold watches was in the form of a multicoloured champlevé enamel jigsaw puzzle on a turquoise background; there was an orange background for the Everose version. This was pretty damned flamboyant by itself, but compared with the two windows in the dial it was practically sedate. Let us remember that this is the Day-Date: it has two windows which tell you those two things – the day and the date. But not on this model. Instead the upper window, normally reserved for the date, displayed one of seven words – Eternity, Faith, Gratitude, Happy, Hope, Love and Peace, while the date window showed one of 30 different emojis or the green Rolex Coronet.

Over the years, the Day-Date had been fitted with a variety of stone dials (see page 240), jewelled dials (see page 304) and, of course, the Stella dials (see page 242). But until now there had never been enamel dials. The cloisonné dials Rolex bought from firms such as Stern Frères back in the 1950s were only ever fitted to Rolex Perpetual watches, never to Datejusts or Day-Dates.

Cloisonné enamel dials are created by attaching thin gold wires to a dial plate in the pattern desired to create a cell for each section of the design. The cells are filled with different coloured enamels, and the dial is fired and then polished (see page 106). Champlevé enamel, on the other hand, is almost the reverse of cloisonné. While cloisonné is built up on a flat dial plate, champlevé is almost excavated from the dial plate. The design is traced onto the blank dial plate, and a grooved tool is used to remove metal from the areas where the enamel will be, leaving metal barriers between the different colours. Like a cloisonné dial, it is then fired and polished to produce a perfectly flat surface before the text is then printed onto it. But that was not the end of the dial's flamboyance. There were no simple batons or Roman numerals as indices. Instead, ten baguette sapphires in rainbow colours were applied to the dial to mark the hours.

This was, by far, the most flamboyant watch ever made by Rolex, it rivalled the output of such enfants terribles as Franck Muller and Richard Mille in the outrageousness stakes.

PEACE
ROLEX

2025

LAND-DWELLER

Rolex shocked everyone by introducing not only a brand new case, bracelet and dial, but also a revolutionary new escapement. The only thing anyone complained about was the name.

- **Model number: 127336**
- **Date: 2025**
- **Dial: Brass, PVD colouring then laser etched, white gold indices**
- **Movement: 7135**
- **Case material: Platinum**
- **Dimensions: 40mm**

I have often joked that MI6 should hire Rolex to handle its security – after all, Rolex is a company from which nothing seems to leak. Not so in 2025. Shockingly accurate rumours, followed by images of a new Rolex model, surfaced weeks before the Watches and Wonders fair in Geneva, where Rolex traditionally unveils its latest creations. Not only did the images spread like wildfire, but the rumour mill buzzed with talk of an entirely new movement featuring a revolutionary escapement.

When the show opened there it was, in the front window of Rolex's massive stand, exactly as the leaks had suggested.

The watch bore more than a passing resemblance to the short-lived Rolex 1630 (see page 206), a quirky two-tone model from the 1970s that combined the Oysterquartz case with the calibre 1535 automatic movement. The similarities were not limited to the angular case and five-link integrated bracelet. What really evokes the 1630 for me is the inner minute track – on both watches it is not printed on the dial's periphery but rather on a sloped inner bezel (known in French as the *rehaut*).

But that is where the resemblance ends. The Land-Dweller is far slimmer than both the Oysterquartz and the 1630, and its bracelet is significantly more flexible – almost sensual – with a concealed clasp. Of course, the real headline is the movement. Not just new, but revolutionary. Coming from the least radical company in Swiss horology, this was unexpected; Rolex had built its reputation on gradual evolution, not sweeping changes. Yet upon closer inspection, while the movement boasts groundbreaking features, its foundation remains evolutionary.

It is based on the Calibre 7140, used in the 1908 dress watch – already a high-tech movement featuring the Chronergy escapement and Syloxi hairspring. Now, the escapement has been replaced by the new Dynapulse system, which takes the best elements of Breguet's double-impulse escapement (later refined by George Daniels, Laurent Ferrier, Charles Frodsham and others) and pairs them with cutting-edge balance assembly technology. The balance wheel is crafted from a Rolex-patented brass alloy containing no ferrous materials, while the balance staff is made from a high-tech ceramic compound. That alone is innovative, but the finishing process is truly groundbreaking: to achieve flawlessly smooth pivots, the staff is 'polished' using the same ultra-precise lasers employed in delicate eye surgery. The hairspring remains Syloxi, but due to the new movement's 5Hz (36,000 bph) beat rate, it has been made significantly more rigid. The result? A balance assembly completely immune to magnetism.

This new movement is more shock-resistant and antimagnetic, and – thanks to its higher frequency – should be more accurate. So, will it replace the 32XX series? When I posed this question, I was told Rolex would roll it out *gradually*. I suspect we might see, for example, a new Datejust with this movement while the 3235-powered version remains available at a lower price. Rolex has done this before: the earliest Explorers (see page 88) came in two versions – the 6350 with a chronometer-certified movement and a finer dial, and the 6150 without. And who could forget the Submariners of the 1960s and 1970s – the 5512 with a superior chronometer movement (see page 160) and the 5513 with a more basic calibre (see page 174)?

↑ When Rolex launched the Oysterquartz in 1997, they did so in a unique case with flat surfaces and sharp angles. They were saying, in effect, 'This isn't your dad's Rolex, this is something new and different'. I think that Rolex were saying pretty much the same thing when they launched the Land-Dweller in a case bearing more than a passing resemblance to the Oysterquartz. This most certainly isn't your dad's Rolex.

The watch is impressive. The case and bracelet aesthetics are stunning, and the feel is exceptional. The dial is a tad too busy for my taste, but the movement proves that – even after 120 years – Rolex remains at the top of its game.

RECOGNITION for important public services, or for distinguished work in commerce, industry, science or medicine, present opportunities to offer the Rolex Prince.
Whenever such occasions arise think of the Prince as a really worthy souvenir.
Its very solid and exceptionally elegant case is inlaid with white and yellow 18 carat gold, and of perfect design. No other watch has ever been so designed.
In 9 carat it is made of yellow gold in a slightly different design, and this same model is also available in sterling silver.
The manufacture of the Rolex Prince is limited to a very small number only, and orders for same will be accepted by a selected few of the very best jewellery establishments in the British Empire, for execution in strict rotation, as such fine watches cannot be made in large quantities.
The Prince will be delivered as and when it leaves the Government Observation Stations, provided with an Official Pedigree of Super-Excellence.
Orders should be placed at an early date ensure delivery this side of Christmas.
867 Rupees
The ROLEX PRINCE
PURE SOLID PLATINUM
Government Hall-Marked
867 Rupees
WHITE & YELLOW GOLD MODEL
18 carat 280 Rupees
ALL GOLD MODEL
9 carat 196 Rupees
ALL SILVER MODEL
112 Rupees
Prices are the same as in England and strictly net for Cash.
SHOWING THE CURVE OF THE ROLEX PRINCE, DESIGNED TO FIT SNUGLY ON THE WRIST.
No. 629
Elegant Lady watch
18 Kt. gold with diamonds
$ 837
ROLEX
"Precision" movements
WATERTIGHT
DUST-PRO
ROLEX
31 WORLD RECORDS
What is a Chronometer?
In accordance with the rules of the Chronometric Societies of Switzerland and France · The title of Chronometer is permitted only if it is a watch of the finest quality and so precisely adjusted in all positions and extremes of temperature that it will pass a 14 days' continuous Observatory test'
ROLEX CHRONOMETERS conform with this Official definition.
ROLEX OYSTER Royal
ROLEX OYSTER Small Models for Ladies
UNBREAKABLE GLASS
۵۵۱۳ سابمرینر (زیردریائی)
۱۶۸۰
۱۶۶۵ سی — دوولر (آبمان)
۱۰

AFTERWORD

Forty-five years ago, I knew next to nothing about watches. My collecting instincts were focused on cars and M-series Leica cameras. I owned two watches, a Rolex GMT-Master (I had a business partner in California on a different time zone) and a Cartier Tank, and they were all I needed. Then, for our first anniversary, I bought my wife a vintage watch as she had admired one on a friend's wrist. In turn she bought me one; it was a Harwood, one of the first automatic wristwatches. The story of John Harwood intrigued me and I began to collect early automatics. There were a lot of them: Autorist, Wig-Wag, Rolls, Wyler and the Rolex Bubbleback (see page 56).

Most were bizarre in one way or the other, the only conventional one was the Rolex and – when I wore it – the only one that worked as intended was also the Rolex. So I concentrated on collecting Bubblebacks, which led me into other areas of early Rolex, including the Prince (see page 50) and the Rebbergs (see page 16).

My natural inquisitiveness made me curious about the company, so I asked around among dealers in vintage watches and other collectors and hit a brick wall. Nature abhors a vacuum, and there was a veritable vacuum of information about Rolex back then. What I encountered were what can best be described as conspiracy theories – it was owned by the Vatican or by the Swiss government, or even wilder theories. So I decided to research it myself. Back in those pre-internet days that involved days at the Public Records Office, the British Library Newspaper Archive in Colindale on the outskirts of London and several trips to Switzerland. I learned about watchmaking from Richard Good, keeper of horology at the British Museum, and about Rolex from John Read, former CEO of Rolex Japan, who knew Hans Wilsdorf well. Slowly but surely, I began to compose a coherent image of the firm, and that was when my friend Jeffrey Hess and I started to write a history of Rolex. In 1996, Schiffer published *The Best of Time*, by which time I had discovered the internet; this led me to a tiny website in Singapore called Timezone. There were around a dozen users on the site at this time, and I think I was the first who was not from Asia. Over the years I regularly posted on the site, became the moderator of the Rolex forum, then of the Vintage Rolex forum when that began, and ended up as editor-in-chief.

Since then, the internet has allowed knowledge about the brand to spread worldwide. If you want to know the difference between all the bezel inserts used on a 5513 Submariner during its production run, the answer is just a search request away. But we do not know everything, and we probably never will. I know that I am still learning, and I hope that you have learned something from this book. Thanks for getting this far.

Nobody is perfect, not Rolex, and certainly not this book; if – despite the best efforts of myself and my editors – you discover any errors, please drop me an email at *TheRolexLegacy@gmail.com* and I will ensure they are corrected in subsequent editions.

INDEX

Page numbers in *italic* refer to the illustrations

ACKNOWLEDGEMENTS

This book, and everything else, is for Minda.

Bibliography

Chapuis, Alfred (1956), *The History of the Self Winding Watch*. London: Batsford.

Dowling, James and Hess, Jeffery (2006), *The Best of Time Rolex Wristwatches: An Unauthorized History*. Pennsylvania: Schiffer Publishing.

Pergola, Carlo (2006), *Rolex Daytona, a Legend is Born*. Rome: Best Edizioni.

Rolex Geneva (1946), *Rolex Vade Mecum*.

Rolex Geneva (various issues), *The Rolex Magazine*.

Trueb, Lucien F., Ramm, Gunther and Wenzig, Peter (2013), *Electrifying the Wristwatch*. Pennsylvania: Schiffer Publishing.

Acknowledgements

It's my name on the cover, but this was a team effort. It would never have happened without Trevor, my publisher, Scarlet, my editor who kept it all on track, and Jonathan, creative director, who made it look good. And, of course, there's Vinny, the best photographer in Shepherd's Bush. Also Alia Hameed for making things make sense for me. I would also like to thank Abdulla Al Shaer, David Boettcher and Ed Delgado for their help, advice and support.

The book would never have happened without the active co-operation of many collectors, dealers and auction houses who unstintingly loaned their watches and their images, including:

Roger Michel, Executive Director of the Institute for Digital Archaeology
Philip Toledano, MisterEnthusiast
Mike Wood, The Old Watch Shop, Southport
Christy and Ed, Subdial, London
Spencer and Josh, BQ Watches, Radlett
Raj and Nino, The Watch Centre, London
Tariq, Momentum Dubai
Jeff Harris
George and Daniel Somlo, Somlo Antiques
Ross and Davide, Monaco Legend Auctions
Paul Boutros, Deputy Chairman, Americas, Phillips Auctions
Carla Filmer, Christie's
And three who choose to remain anonymous.

I would also like to acknowledge a sincere debt of gratitude to the late Dominique Tadion from Rolex Geneva, who had faith in what I was doing and who always had time. Gone too soon.

About the author

James is an avid collector with a passion for horology. His fascination with watches began more than four decades ago, sparking a journey that led him into the world of timepiece collecting and trading, earning him the sobriquet 'Mr Rolex'.

This deep dive into the intricacies of timepieces not only honed his discerning eye for quality and craftsmanship, but also fostered a profound appreciation for the creativity and innovation inherent in watchmaking and in its history. With each acquisition and transaction, James's knowledge and expertise in the realm of watches grew, solidifying his reputation as a seasoned collector and connoisseur in the horological community, with a passion for research and a dedication to spreading the results of his research as widely as possible.

His areas of interest are vintage and military timepieces and he is acknowledged as an authority on Rolex within the industry. He has been a moderator of several online watch forums and has written on watches and collecting for magazines and newspapers on every continent except South America and Antarctica. He gave the 1999 Dingwall Beloe, Worshipful Company of Clockmakers Lecture at the British Museum, he is a Member of the Academy of the Grand Prix d'Horlogerie de Genève and a member of the committee of the 2023/24 and 2025/26 Louis Vuitton Prize for Independent Watchmaking.

Picture credits

Slipcase:
Front: Sea-Dweller 16660, Vinny Whiteman.
Back: Yacht-Master, Rolex.

Cover:
Front: Daytona, Rolex.
Back: Day-Date, Momentum Dubai.

Vinny Whiteman: 1, 4, 13, 14, 15, 22, 23, 25, 28, 33, 34, 35, 36, 37, 39, 42, 45, 46, 47, 49, 50, 51, 52, 53, 54, 55, 62, 66, 67, 69, 70, 71, 72, 73, 76, 77, 78, 79, 80, 81, 82, 89, 91, 96, 97, 99, 100, 113, 119, 131, 144, 145, 150, 154, 157, 163, 169, 172, 174, 178, 179, 180, 190, 191, 198, 201, 209, 213, 214, 215, 217, 218, 219, 257, 259, 326, 336.

Subdial: 2, 103, 121, 143, 153, 166, 171, 173, 175, 183, 189, 205, 221, 222, 223, 230, 237, 240, 252, 255, 261, 263, 265, 267, 274, 277, 283, 285, 286, 287, 293 (right), 296, 301, 303, 305, 309, 311, 312, 313, 314, 315, 317, 319, 320, 321.

James Dowling: 10, 17, 19, 21, 38, 57, 59, 65, 83, 86, 90, 101, 105, 107, 115, 127, 134, 151, 155, 159, 161, 195, 207, 211.

Christie's Images Limited: 122, 123, 137, 192, 193, 293 (left).

Retro AdArchives/Alamy Stock Photo © 31.

Phillips: 75, 92, 93, 94, 95, 110, 117, 128, 129, 133, 149, 202, 225, 227, 269, 271, 279, 307.

Momentum Dubai: 125, 132, 135, 138, 139, 146, 147, 177, 184, 185, 187, 203, 235, 239, 241, 243, 248, 249.

Rolex: 141, 188, 247, 289, 299, 323, 324, 325.

Monaco Legend Auctions: 233, 245.

Watch Centre: 281, 291.

First published in Great Britain in 2025 by
Cassell, an imprint of
Octopus Publishing Group Ltd
Carmelite House, 50 Victoria Embankment,
London EC4Y 0DZ
www.octopusbooks.co.uk

An Hachette UK Company
www.hachette.co.uk

This edition published by ACC Art Books in 2025 for distribution in North America by agreement with Cassell

ISBN: 978-1-78884-341-6

A CIP catalogue record for this book is available from the British Library

The author and publisher gratefully acknowledge the permission granted to reproduce the copyright material in this book. Every effort has been made to trace copyright holders and to obtain their permission for the use of copyright material. The publisher apologises for any errors or omissions in the text and would be grateful if notified of any corrections that should be incorporated in future reprints or editions of this book.

For Cassell
Publisher: Trevor Davies
Creative Director: Jonathan Christie
Editor: Scarlet Furness
Copy Editor: Julie Brooke
Senior Production Manager: Peter Hunt

For ACC Art Books
Publisher: James Smith
Editor: Sue Bennett
Technical Production: Steve Farrow

EU GPSR Authorised Representative:
Easy Access System Europe Oü, 16879218
Address:Mustamäe tee 50, 10621 Tallinn, Estonia
Email: gpsr@easproject.com Tel: +358 40 500 3575

FSC www.fsc.org MIX Paper | Supporting responsible forestry FSC® C008047

Printed in China by C & C Offset Printing Co. Ltd for ACC Art Books Ltd, Woodbridge, Suffolk, UK
www.accartbooks.com

ACC ART BOOKS

ROLEX OYSTER
PERPETUAL